1 MONTH OF
FREE
READING

at

www.ForgottenBooks.com

By purchasing this book you are eligible for one month membership to ForgottenBooks.com, giving you unlimited access to our entire collection of over 1,000,000 titles via our web site and mobile apps.

To claim your free month visit:

www.forgottenbooks.com/free815535

ISBN 978-0-364-55881-2
PIBN 10815535

THE MUSES RECREATION,

WIT RESTOR'D,

AND

WITS RECREATIONS.

Facetiae.

MUSARUM DELICIÆ:

OR,

The Muses Recreation.

CONTEINING SEVERALL PIECES OF POETIQUE WIT.

BY Sr. J. M. AND JA: S. 1656.

AND

WIT RESTOR'D,

IN SEVERALL SELECT POEMS, NOT FORMERLY PUBLISH'T. 1658.

ALSO

WITS RECREATIONS,

SELECTED FROM THE FINEST FANCIES OF MODERNE MUSES.

WITH

A Thousand Out-landish Proverbs.

Printed from Edition 1640, with all the Wood Engravings, and Improvements of subsequent Editions.

TO WHICH ARE NOW ADDED

MEMOIRS OF SIR JOHN MENNIS AND DR. JAMES SMITH.

WITH

A PREFACE.

IN TWO VOLUMES.

VOL. II.

LONDON:

PRINTED BY T. DAVISON, WHITEFRIARS;

FOR LONGMAN, HURST, REES, ORME, AND BROWN,

PATERNOSTER-ROW.

1817.

Epigrams.

On Battus.

I PRAY thee *Battus*, adde unto thy store
This booke of mine to make thy number more;
It is well bound, well printed, neatly strung,
And doth deserve to have a place among
Th' inhabitants of thy Vatican, if thou
Wilt so much favor to its worth allow.

Gender and Number.

Singular sins and plurall we commit;
And we in every gender vary it.

To Sr John Suckling.

If learning will beseem a courtier well,
If honour waite on those who dare excell,
Then let not poets envy but admire,
The eager flames of thy poetique fire;
For whilst the world loves wit, Aglaura shall,
Phœnix-like live after her funerall.

To Mr. George Sands.

Sweet-tongued *Ovid*, though strange tales he told,
Which gods and men did act in dayes of old,
What various shapes for love sometimes they took
To purchase what they aym'd at: could he look
But back upon himself he would admire
The sumptuous bravery of that rich attire;
Which *Sands* hath clad him with, and then place this
His change amongst their metamorphosis.

To Mr. William Habbington on his Castara, a Poem.

Thy muse is chaste and thy Castara too,
'Tis strange at court, and thou hadst power to woo
And to obtain (what others were deny'd)
The fair *Castara* for thy vertuous bride:
  Enjoy what you dare wish, and may there bee
  Fair issues branch from both, to honor thee.

To Mr. Francis Beaumont, and Mr. John Fletcher, gent.

Twin-stars of poetry, whom we justly may
Call the two-tops of learn'd Pernassus-Bay,
Peerlesse for freindship and for numbers sweet,
Whom oft the muses swaddled in one sheet:
  Your works shall still be prais'd and dearer sold,
  For our new-nothings doe extoll your old.

To Mr. Benjamin Johnson.

Had Rome but heard her worthies speak so high,
As thou hast taught them in thy poesie;

She would have sent her poets to obtain,
(Tutour'd by thee) thy most majestique strain.

To Mr. George Chapman on his Translation of Homers works into English meeter.

Thou ghost of Homer 'twere no fault to call
His the translation, thine the originall,
Did we not know 'twas done by thee so well;
Thou makest *Homer*, *Homers* self excell.

To William Shake-spear.

Shake-speare we must be silent in thy praise,
'Cause our encomions will but blast thy bayes,
Which envy could not, that thou didst so well;
Let thine own histories prove thy chronicle.

To Mr. Thomas Randolph.

Thou darling of the Muses for we may
Be thought deserving, if what was thy play
Our utmost labours can produce, we will
Freely allow thee heir unto the hill,
The Muses did assign thee, and think't fit
Thy younger yeares should have the elder-wit.

Man.

Man's like the earth, his hair like grasse is grown,
His veins the rivers are, his heart the stone.

Vita via.

Well may mans life be likened to a way,
Many be weary of their life they'll say.

To Mr. Thomas May.

Thou son of *Mercury* whose fluent tongue
Made Lucan finish his Pharsalian song,
Thy fame is equall, better is thy fate,
Thou hast got *Charles* his love, he *Nero's* hate.

To Mr. George Wythers.

Th' hast whipp'd our vices shrewdly and we may
Think on thy scourge untill our dying-day:
Th' hast given us a remembrancer which shall
Outlast the vices we are tax'd withall,
Th' hast made us both eternall, for our shame
Shall never Wyther, whilst thou hast a name.

To Mr. Thomas Middleton.

Facetious *Middleton*, thy witty Muse
Hath pleased all, that books or men peruse.
If any thee dispise, he doth but show
Antipathy to wit, in daring so:
Thy fam's above his malice, and 'twill be
Dispraise enough for him to censure thee.

To Mr. James Shirly on his Comedy, viz, the young Admirall.

How all our votes are for thee (*Shirly*) come
Conduct our troops, strike up Apollo's drum,
We wait upon thy summons and do all
Intend to choose thee our yong admirall.

To Mr. Philip Massinger.

Apollo's Messenger, who doth impart
To us the edicts of his learned art,
We cannot but respect thee, for we know
Princes are honour'd in their Legats so.

To Mr. John Ford.

If e're the Muses did admire that Well
Of Hellicon, as elder times do tell,
I dare presume to say upon my word,
They much more pleasure take in thee, rare *Ford*.

To Mr. Thomas Heywood.

Thou hast writ much and art admir'd by those,
Who love the easie ambling of thy prose;
But yet thy pleasingst flight was somewhat high,
When thou did'st touch the angels Hyerarchie:
Fly that way still, it will become thy age,
And better please then groveling on the stage.

To Mr. Thomas Goffe on his tragedies

When first I heard the Turkish Emperours speak
In such a dialect, and *Orestes* break
His silence in such language, I admir'd
What powerful favorite of the nimphs inspir'd
Into their souls such utterance, but I wrong
To think 'twas learnt from any but thy tongue.

On a dying Usurer.

With greater grief non doth death entertain
Then wretched *Chrysalus*, he sighs a mayn,

Not that he dyes, but 'cause much cost is spent
Upon the sexton and his regiment
The joviall ringers, and the curate must
Have his fee too, when dust is turn'd to dust,
And which is greater then the former sum,
Hee'l pay an angell for a moor-stone-tomb.

On Sextus.

What great reuenews *Sextus* doth possesse,
When as his sums of gold are numberlesse,
What cannot *Sextus* have? I wonder then,
Sextus cann't live as well as other men.

On Celsus his works.

Celsus to please himselfe, a book hath writ:
It seems so, for there's few that buyeth it.
He is no popular man, it thereby seems,
Sith men condemn, what he praise worthy deems,
Yet this his wisdome and his book prefer,
Disprais'd by all, they think both singular.

The Devill and the Fryar.

The devill was once deceived by a fryar,
Who, though he sold his soul, cheated the buyer,
The devill was promist, if he would supply
The fryar with coyn at his necessity,
When all the debts he ow'd discharg'd were quite,
The devill should have his soul as his by right.
The devill defray'd all scores, payd all, at last
Demanded for his due his soul in haste:

The fryar return'd this answer, if I ow
You any debts at all, then you must know
I am indebted still, if nothing be
Due unto you, why do you trouble me?

On Wine.
What? must we then on muddy tap-lash swill,
Neglecting sack? which makes the poet's quill
To thunder forth high raptures, such as when
Sweet-tongued *Ovid* erst with his smooth pen,
In flourishing Rome did write; frown god of wines
To see how most men disesteem thy vines.

On a land-skip in the lid of his Mrs. Virginals.
Behold Don *Phœbus* in yon shady grove,
On his sweet harp plaies roundelaies of love,
Mark how the satyr grim *Marsyas* playes
On his rude pipe, his merry-harmlesse layes,
Mark how the swaines attentively admire,
Both to the sound of pipe and tang of lyre;
But if you on these virginals will play,
They both will cast their instruments away,
And deeming it the musique of the spheares,
Admire your musique as the swains do theirs.

On a Tennis-court haunter.
The world's a court, we are the bals, wherein
We bandied are by every stroke of sin,
Then onely this can I commend in thee,
Thou actest well our frail mortalitie.

On Balbulus.

Thou do'st complaine poets haue no reward
And now adayes they are in no regard:
Verses are nothing worth, yet he, that buyes
Ought that is thine, at a three-farthings price,
Will think it too too dear, and justly may
Think verses are in price, since th' other day,
Yea who ere buies 'em at a farthings rate,
At the same price can neuer sell 'em at.

To his Mistris.

Hyperbole of worth should wit suggest
My will with epithites, and I invest
That shrine but with deserved paraphrase,
Adulatory poetry would praise,
And so but staine your worth: your vertues (or
Else none at all) shall be my orator.

On his Mistris.

I saw faire *Flora* take the aire,
When *Phœbus* shin'd and it was faire;
The heavens to allay the heat,
Sent drops of raine, which gently beat,
The sun retires, asham'd to see
That he was barr'd from kissing thee;
Then *Boreas* took such high disdaine,
That soon he dri'd those drops again.
Ah cunning plot and most divine!
Thus to mix his breath with thine.

On an houre glasse.

Do thou consider this small dust
Here running in this glasse
    By atomes mov'd?
Canst thou beleeve that this the body was
    Of one that lov'd;
And in his mistrisse playing like a fly
    Turn'd to cinders by her eye?
Yes, and in death as life, have it exprest
    That lovers ashes take no rest.

On the picture of Cupid in a jewell worn by his Mrs. on her breast.

Little *Cupid* enter in and heat
Her heart, her brest is not thy seat;
Her brests are fitted to entice
Lovers, but her heart's of ice.
Thaw *Cupid*, that it hence forth grow
Tender still by answering, no.

How to choose a wife.

Good sir, if you will shew the best of your skill
    To picke a vertuous creature,
Then picke such a wife, as you love a life,
    Of a comely grace and feature;
The noblest part, let it be her heart,
    Without deceit or cunning,
With a nimble wit, and all things fit,
    With a tongue that's never running, .

The haire of her head, it must not be red,
     But faire and brown as a berry;
Her fore-head high, with a christall eye,
     Her lips as red as a cherry.

Claudianus de Sphærâ Archimedis.

When *Jove* within a little glasse survay'd
The heavens, he smil'd, and to the gods thus sayd,
Can strength of mortall wit proceed thus far?
Loe in a fraile orbe, my works mated are,
Hither the Syracusians art translates
Heavens form, the course of things and humane fates,
Th' including spirit serving the star-deck'd signes,
The living work in constant motion windes,
Th' adult'rate zodiaque runs a naturall yeere,
And *Cynthias* forg'd horns monethly new light bear,
Viewing her own world, now bold industry
Triumphs and rules with humane power the sky.

On Cælia.

In *Cælia*'s face a question did arise,
Which were more beautifull, her lips or eyes;
We, say the eyes, send forth those pointed darts,
Which pierce the hardest adamantine hearts,
From us, reply the lips, proceed those blisses,
Which lovers reap by kind words and sweet kisses:
Then wept the eyes, and from their eyes did pow'r
Of liquid orientall pearle a shower;
Where at the lips mov'd with delight and pleasure
Through a sweet smile unlock'd their ivory treasure,

And bad love judge, whether did ad more grace,
Weeping or smiling pearls to *Cælia's* face?

A plain Sutor to his love.
Faire I love thee, yet I cannot sue,
And shew my love as masking courtiers doe,
Yet by the smocke of *Venus*, for thy good,
I'le freely spend my thrice concocted blood.

A gentleman in love.
Tell her I love, and if she aske how well,
Tell her my tongue told thee no tongue can tell.

Her answer.
Say not you love, unlesse you doe
For lying will not honor you.

His answer.
Maddam I love, and love to doe,
And will not lye, unlesse with you.

On a Musitian and his Scholler.
A man of late did his fair daughter bring
To a musitian for to learne to sing,
He fell in love with her, and her beguil'd,
With flattering words, and she was got with child.
Her father hearing this was griev'd and said,
That he with her but a base-part had play'd,
For wch he swore that he would make him smart
For teaching of his daughter such a part:

But the musitian said, he did no wrong,
He had but taught her how to sing prick-song.

On his Mrs.

Shall I tell you how the rose at first grew red,
And whence the lilly whiteness borrowed?
You blusht, and straight the rose with red was dight,
The lilly kist your hand, and so was white.
Before such time, each rose had but a stain,
And lillies nought but palenes did contayne:
You haue the native colour, these the dy,
And onely flowrish in your livery.

To his Mrs.

Think not, deare love, that I'le reveale
Those houres of pleasure we do steale,
No eye shall see, nor yet the sun
Descrie what thee and I have done;
The god of love himself, whose dart
Did first peirce mine, and next thy heart,
He shall not know, that we can tell
What sweets in stoln embracements dwell,
Onely this meanes may find it out,
If when I dy, phisians doubt
What caus'd my death, and they to view
Of all the judgements that are true,
Rip up my heart, oh then I feare
The world will find thy picture there.

Tempus edax rerum.

The sweetest flower in the summers prime,
By all agreement is the damaske rose,
Which if it grow, and be not pluck'd in time,
She sheds her leaves, her buds their sent do loose;
  Oh let not things of worth, for want of use
  Fall into all consuming times abuse:
The sweetest work that ever natur'd fram'd,
By all agreement is a virgins face,
Which not enjoy'd, her white and red will fade,
And unto all worm eating time give place:
  Oh let not things of worth, for want of use,
  Fall into all consuming times abuse.

To his Mrs.

Thou send'st to me a heart was crown'd,
I tooke it to be thine,
But when I saw it had a wound,
I knew that heart was mine.
A bounty of a strange conceit,
To send mine own to me,
And send it in a worse estate,
Then when it came to thee;
The heart I gave thee had no staine,
It was intire and sound;
But thou hast sent it back againe,
Sick of a deadly wound.
Oh heavens! how wouldst thou use a heart
  That should rebellious be,
When thou hast kill'd me with a dart,
  That so much honor'd thee?

On a charming beauty.

I'le gaze no more on that bewitched face,
Since ruin harbors there in every place,
For my inchanted soul alike she drowns,
With calms and tempests of her smiles and frowns.
I'le love no more those cruell eyes of hers,
Which pleas'd or anger'd still are murtherers;
For if she dart like lightning through the ayre,
Her beames of wrath, she kils me with despaire;
If she behold me with a pleasing eye,
I surfet with excesse of joy, and dy.

In Mincam.

Fine *Minca* lisping yea and no forsooth,
Though little eats, yet keeps a dainty tooth:
Minca that longs for apples on the tree,
In May, before the blossomes fallen be,
Or will not eate a Kentish cherry down,
But for a couple, when she payes a crown;
And cares not for a straw-berry or peare,
In truth because th'are common every where;
Yet what is that, which may be had for reason,
And never comes to *Minca* out of season?

Clericus absque libro.

When *Crassus* in his office was instal'd,
For summs of money, which he yet doth ow,
A client by the name of Clerke him call'd,
As he next day to Westminster did go;
Which *Crassus* hearing whispers thus in 's eare,
Sirrah you now mistake, and much do erre,

That henceforth must the name of Clerk forbear,
And know I am become an officer.

    Alas (quoth he) I did not so much marke,
    Good Mr. officer, that are no Clerke.

To his Mrs.

Your lips (faire lady) if 't be not too much,
I beg to kisse, your hand I crave to touch,
And if your hand deny that courtesie,
(Sweet mistris) at your feet I prostrate ly;
But if your foot spurn my humility,
Or that your lips think I do aime too high,
Then let your hand, in token of consent,
Point at the meane, the maine of all content,
And I shall leave extreames, and to be blist,
Rest in your midst, where vertue doth consist.

Umbras non certus metuit.

Mistrisse *Maryna* starts to see a frog,
A naked rapier, or a creeping mouse:
To hear a gun, or barking mastive dog,
Or smell tobacco, that defiles her house,
    To taste of fish, no man alive shall woe her,
    Yet feares she not what flesh can doe unto her.

On Women.

Although they seeme us onely to affect,
'Tis their content, not ours, they most respect:
They for their own ends cunningly can feigne,
And though they have 't by nature, yet they'll strain:

Sure if on earth, by wiles gain'd might be blisse,
Staight that I were a woman I would wish.

Women are mens shadowes.

Follow a shaddow, it still flies you,
Seeme to fly, it will pursue:
So court a mistrisse, she denies you,
Let her alone, she will court you.
    Say are not women truely then
    Stil'd but the shadwoes of us men?
At morne and even shades are longest,
At noone they are, or short or none:
So men at weakest, they are strongest;
But grant us perfect, they're not known.
    Say are not women truely then
    Stil'd but the shadowes of us men?

To his Mistrisse.

Take, oh take those lips away,
That so sweetly were for-sworne:
And those eies like breake of day,
Lights that doe mislead the morne:
    But my kisses bring againe,
    Seales of love, though seal'd in vaine.
Hide, oh hide those hills of snow,
Which thy frozen bosome beares:
On whose tops the pinkes that grow,
Are of those that Aprill weares:
    But first set my poor heart free,
    Bound in those icie chaines by thee. .

In Diogenem & Crœsum.

When the tubb'd *Cynicke* went to hell, and there
Found the pale ghost of golden *Crœsus* bare,
Hee stops; and jeering till he shrugges againe,
Sayes O! thou richest king of kings, what gaine
Have all thy large heapes brought thee, since I spie
Thee here alone, and poorer now then I?
For all I had, I with me bring; but thou
Of all thy wealth hast not one farthing now.

Unde venis, memora.

With earthen plate, *Agathocles*, they say,
Did use to meal; so serv'd with Samo's clay,
When jewell'd plate, and rugged earth was by,
He seem'd to mingle wealth and poverty.
One ask'd the cause: he answers, I that am
Sicilia's King, from a poor Potter came.
Hence learn, thou that art rais'd from mean estate,
To sudden riches, to be temperate.

To young men.

Yong men fly, when beauty darts
Amorous glances at your hearts,
The fixt marke gives your shooter aime,
And ladyes lookes have power to maime,
Now 'twixt their lips, now in their eyes
Wrapt in a kisse or smile love lyes,
Then fly betimes, for onely they
Conquer love, that run away.

The pens prosopopeia to the Scrivener.

Thinke who, when you cut the quill,
Wounded was, yet did no ill;
When you mended me, thinke you must
Mend yourselfe, else you're unjust.
When you dip my nib in inke,
Thinke on him that gall did drinke,
When the inke sheds from your pen,
Thinke who shed his blood for men;
When you write, but thinke on this,
And you ne're shall write amisse.

A raritie.

If thou bee'st born to strange sights,
Things invisible to see,
Ride ten thousand dayes and nights,
Till age snow white haires on thee.
  And thou, when thou return'st will tell me
  All strange wonders that befell thee,
And thou 'lt sweare that no where
Liues a maiden true and faire.

On the Queene of Bohemia.

You meaner beauties of the night,
Which poorely satisfie our eyes;
More by your number then your light;
The common people of the skies:
  What are you, when the moon shall rise?

You violets that first appeare,
By your purple mantle known, ,
Like proud virgins of the yeere,
As if the spring were all your own ;
　　What are you, when the rose is blown ?
You wand'ring chaunters of the wood,
That fill the ayre with natures layes,
Thinking your passions understood,
By weak accents, where's your praise,
　　When *Philomell* her voice shall raise ?
So when my Princesse shall be seen,
In sweetnes of her lookes and mind,
By vertues first, then choyce a Queen,
Tell me, was she not design'd
　　Th' eclipse and glory of her kind ?

To his noble friend.

There's no necessity that can exclude
The poorest being from a gratitude ;
For when the strength of Fortune lends no more,
He that is truely thankefull is not poore :
Yours be the bounty then, mine the great debt,
On which no time, nor power can ransome set.

On his Mrs death.

Unjustly we complain of fate,
　　For short'ning our unhappy dayes,
When death doth nothing but translate
　　And print us in a better phrase ;

Yet who can choose but weep? not I,
  That beautie of such excellence,
And more vertue then could dy;
  By deaths rude hand is ravish'd hence,
Sleepe blest creature in thine urne,
  My sighes, my teares shall not awake thee,
I but stay untill my turne
  And then, oh then! I'le overtake thee.

Æquè facilitas ac difficultas nocet amoris.

I love not her, that at the first cries, I;
I love not her, that doth me still deny;
Be she too hard, shee'll cause me to despaire,
Be she too easie, shee's as light as faire;
'Tis hard to say whether most hurt procure,
She that is hard or easy to allure;
If it be so, then lay me by my side
The hard, soft, willing and unwilling Bride.

Quidam erat.

A preaching fryar there was, who thus began,
The Scripture saith there was a certaine man:
A certain man? but I do read no where
Of any certaine woman mention'd there:
A certaine man a phrase in Scripture common,
But no place shewes there was a certaine woman.
And fit it is, that we should ground our faith
On nothing more then what the Scripture saith.

On the marriage of one Turbolt with Mrs. Hill.

What are *Deucalions* dayes return'd, that we
A *Turbolt* swimming on a *Hill* do see ?
What shall we in this age so strange report,
That fishes leave the sea on hils to sport ?
And yet this *hill*, though never tir'd with standing,
Lay gently down to give a *Turbolt* landing.

Barten Holiday to the Puritan on his Technogamia.

'Tis not my person, no my play,
But my sirname, *Holiday*,
That does offend thee, thy complaints
Are not against me, but the Saints ;
So ill dost thou endure my name,
Because the Church doth like the same,
A name more awfull to the puritane
Then *Talbot* unto France, or *Drake* to Spaine.

In meretrices.

The law hangs theeves, for their unlawfull stealing,
The law carts bawds, for keeping of the doore,
The law doth punish rogues, for roguish dealing,
The law whips both the pander and the whore:
But yet I muse from whence this law is grown ;
Whores must not steal, yet must not use their own.

Quicquid non nummus.

The mony'd man can safely saile all seas,
And make his fortune as himselfe shall please ;

He can wed *Danae*, and command that now
Acrisius selfe that fatall match allow :
He can declaime, chide, censure verses, write,
And do all things better than *Cato* might;
He knows the law, and rules it, hath and is
Whole *Scrvius*, and what *Labeo* can possesse ;
In briefe, let rich men wish what e're they love,
'Twill come; they in a lock'd chest keep a *Jove*.

A poore Peasant.

A poore man being sent for to the king,
Began to covet much a certaine thing
Before he went : being but an iron naile,
His friend did aske him, what it would availe ?
(Quoth he) this is as good as one of steele,
For me to knock now into fortunes wheele.

Three Pages.

Three pages on a time together met,
And made a motion, that each one would let
The other know, what hee'd desire to be,
Having his wish; thereto they did agree.
Quoth one, to be a melon I would chuse,
For then I'm sure, none would refuse
To kisse my breech, although the sent were hot,
And so they'd know whether I were good or not.

A peasant and his wife.

A peasant and his wife was almost wilde
To understand his daughter was with childe,

And said, if to the girle sh'ad taken heed,
Sh'ad not been guilty of so foule a deed.
Husband (said she) I swear by cock,
   (Welfare a good old token)
The dev'll himselfe can't keep that lock
   Which every key can open.

An evill age.

Virgil of *Mars* and ruthfull warres did treat,
Ovid of *Venus* love and peace did write,
Yet *Virgil* for his straine was counted great,
And *Ovid* for his love was banished quite;
  No marvell then if courtesie grow cold,
  When hate is prais'd, and love itself controll'd.

Of a Judge.

Were I to choose a captaine, I would than
Not choose your courtier, or a youthfull man,
No; I would choose a Judge; one grim and grave,
To make a captaine such a man I'de crave;
Give me that mã, whose frowning brow is death,
I, such an one, as can kill men with breath.

Asperum nimis condimentum.

Monsieur *Albanus* new invested is
With sundry suits and fashions passing fit,
But never any came so nigh as this,
For joy whereof *Albanus* frollicks it,
  Untill the taylors bill of *solvi fäs*
  Diverts his humour to another bias.

Atheists pastimes.

Grammarians talk of times past and hereafter :
I spend time present in pastime and laughter.

On Paulus.

Because thou followest some great peer at court,
Dost think the world deems thee a great one for't ?
Ah no ! thou art mistaken *Paulus,* know
Dwarfs still as pages unto gyants goe.

On a cowardly Souldier.

Strotzo doth weare no ring upon his hand,
Although he be a man of great command ;
But gilded spurres do jingle at his heeles,
Whose rowels are as big as some coach wheeles.
He grac'd them well, for in the Netherlands
His heeles did him more service then his hands.

Auri sacra fames—quid non ?

A smooth-fac'd youth was wedded to an old
Decrepit shrew, such is the power of gold :
That love did tye this knot, the end will prove,
The love of money, not the god of love.

On Lepidus and his wife.

Lepidus married some while to a shrew,
She sick'ned, he in jesting wise to shew
How glad her death would make him; said sweetheart,
I pray you e'r you sing loth to depart,

Tell who shall be my second wife, and I
After your death will wed her instantly;
She somewhat vext hereat, straightway replide,
Then let grim *Pluto's* daughter be your bride:
He answer'd, Wife I would your will obey,
But that our lawes my willingnesse gain-say;
For he, who *Pluto's* sister takes to wife,
Cannot his daughter too, upon my life.

To Phillis.

Aske me not *Phillis* why I doe refuse
To kisse thee as the most of gallants use,
For seeing oft thy dogge to fawne and skip
Upon thy lap, and joyning lip to lip,
Although thy kisses I full faine would crave,
Yet would I not thy dogge my rivall have.

Of Caridemus.

Although thy neighbor have a handsome horse,
Matchlesse for comely shape, for hue and course,
And though thy wife thou knowst ill-shapen be
Yet *Caridemus* praises mightily
His ugly wife, and doth the horse dispraise;
How subtilly the fox his engin layes,
For he desires his neighbours horse to buy,
And sell his wife to any willingly.

On beere.

Is no juice pleasing but the grapes? is none
So much beloved? doth perfection

Onely conjoyne in wine? or doth the well
Of Aganippe with this liquor swell,
That poets thus affect it? shall we crowne
A meere exotique? and contemn our owne,
Our native liquor? haunt who list the grape
I'le more esteem our oate, whose reed shall make
An instrument to warble forth her praise,
Which shall survive untill the date of daies
And eke invoke some potent power divine
To patronize her worth above the vine.

On a vaunting Poetaster.

Cæcilius boasts his verses worthy bee,
To be engraven on a cypresse tree,
A cypresse wreath befits 'em well; 'tis true
For they are neer their death, and crave but due.

On a valiant Souldier.

A Spanish Souldier in the Indian warre
Who oft came off with honour, and some scarre,
After a tedious battell, when they were
Enforc'd for want of bullets to forbeare
Farther to encounter, which the savage Moore
Perceiving, scoff'd, and neerer then before
Approach'd the Christian host, the soldier griev'd
To be out-brav'd, yet could not be reliev'd,
Beyond all patience vex'd, he said although
I bullets want, myselfe will wound the foe;
Then from his mouth took he a tooth, and sent
A fatall message to their regiment:

What armes will fury steed men with, when we
Can from ourselves have such artillerie?
Samson thy jaw bone can no trophy reare
Equall to his, who made his tooth his speare.

On Aurispa.

Why doth the world repute *Aurispa* learn'd?
Because she gives men what they never earn'd.

On Alexander the Great.

If *Alexander* thought the world but small,
Because his conquering hand subdu'd it all,
He should not then have stil'd himselfe the Great,
An infants stoole can be no gyants seat.

On sore eyes.

Fuscus was councell'd if he would preserve
His eyes in perfect sight, drinking to swerve;
But he reply'd, 'tis better that I shu'd
Loose thē, then keep them for the worms as food.

On an inevitable Cuckold.

Two wives th' hast buried and another wed,
Yet neither of three chaste to thy bed,
Wherefore thou blam'st not onely them, but all
Their sex into disgrace and scorne dost call,
Yet if the thing thou wilt consider well
Thou wilt thy malice, and this rage expell,
For when the three were all alike 't should seem
Thy stars gave thee the Cuckolds anadem:

If thou wert borne to be a wittoll, can
Thy wife prevent thy fortune? foolish man!
That woman which a *Hellen* is to thee,
Would prove another mans *Penelope.*

On the ensuring Office.

Linus met *Thuscus* on the Burse by chance,
And swore he'd drink a helth to th'heir of France
For on th'Exchange for currant news 'twas told
France had a Dolphin not yet seven dayes old:
Thuscus excus'd himselfe, and said he must
By all meanes go to th'Ensuring Office first,
And so ensure some goods, he doubted were
Unlikely else e're to his hands appeare;
Linus reply'd, Ile with thee then, for I
Would have my lands ensur'd to me in fee
Which otherwise I doubt I never shall
From debt and morgage e're redeem at all.

On Clodius Albinus.

Clodius great cheere for supper doth prepare,
Buyes chickens, rabbets, phesants, and a hare,
Great store of fowle, variety of fish,
And tempting sawce serv'd in, in every dish,
To this great feast, whom doth he meane t'invite?
Albinus onely sups with him to night.

To Lycus.

That poetry is good and pleasing thou dost cry,
Yet know'st not when 'tis right or when awry,

Thou know'st great *Ovids* censure, to abstaine
From pleasing good is vertues chiefest aime.

Of one praising my Book.

Harpax doth praise my Book I lately writ,
Saith it is short and sweet, and full of wit;
I knew his drift, and said, Be silent pray
For in good faith, I've given 'em all away.

On Women.

Women are bookes, and men the readers be,
In whom oft times they great errata's see;
Here sometimes we a blot, there we espy
A leafe misplac'd, at least a line awry;
If they are books, I wish that my wife were
An almanack, to change her every yeare.

On Tobacco.

Nature's idea, physicks rare perfection,
Cold rheumes expeller, and the wits direction,
O had the gods known thy immortall smack,
The heavens ere this time had bin colored black.

On a beloved lye.

I hate a lye, and yet a lye did run
Of noble *Goring's* death and *Kensington*,
And for that they did not untimely dye,
I love a lye, because that was a lye,
For had it been an accident of ruth,
'T had made me grow in hatred of the truth,

Though lyes be bad, yet give this lye its due,
'Tis ten times better, then if't had bin true.

On a fiddle-sticke.

Am I an instrument to make you sport,
A Fiddle stick I am, ye shan't report
That ere ye hand'led me in such a case;
To make me strike up fiddles mean and base,
Nay, you shall never bend me to your bow,
It goeth against the haire, you should doe so,
Nor shall you curbe me in thus every day,
I'le but my pleasure, I was made to play;
But here I must not play upon another,
Why have I then a fiddle for my brother?
If I were gone, you'd be compel'd my friends
To make your musicke on your fingers ends:
My brother Fiddle is so hollow-hearted
That ere't be long, we must needs be parted,
And with so many frets he doth abound
That I can never touch him but he'l sound:
When he's reviv'd, this poore excuse he puts,
That when I play, I vex him to the guts;
But since it is my nature, and I must,
I'le crowd and scrape acquaintance for a crust;
I am a gentleman of high descent,
Come from *Apollo*'s glorious element;
Above the bridge I alwayes use to keep,
And that's my proper spheare when I do sleep
So that I cannot be in tune or towne,
For all my scraping, if the bridge be downe;

But since without an end, nought can endure,
A Fiddle-sticke hath two ends to be sure.

On hopes of preferment.

I saw my fortune goe before,
As *Palinurus* saw the shore,
If that I dye, before it hitch,
Well fare mine eyes for they are rich.

On a Gentleman that married an Heire privately at the Tower.

The angry father hearing that his childe
Was stolne, married, and his hopes beguild,
('Cause his usurious nature had a thought
She might have bin to greater fortunes brought)
With rigid lookes, bent brows, and words austere,
Ask'd his forc'd son in law, how he did dare
(Without a full consenting from him carried)
Thus beare his onely daughter to be married,
And by what cannons he assum'd such power?
He said, the best in *England* sir—the Tower.

A Gentlemans satisfaction for spitting in another mans face.

A gentleman (not in malice nor disgrace,
But-by chance) spet in anothers face,
He that receiv'd it, knowing not the cause
That should produce such rashnesse ('gainst the laws
Of Christian man-hood or civility)
In kindling anger, ask'd the reason why ;

Pray sir, sayes he, what thing that doth but sound
Like to an injury have you ere found
By me at any time ? or if you had
It never would deserve contempt so bad,
'Tis an inhumane custome none ere use,
But the vile nation of contemned Jewes :
Pray sir, cryes th' other, be not so unkinde,
Thus with an accident to charge my minde,
I meant it not, but since it falls out so,
I'm sorry, yea, make satisfaction too ;
Then be not mov'd, but let this ease your doubt,
Since I have spet, please you, I'le tread it out.

On a little Gentleman and one Master Story.

The little man, by th'other mans vain glory,
It seemes was roughly us'd (so sayes the story)
But being a little heated and high blowne,
In anger flyes at *Story*, pulls him downe ;
And when they rise (I know not how it fated)
One got the worst, the *Story* was translated
From white to red, but ere the fight was ended
It seemes a gentleman, that one befriended,
Came in and parted them ; the little blade
There's none that could intreat, or yet perswade,
But he would fight still, till another came,
And with sound reasons councel'd 'gainst the same
'Twas in this manner, friend ye shall not fight
With one that's so unequall to your height,
Story is higher, th'other made reply,
I'd pluck him downe, were he three *Stories* high.

On a faire Gentlewoman whose name was Browne.

We praise the faire, and our inventions wrack,
In pleasing numbers to applaud the black,
We court this ladies eye, that ladies haire,
The faire loves black, the black best like the faire,
Yet neither sort I court, I doat upon
Nor faire, nor black, but a complexion
More rare than either; she that is the crowne
Of my entire affection is browne,
And yet she's faire, 'tis strange, how can it be,
That two complexions should in one agree?
Do I love *Browne,* my love can please mine eye,
And sate my narrowest curiosity,
If I like faire, she hath so sweet a grace,
That I could leave an angel for her face,
Let any judge then, which complexion's rarest,
In my opinion, she is *Browne* that's fairest.

On the word intollerable.

Two gentlemen did to a taverne come,
And call'd the drawer for to shew a roome,
The drawer did, and what room think ye was't?
One of the small ones, where men drink in haste;
One gentleman sate downe there, but the other
Dislik'd it, would not sit, call'd for another:
At which his friend, rising up from the table,
Cryes, friend let's stay, this room is tollerable:
Why that's the cause (quoth he) I will not stay,
Is that the cause, quoth th'other? why I pray?

To give a reason to you I am able,
Because I hate to be in—tollerable.

On Womens inconstancie.

Goe catch a star that's falling from the skye,
Cause an immortall creature for to dye,
Stop with thy hand the current of the seas,
Poste ore the earth to the Antipodes;
Cause times returne, and call back yesterday;
Cloath January with the month of May,
Weigh out an ounce of flame, blow back the wind
And then find faith within a womans mind.

On Women.

Why sure these necessary harmes were fram'd,
That men as too too heedlesse might be blam'd,
His weaknesse cannot greatest weaknesse fly,
In her strong drawing, fraile necessity;
Then happy they, that know what women are,
But happier, which to know them never care.

Satis est quod sufficit.

Weep no more, sigh nor groane,
Sorrow recalls not, times are gone,
Violets pluck'd, the sweetest raine,
Makes not fresh or grow againe,
Joyes are windy, dreames flye fast,
Why should sadnesse longer last?
Griefe is but a wound to woe,
Gentle faire, mourne no moe.

Of Women.

Commit the ship unto the wind,
But not thy faith to woman kind,
There is more safety in a wave,
Then in the faith that women have;
No woman's good, if chance it fall,
Some one be good amongst them all,
Some strange intent the dest'nies had,
To make a good thing of bad.

On Musick.

I want a quill out of an angels wing,
To write sweet Musickes everlasting praise,
I likewise want an angels voyce to sing
A wished anthem to her happy dayes,
   Then since I want an angels voyce and pen,
   Let angels write and sing, I'le say *Amen*.

On Tobacco.

Times great consumer, cause of idlenesse,
Old whorehouse hunter, cause of drunkennesse,
Bewitching smoake, vainest wealths consumer;
Abuse of wit, stinking breath's perfumer,
Cause of entrailes blacknesse, quenching her fire,
Offence to many, bringing good to none,
Ev'n be thou hack'd till thou art burnt and gone.

Womens properties.

To weep oft, still to flatter, sometimes spin,
Are properties, women excell men in.

Womens teares.

When women weep in their dissembling art,
Their teares are sauce to their malicious heart.

On Gervase.

A double gelding *Gervase* did provide,
That he and's wife to see their friends might ride
And he a double gelding prov'd indeed;
For he so suddenly fell to his speed,
That both alight, with blows and threats among
He leads him, and his wife drives him along.

To A. S.

Rich *Chremes* whilst he lives will nought bestow
On his poore heires, but all at his last day,
If he be halfe as rich I trow,
He thinks that for his life they seldome pray.

On Claret Wine spilt.

What's this that's spilt? 'tis Claret Wine,
'Tis well 'tis spilt, its fall sav'd mine.

Of Women.

Are Women saints? no saints, and yet no devils,
Are Women good? not good but needfull evils,
So angel-like that devils you need not boubt,
Such needfull evils, that few can be without.

Liber too wary to thrive.

Liber is late set up and wanteth custome,
Yet great resort hath got, but will not trust 'em:

Is not his love unto his friend the greater,
He'l want himselfe, e're hee'l see him a debtor.

On Venus and Vulcan.

I muse, why *Venus* hath such fiery holes,
I thinke that *Vulcan* once there blow'd his coales.

Sorte tua contentus.

Bartus being bid to supper to a lord,
Was marshall'd at the lower end of the boord,
Who vext thereat 'mongst his comrades doth fret
And sweares that he below the salt was set;
But *Bartus* th'art a fool to fret and sweare,
The salt stands on the bord wouldst thou sit ther?

Fovent pejuria furtum.

Piso hath stoln a silver bole in jest,
For which suspected only, not confest,
Rather then *Piso* will restore your bole,
To quit the body, he will cast the soule.

Virescit vulnere Venus.

Susan's well sped and weares a velvet hood,
As who should know, her breeding hath been good
'Tis reason she should rise once in her life,
That fell so oft before she was a wife.

On a rich country Gentleman.

Of woods, of plaines, of hils and vales,
Of fields, of meades, of parks and pales,

Of all I had, this I possesse,
I need no more I have no Issue.

In Octavium.

Octavius lying at the point of death,
His gelding kindly did to me bequeath :
I wanted one, and was in haste to ride,
In better time he never could have di'd.

Love's Lunacy.

Before I knew what might belong to war,
I was content to suffer many a scarre ;
Yet none could hurt me, 'till at length a boy,
Disgrace to manhood, wrought my sad annoy,
This lad though blind, yet did he shoot a dart
Which pierc'd my brest and lighted on my heart
Yet did I feele no hurt till from above,
I heard a voyce say souldiers you must love,
I lik't it well and in this pleasing vaine :
I lost my wits to get my heart againe.

Most men mistaken.

Good, bad, rich, poore, the foolish and the sage,
Doe all cry out against the present age :
Ignorance make us thinke our young times good
Our elder dayes are better understood :
Besides griefes past, we easily forget,
Present displeasures make us sad or fret.

An idle houswife.

Fine, neat, and curious mistresse butterfly,
The idle toy, to please an ideots eyes :
You, that wish all good houswifes hang'd, for why,
Your daies work's done, each morning as you rise :
Put on your gown, your ruff, your mask, your chain,
Then dine, and sup, and goe to bed againe.

To Women.

You were created angels pure and faire,
But since the first fell, tempting devils you are :
You should be mens blisse, but you prove their rods
Were there no women men might live like gods.

On a Bed-rid man.

A bed-rid man before the judge was brought,
The judge bids stand up sirrah as you ought ;
Oh sir, nor goe, nor sit, nor stand can I,
I am your friend, pray give me leave to lie :
Art thou my friend quoth he ? then lie thy fill,
A judge gives all his friends leave to lie still.

In procos.

Who woes a wife, thinkes wedded men do know,
The onely true content, I thinke not so :
If woe in wooers be, that women court,
As the word woe in wooers doth import :
And woe in women too, that courted be,
As the word woe in women we do see.
I thinke 'tis better lead a single life,
Than with this double woe to wooe a wife.

On Promises.

My mistresse sweares she'd leave all men for mee,
Yea though that Jove himselfe should rivall be,
She sweares it, but what women sweare to kind-
Loves, may be writ in rapid seas and wind.

On a barbar.

Suppose my Barber when his razors nigh
My throat, should then aske wealth and liberty :
I'de promise sure, the Barber askes not this,
No, 'tis a theefe, and feare imperious is.

On Durus.

A friend of *Durus* comming on a day
To visit him, finding the doores say nay ;
Being lock'd fast up, first knocks, & then doth pause,
As Lord have mercy on's had beene the cause ;
But missing it, he ask't a neighbour by
When the rich *Duru's* were lock't, and why ?
He said it was a custome growne of late
At dinner time, to locke your great men's gate.
Duru's his poore friend admir'd, and though the door
Was not for state lock'd up, but 'gainst the poore,
And thence departing empty of good cheere,
Said, Lord have mercy on us is not here.

Leucus.

Leucus loves life, yet liveth wickedly ;
He hateth death, yet wisheth he may dy
Honestly and well : so what is naught he loves,
And what hee would have good, hee naught approves.

In Thrasonem.

Since *Thraso* met one stoutly in the field,
He crakes his spirit, and knows not how to yeeld,
Looks big, swears, strouts with set-side-armes the streets,
Yet gently yeelds the wall to all he meets
And to his friends that asks the reason, why?
His answer's this, My self I grace thereby:
For every one the common proverb knows,
That alwayes to the wall the weakest go's.

On a Wittall.

I know my fate, and that must bear;
And since I know, I need not feare.

On Mopsus.

Mopsus almost, what e're he means to speak,
Before it, sir-reverence the way must break:
Such maners hath sir-reverence learnt at school,
That now sir-reverence *Mopsus* is a fool.

Turpe lucrum Veneris.

Will in a wilfull humour, needs would wed
A wench of wonder, but without a stock,
Whose fame no sooner through the street was spred,
But thither straight our chiefest gallants flock.
  Put case she's poor, brings she not chapmen on?
  I hope his stock may serve to graff upon.

Si hodie tibi, cras mihi.

A scornfull dame, invited over-night,
To come and dine next morrow with a knight,

Refus'd his sudden bidding with disdain,
To whom this message was return'd again;
Sith with so short time she could not dispence,
To pray her come at that day twelve-moneth hence.

Better lost then found.

Lo here's a Coyner, yet he fears no death,
For he ne'r stamps in mettall, but in breath :
Swears from Believe me, and Good-faith & troth,
Up to God-damn-me; and without an oath
Protests in nothing, be he ne'r so bare,
He's brave in this, that he can bravely swear.

Fronti nulla fides.

Cantus that wooll-ward went, was wondred at;
Which be excus'd, as done through pure contrition.
But who so simple, *Cantus*, credits that?
Tis too well known, thou art of worse condition.
And therefore if no linnen thee begirt,
The naked truth will prove, thou hast no shirt.

Against Cajus.

Twenty small pieces I'd have borrowed late,
Which, if bestow'd, had been a gift not great :
For, t'was a rich friend whom I ask'd, and old ;
Whose crowded chests would scarce his riches hold.
He cry's turne lawyer, and thou'lt thrive : I'd have
No councell, *Cajus*, give me what I crave.

Fama mendax.

Report, thou sometime art ambitious,
At other times, too sparing, covetous;
But many times exceeding envious,
And out of time most dev'lish, furious.
   Of some, or all of these, I dare compound thee;
   But for a lyer ever I have found thee.

On Otho.

Three daughters *Otho* hath, his onely heirs,
But will by no means let them learn to write;
'Cause, after his own humour, much he fears,
They'l one day learn, love-letters to indite.
The yongest now's with childe; who taught her then,
Or of her self learn'd she to hold her pen?

On a Thief.

A thief condemned for a hainous crime,
Was for to lose his tongue at the same time:
But he the court intreats with feigned tears,
To spare his tongue, and cut off both his ears.
To this, the judge, and all the bench agreed,
And for th'executioner sent with speed:
Who being come, and searching, there was found
No ears, but hairs, at which, all laughed round.
Saith th'judge, thou hast no ears. Sir (quoth the wight)
Where there is naught, the king must lose his right.

On Dare, an up-start Poet.

Dare, a fresh author to a friend did boast,
Hee'd shew in cheap, his name upon a post,

But did *Dare's* friend to's hostes house but walk,
Sheel'd shew't him there on every post in chalk.

Ambo-dexter.

Two gentlemen of hot and fiery sp'rite,
Tooke boate and went up westward to goe fight;
Embarked both, for Wend-worth they set sail,
And there ariving with a happy gale:
The water-men discharged for their fare,
Then to be parted, thus their minds declare:
Pray Oares, say they, stay here, and come not nigh,
We go to fight a little, but here by:
The water-men, with staves did follow then,
And cry'd, oh hold your hands, good gentlemen,
You know the danger of the law, forbeare;
So they put weapons up, and fell to sweare.

Vpon Indeedla.

Indeedla grumbles much, that he a penny,
Is levied in collection to the poore;
Indeedla but you are the first of any,
Will contribute unto a handsome——

Ictus piscator sapit.

Brutus at length escap'd the surgeons hands,
Begins to frollique as if all were well;
And would not for the worth of thrice his lands,
Endure the brunt of such another hell;
  But leaves this farewell for his physickes hire;
  The child that's burnt, for ever dreads the fire.

On a woman.

All women naturally are called *Eves*
Because from *Eve* all women do proceed,
And by TH. are women turn'd to theeves,
Then unto *Eve* if.you put *l.* behind,
Your woman's turn'd quite from *Eve* to *Evel:*
But place a *D.* before, and you shall find
That shee by doing Evell is turned Devel,
    So that from *Eves* to Theeves, from Theeves to Evel,
    Women do runne untill they come to'th Devel.

Humors.

Aske *Humors* why a feather he doth weare?
It is his humor (by the Lord) he'le sweare.
Or what he doth with such a horse-taile locke?
Or why upon a whore hee spends his stock?
Onely a humor: if you question why,
His tongue is ne're unfurnisht with a lye.
If you perceive his wits in wetting shrunke,
It commeth of a humor to be drunke:
When you behold his lookes, pale, thin, and poor,
Th'occasion is, his humor and a whore.

Into a barbars shop there came
A carret-colour'd bearded man,
And asking for the boy *Tom Baret*,
Said, give me a *Turn-up* to my *Carret*.

Friendship.

A reall friend a cannon cannot batter.
With nominall friends a squib's a perilous matter.

On Giles and Ioane.

Who sayes that *Giles* and *Joane* at discord be?
Th'observing neighbours, no such mood can see:
Indeed poore *Giles* repents he married her,
But that his *Joane* doth too, & *Giles* would never,
By his good will, be in *Joanes* company,
No more would *Joane* he should.   *Giles* riseth early,
And having got him out of dores is glad:
The like is *Joane*.   But turning home is sad,
And so is *Joane*.   Oft times when *Giles* doth find
Harsh sighs at home, *Giles* wishes he were blind:
All this doth *Joane :* or that his long-yearn'd life
Were quite out spun, the like wish hath his wife.
The children that he keepes, *Giles* sweares are none
Of his begetting, and so sweares *Joane.*
In all affections she concurreth still;
If now with man and wife to will and nill
The selfe same things, a note of concord be;
I know no couple better can agree.

To Gentlewomen with black bags.

Tell mee, who taught you to give so much light
As may entice, not satisfie the sight?
Betraying what may cause us to admire,
And kindle onely lust, not quench desire.

Among your other subtilties this is one,
That you see all, and yet are seene of none.
'Tis the darke lanthorne to the face : oh then
I may conclude there's treason against men.
Whil'st thus you onely do expose your lips,
'Tis but a faire and wantoner eclipse.
    Meant how you will, at once to shew and hide,
    At best its but the modestie of pride.

To a proud Lady.

Is it birth puffes up thy mind ?
Women best borne, are best inclin'd.
Is it thy breeding ? no, I ly'd ;
Women well bred are foes to pride.
Is it thy beauty foolish thing ?
Lay by thy clothes there's no such thing.
Is it thy vertue, that's deny'd,
Vertue is an opposite to pride.
Nay then walke on, I'le say no more,
Who made thee proud can make thee poore.
    The devill onely hath the skill,
    To draw faire fooles to this fowle ill.

On Panurgus.

Panurgus pryes in high and low affaires,
He talks of forraigne, and our civill state :
But for his own, he neither counts nor cares ;
That he refers to fortune and his fate,
    His neighbors faults straight in his face he'l find
    But in a bag he laps his own behind.

On Misus.

They say the unsurer *Misus* hath a mill,
Which men to powder grindeth cruelly ;
But what is that to me ? I feare no ill,
For smaller than I am, I cannot bee.

On a swearing Gallant.

What God commands, this wretched creature loaths,
He never names his Maker, but by oaths.
And weares his tongue, of such a damned fashion,
That swearing is his only recreation.
In morning, even assoon as he doth rise,
He swears his sleep is scarcely out of's eyes ;
Then makes him ready, swearing all the while,
The drowzy weather did him much beguile.
Got ready, he, to dice or tables goes,
Swearing an oath at every cast he throws .
To dinner next, and then in stead of grace,
He swears his stomack is in hungry case.
No sooner din'd, but cals, come take away,
And sweares 'tis late, he must go see a play.
There sits and swears, to all he hears and see's,
This speech is good, that action disagrees.
So takes his oars, and swears he must make hast,
His houre of supper-time is almost past.

On a Mother and her son having but two eyes betwixt them, each one.

A half blind-boy, born of a half blind mother.
Peerelesse for beauty, save compar'd to th'other ;

Faire boy, give her thine eye and she will prove
The queen of beauty, thou the god of love.

To his quill.

Thou hast been wanton, therefore it is meet,
Thou shouldst do penance do it in a sheet.

Of Christ crucified.

When red the sun goes down, we use to say
It is a signe, we shall have a faire day :
Blood red the Sun of Heaven went down from hence
And we have had faire weather ever since.

Vpon Thorough-good an unthrift.

Thy sir name *Thorough-good* befitteth thee,
Thou *Thorough-good*, and good goes thorough thee
Nor thou in good, nor good in thee doth stay,
Both of you, thorough go, and passe away.

In Amorem.

Love, if a god thou art, then evermore thou must
     Be mercifull and just,
If just thou be, O wherefore doth thy dart,
Wound mine alone, and not my mistrisse heart ?
If mercifull, then why am I to paine reserv'd,
Who have thee truly serv'd ?
While shee that for thy power cares not a fly,
Laughs thee to scorn, and lives at liberty :
Then if a god thou wilt accounted be,
Heale me like her, or else wound her like me.

On the new dressings.

Ladyes that weare black cypresse vailes,
Turn'd lately to white linnen railes,
And to your girdle weare your bands;
And shew your armes in stead of hands:
What can yo do in Lent more meet,
As fittest dresse, than weare a sheet:
'Twas once a band, 'tis now a cloake,
An acorne one day proves oake,
Weare but your lawn unto your feet,
And then your band will prove a sheet:
By which device and wise excesse,
You do your pennance in a dresse,
And none shall know, by what they see,
Which lady's censur'd, which goes free.

Thus answered.

Black cypresse vailes are shrouds of night,
White linnen railes are railes of light;
Which though we to our girdles weare,
W'have hands to keep your armes off there;
Who makes our band to be a cloake,
Makes *John* a *Stiles* of *John* an *Oke:*
We weare our linnen to our feet,
Yet need not make our band a sheet.
Your clergie wears as long as we,
Yet that implyes conformitie:
Be wise, recant what you have writ,
Lest you do penance for your wit:

Love-charmes have power to weave a string
Shall tye you, as you ty'd your ring,
Thus by loves sharpe, but just decree
You may be censur'd, we go free.

Amicitia.

What's friendship? 'tis a treasure,
    'tis a pleasure:
Bred 'twixt two worthy spirits,
    by their merits:
'Tis two minds in one, meeting,
    never fleeting:
Two wils in one consenting,
    · each contenting,
One brest in two divided, yet not parted;
A double body, and yet single hearted;
Two bodies making one, through self election,
Two minds, yet having both but one affection,

To Sextus.

Sextus thy wife is faire, that's not amisse,
But she's a scould, tell me how lik'st thou this.

Vxor Fortior.

Will by the warre would seeme a domineerer,
But *Anne* his wife hath beene the ancient-bearer.

There was a man that lost his purse,
And that was a shrewd disaster:

But was it ever knowne before,
That a purse should lose his master?

Fælix donec——

While *Turnus* feasted, not a guest durst faile him,
But being arested, not a guest durst baile him.

In Gallum.

Gallus hath beene this summer in Freezeland,
And now return'd, he speaks such war-like words,
As if I could their English understand,
I feare me they would cut my throat like swords.
He talkes of counter-scarpes and casamates,
Of parapets, curteynes, and palizadoes,
Of flankers, raveling, gabions he prates,
And of false brags, and salleys, and scabadoes:
But to requite such gulling termes as these,
With words of my profession I reply,
I tell of sourching, vouchers, counter-pleas,
Of *Withernams* essoynes, and champertine,
So neither of us understanding the other,
We part as wisely as we came together.

A Farrier Physitian.

A neate Physitian for a Farrier sends,
To dresse his horses, promising him amends:
No (quoth the Farrier) amends is made,
For nothing do we take of our owne trade.

Verbositus.

Verbositus at words from Latine carv'd,
Du's snatch, as if his wits were hunger-starv'd:
And well he du's; for sure so leane 'tis growne,
That from anatomy 'tis hardly knowne.
It is so weake, as (truely) I protest,
Fine phrase rhetoricall 'twill not digest.
   Hark wouldst be wise? by good words ill apply'd
   The asse to be a foole by's own tongue's try'd;
   Then if th'art wise, thy tongue hath the bely'd.

Fatum Supremum.

All buildings are but monuments of death,
All clothes but winding sheets for our last knell,
All dainty fattings for the worms beneath,
All curious musique, but our passing bell;
   Thus death is nobly waited on, for why?
   All that we have is but deaths livery.

In Cupidinem.

Who grafts in blindnesse may mistake his stock,
Love hath no tree, but that whose bark is smock.

On a Picture.

This face here pictur'd time shall longer have,
Then life the substance of it, or the grave,
Yet as I change from this by death I know,
I shall like death, the liker death I grow.

On the City Venice.

When in the Adriatick Neptune saw
How Venice stood, and gave the seas their law,
Boast thy Tarpeian towers, now *Jove* said he,
And *Mars* thy wals, if Tiber 'fore the sea
Thou dost prefer, view both the cities ods,
Thou'lt say that men built Rome, Venice, the gods.

To a Lady that every morning used to paint her face.

Preserve what nature gave you, nought's more base,
Then Belgian colour on a Roman face,
Much good time's lost, you rest your faces debtor,
And make it worse, striving to make it better.

On a Cuckold.

My friend did tax me seriously one morne,
That I would weare, yet could not winde a horne,
And I reply'd he perfect truth should finde it,
Many did weare the horne that could not wind it,
Howe're of all, that man may weare it best,
Who makes claime to it as his ancient crest.

On Taurus.

Ist true that *Taurus* late hath lost his wit?
How can that be, when never he had it?
I could beleeve it, had he fought a fray,
And so perhaps his fingers cut away.

On Man.

What shall I like man to, man so proud,
And yet so miserable? to a cloud,
A vapour vild, and of an abject birth,
Extracted from the humble wombe of earth;
Yet proud, and still aspiring, soares upright,
Till heaven it selfe lookes angry at the sight.
Now 'tis dispersed by the scorching sunné,
New frozen up in some cold region.
Here, and then there, it can no resting find,
But lightly fleetes before each gale of wind:
Each tempest hurries it about, each stormes
Mangles, and rends it into a thousand formes:
Till at length tost by night, consum'd by day,
It melts in teares and vanishes away.

To Coracine.

If so be, *Coracine*, thou had'st disburst
But twenty nobles when I ask't them first,
Th'adst done a timely courtesie, and then
I should have ow'd thee twenty more for 'em.
But since thou did'st it with such strange delay,
After some ten long months, or twelve months stay;
Shall I tell truth? why by you starres that shine,
Th'ast lost thy twenty nobles, *Coracine*.

On Tasso.

Tasso writes verses, and imagines them
Farre longer-liv'd than old *Methusalem*:

When I say nay, he straight sweares in his rage;
Th'are stronger than the iron teeth of age.
Trust thy friends, *Tasso*, when they tell right;
Why should'st thou think so? since in a short nig
Neither the spite of fury, fire, nor flames,
But one poore rat devour'd ten epigrams.

On Stella.

As the pale moon, and stars shin'd clearly bright,
My fairest faire stood gazing on the skyes:
O that I had beene heaven then, that I might?
Have view'd my *Stella* with so many eyes.

Who best friend.

A louse I say: for when a man's distrest,
And others fall off, she stickes surest.

A lecherous gallants blood, a Jesuites
Devisefull braine, the teares of hypocrites,
Salted with jeasts, and scurrill wantonnesse,
Saint *Kitts* tobacco, chopt for herbes all these,
Sod with the fop'ries of Arminian,
Ith' scull of a profound magitian,
And peppar'd well with every seed of evill,
Would make a messe of pottage for the devill.

To fortune.

Thou art a froward jade, and being such,
I cannot scold or raile at thee too much:

Doting on fooles, thou hid'st thee from the wise,
Thou prostitut'st thy selfe to avarice.
Thou runn'st a whoring with the world, and sinne;
Thou cramm'st bold buzzards & lett'st eagles pine;
Thou bowl'st thy golden pieces, where I can
Not get a mite: by the Justitian.
Mantles his students all in robes of state,
And by the gallon makes his fortunate:
Yet I live poore, and while base ideots ride,
Marullo footes in *Cuerpo* by their side.
Untoward trull, could but this hand attatch thee,
Could all my skill, and best endeavours reach thee:
On thy owne wheele (proud dame) I'de make thee spin
Tissues, and Tyrian silkes to clothe mee in:
I'de make thee (blindfold as thou art) find out
All that is rare, and good, the world about,
To make mee happy, and for the least frowne,
I'de braine thee, with the ball thou stand'st upon.

To Momus.

Thou that dost wrest thy wrinkled face awry,
And canst not read these trifles willingly;
May'st thou for ever envy other men,
But none have cause, to envie thee agen.

On Phaulo.

Phaulo weares brave clothes, yet his spirits faile;
Phaulo eates wholsome meate, and yet he's pale,
Phaulo takes physicke, yet his spirits faile;
Phaulo hath good attendance, yet he's pale.

Phaulo's a glutton, yet his spirits faile;
Phaulo drinks deepe, and whores, and yet he's pale.

To Susa.

Why do I scorne to kisse thee? thy nose runnes,
Thy teeth are blacke and rotten in thy gummes:
Why do I scorne to kisse thee? thy breath stinks
Farre worse than twenty fish-stalls, or town sinkes:
Why do I scorne to kisse thee? thou art all
Surfeited, nastie, ill-complexion'd, pale,
Who scornes not (*Susa*) to kisse thee will scarce
Scorne to kisse (I thinke) a sick hang-mans arse.

On Quacksalve.

This man is brother to the wormes, and can
Not live, but by corruption of man:
Deaths harbinger, that for bare one he saves,
Sends hundreds young, and old to people graves.
Yet still he lives in repute; he hath pelfe,
And each good deed he does, proclames it selfe,
But every bad one (as perforce it must)
With the dead corse lyes buried in the dust.
Diseases are his health, and Quacksalve thrives
By purchasing ill fame, and selling lives.
'Tis well he knowes me not: for I must think.
If I come in his hands, hee'l make me stink.

On Saint Bernard.

Saint *Bernards* painted halfe, and ever shall:
For not a man a live can paint him all.

On Captaine Drad-nought, and Lieutenant Slaughter.

Slaughter he swels, and proudly gives the lye,
Which *Drad-nought* vowes to make him justifie.
Slaughter will kill, or else be kill'd ith' place:
Lieutenant curses, Captaine sweares apace.
Lieutenant *Slaughter* belches out disdaine,
And Captaine *Drad-nought* breathes all fire againe
The rest, good gentlemen, stand trembling there,
Ready to quit the taverne all, for feare:
There's not a man, but sues, and wooes, and sends
For what the house can yeeld, to make 'em friends.
Anchovise, wine, dry'd tongues, are brought in hast,
Which sight perswades their stubborne soules at last.
Anger abates, the storme is over-blowne,
And in rich sack they drinke the quarrell downe.

Why do the clouds showr rain so fast down? why,
Blusters the north-winde so impetuously?
This is the reason, as divines give out,
Heaven sighs, and weeps for us, since we cannot.

On Poets.

Why do I climb Parnassus, since my hope
Can but expect cold water at the top?
Why do I like a taper in the night,
Consume my selfe still, to give others light?
If fortunes minions I should celebrate,
All my reward were, to be flouted at.

Wit, as a thing above them, they cry downe,
Rather they'll saginate a beefe braind clowne.
To laugh at 'em, or like fond easie snites,
Be flatter'd out of all by parasites.
Cock-pits and revels share their store; cards may
Shuffle away whole lordships in a day:
But to a poet charity's so cold,
They'le not afford the rust wip'd from their gold.
He that can frame a morall glasse, whereby
To dresse them in the trim of honesty;
He that can stick them in the starry skie,
And mate their glories with eternity,
Must live a recluse to all happinesse,
His vertues checkt, and clouded in distresse.
Avaunt then Muses nine, avaunt quick from me,
Now whilst my blooming yeers are growing on me
Phœbus his barren laurell Ile refuse,
And the fat olive with *Minerva* chuse.

To Tasso.

Well *Tasso* shalt thou dine with me,
If thou wilt bring good meat with thee,
And lusty wine, and pleasant wit,
And lests, and mirth to season it.
Well shalt thou dine with me to day,
If thou wilt bring but what I say:
For thy Marulloes purse, heavens know,
Lies full of dust, and spiders now.
But I will have my Doxy here,
And True-wit too, and Chanteclere

Shall runne division on his lute,
And make his voice together sute
In tunes of love, with other things,
As he can well : who when he sings,
Thou'lt wish (although thine owne be long)
An asses eares to heare his song.

On Pæto.

Pæto came by me like a man possest,
Lugging his locks, and beating on his brest.
And O ! he cryed, is any man like me ?
I've buried my rich wife, yet lives you see.
My *Pæto* is right valiant ; his wife gives
Two thousand pounds, and leaves him : yet he lives.

On Torquato.

Torquato now drinks nothing but small beere,
Sack (he sayes) kils us : why what need we feare ?
The Scots will cut our throats, if we dye not :
We shall but put a trick upon a Scot.

To the Reader.

Excuse me Reader, though I now and than,
In some light lines, do shew my selfe a man ;
Nor be so sowre, some wanton words to blame,
They are the language of an Epigramme.

On Battus.

Battus doth brag he hath a world of books,
His studies maw holds more then well it may,

But seld' or never, he upon them looks,
And yet he looks upon them every day.
He looks upon their outside, but within
He never looks, nor never will begin :
Because it cleane against his nature goes
To know mens secrets, so he keeps them close.

On Prue.

Prues nose hangs down so low, one would suppose
When ere she gapes, that *Prue* would eat her nose.

To Gripe.

Gripe keeps his coyn well, and his heaps are great,
For which he seems wise in his own conceit;
Be not deceiv'd *Gripe*, for ought I can see,
Thy bags in this sence are as wise as thee.

On Man and Woman.

When man and woman dyes, as poets sung,
His heart's the last that stirs, of hers the tongue.

On Womans will.

How dearly doth the honest husband buy,
His wives defect of will when she doth dy ?
Better in death by will to let her give,
Then let her have her will while she doth live.

Spangle the spruce Gal:

Spruce Spangles like to a cynamon tree ?
His outside is of much more worth then he.

To Chærilus.

Eat toste and oyl, eat supple herbs and loos,
For thou loo'st wondrous costive *Chærilus*.

In Paulum.

By lawful mart, and by unlawfull stealth,
Paulus from th'ocean hath deriv'd much wealth :
But on the land, a little gulfe there is,
Wherein he drowneth all that wealth of his.

Vestitus peritus.

Clitus goes oft time clad in suits of scarlet,
That els no colour had to play the varlet.

Of Poetus.

Poetus with fine sonnets painted forth
This and that foul ladies beauties worth :
He shews small wit therein, and for his pains,
By my consent, he never shall reap gains ;
Why, what needs *Poets* paint them, O sweet elves !
When ladies paint their beauties best themselves.

Of Shift the Sharker.

Shift swears he keeps none but good company,
For, though th'are such as he did never see,
Worse than himself he's sure they cannot be.

On an Vpstart.

Pray wrong not (*late coyn'd*) give the man his right,
He's made a gentleman although no knight,

For now 'tis cloaths the gentleman doth make;
Men from gay cloaths their pedigree do take;
But wot you what's the arms to such mens house?
Why this—hands chancing of a rampant louse.

Volens Nolens.

Will with provisio wills you testifie,
Has made his will, but hath no will to dye.

Ad Clodium.

Wit, once thou said'st was worth thy weight in gold,
Though now't be common for a trifle sold;
It dearer seems to thee that get'st not any,
(When thou shouldst use it) for thy love or money.

In Getam.

Geta from wool and weaving first began,
Swelling and swelling to a gentleman;
When he was gentleman and bravely dight,
He left not swelling till he was a knight:
At last (forgetting what he was at first)
He sweld to be a lord, and then he burst.

To Emson.

Emson thou once in Dutch wouldst court a wench,
But to thy cost she answered thee in French.

In Fimum.

Fimus is coach'd, and for his farther grace
Doth ask his friends how he becomes the place;

Troth I should tell him, the poor coach hath wrong
And that a cart would serve to carry dung.

In Flaccum.

The false knave *Flaccus* once a bribe I gave;
The more fool I.to bribe so false a knave:
But he gave back my bribe, the more fool he,
That for my folly did not cousen me.

Of womens naked breasts.

In open shops flyes often blow that flesh,
Which in close safes might be kept longer fresh,
They but invite flesh-flyes, whose full spread paps
Like road wayes lye between their lips and laps.

On Morcho.

Morcho for haste was married in the night,
What needed day? his fair young wife is light.

On a Bragadocio.

Don *Lollus* brags, he comes from noble blood,
Drawn down from *Brutus* line; 'tis very good,
If this praise-worthy be, each flea may then,
Boast of his blood more then some gentlemen.

Edens vomens.

Cacus that sups so duly at the Rose,
Casts up the reckning truly ere he goes.

On a Pump stopt with stones.

M. I'le cut it down, I swear by this same hand,
  If 'twill not run, it shall no longer stand.
R. Pray sir be patient, let your pump alone,
  How can it water make when't hath the stone?
Yet did he wisely when he did it fell,
For in so doing he did make it well.

Of Prittle-prattle.

Though th'danger be not great, of all tame cattle,
Yet the most troublesome is Prittle-prattle.

In Aulum.

Thou still art muttring *Aulus* in mine eare,
Love me and love my dog: I will I swear,
Thou ask'st but right; and *Aulus*, truth to tell,
I think thy dog deserves my love as well.

Ad Tilenum.

Tilens 'cause th'art old, fly not the field
Where youthfull *Cupid* doth his banner wield;
For why? this god, old men his souldiers stil'd;
None loves but he who hath been twice a child.

To Vellius.

Thou swearst I bowl as well as most men do,
The most are bunglers, therein thou say'st true.

Three Genders.

A wife although most wise and chast,
  is of the *doubtfull* gender;
A quean o'th'*common:* feminines,
  are women small and tender.

Of Brawle.

Brawle loveth brabling, as he loves his life,
Leave him for dead, when he leaves stirring strife.

In Paulum.

Paul, what my cloak doth hide thou fain wouldst know
Wer't to be seen I would not cover't so.

Of sleep and death.

That death is but a sleep I not deny,
Yet when I next would sleep, I would not dye.

Vpon Methusus.

Methusus ask'd me why I call'd him sot,
I answer made, because he lov'd the pot,
For while *Methusus* busie is with it,
The fool I'm sure's as busie with his wit.

On Thraso.

Thraso goes lame with blows he did receive
In a late duell, if you'l him believe.

News.

When news doth come, if any would discusse
The letter of the word, resolve it thus:
News is convey'd by letter, word, or mouth,
And comes to us from *North, East, West,* and *South.*

Of Rufus.

Rufus had rob'd his host, and being put to it,
Said, I am an arrant rogue if I did do it.

Of Marcus.

When *Marcus* fail'd, a borrowed sum to pay
Unto his friend at the appointed day;
'Twere superstition for a man, he sayes,
To be a strict observer of set dayes.

Of a Thief.

A thief arrested, and in custody
Under strong guards of armed company,
Askt why they held him so; Sir, quoth the chief
We hold you for none other then a thief.

Of Motion.

Motion brings heat, and thus we see it prov'd,
Most men are hot and angry when they'r mov'd.

Formall the Fashionist.

Formall all form and fashion is, for matter,
Who sayes he sees it in him, doth but flatter;

Open and search him, you shall quickly find
With what course canvas his soft silks are lin'd.

Ad Scriptorem quend.

Half of your book is to an index growne,
You give your book *contents,* your reader none.

Riches. -

Gold's th'onely God, rich men bear rule,
  Money makes majesty:
Rich *Pluto,* not plain *Plato* now,
  Speaks with applause most high.

On Sextus.

Sextus doth wish his wife in heaven were,
Where can she have more happinesse then there?

Secreta nobis.

Tassus from Temple-stairs by water goes,
To *Westminster,* and back to Temple rowes,
Belike he loves not trot too much the street
Or surbait on the stones his tender feet:
Tut! come, there's something in't must not be known,
But sir beleev't, *The debt is not his own.*

Of Text-corrupters.

Bad commentators spoyl the best of books;
So God gives meat, (they say) the devil sends cooks.

On a Drawer drunk.

Drawer with thee now even is thy wine,
For thou hast pierst his hogs-head, and he thine.

Vpon the weights of a Clock.

I wonder times so swift, when as I see,
Upon her heels, such lumps of lead to be.

On Cynna.

Because I am not of a gyants stature,
Despise me not, nor praise thy liberall nature,
For thy huge limbs; that you are great 'tis true,
And that I'm little in respect of you:
The reason of our growths is eas'ly had,
You, many had perchance; I but one dad.

On Alastrus.

Alastrus hath not coyn, nor spirit, nor wit,
I think hee's only then for Bedlam fit.

Of Mendacio.

Mendacio pretends to tell men news:
And that it may be such, himselfe doth use
To make it: but that will no longer need,
Let him tell truth, it will be news indeed.

On Landanno.

Landanno in his gallant bravery,
Ruffled his silks, lookt big, and thrust me by:

And still as often as he meets me so,
My home-spun cloth must to the channell go.
Advise thee well *Landanno*, children note,
And fools admire thee for thy velvet coat :
I keep (*Landanno*) in repute with such,
As think they cannot scorn poor thee too much.
But thou canst squire fine madams, thou canst vail
Thy cap and feather, cringe, and wag thy tail
Most decently : Now by you stars that shine,
So thou transcend'st me : Take the wall, 'tis thine.

On Shanks.

Shanks swears he fasts ; and always cryes for beef :
O how he fasts ! that's how fast eats the theef !

Cito bene.

Sir *John* at *Mattins* prayes he might dispatch,
Who by true promise is to bowl a match.

Of Pertinax.

It will, it must, it shall be so,
Saith *Pertinax;* but what's the reason trow ?
Nay, that I cannot tell, nor doth he know.

To valiant Dammee.

Dammee thy brain is valiant, 'tis confest ;
Thou more, that with it every day dar'st jest
Thy self into fresh braules ; but call'd upon,
With swearing *Damme*, answer'st every one.
Keep thy self there, and think thy valour right,
He that dares *damne* himself, dares more then fight.

On Cornuto.

Cornuto is not jealous of his wife,
Nor e're mistrusts her too lascivious life,
Ask him the reason why he doth forbear,
Hee'l answer straight, it cometh with a fear.

On a Shrew.

A froward shrew being blam'd because she show'd
Not so much reverence as by right she ow'd
Unto her husband, she reply'd he might
Forbear complaint of me, I do him right ;
His will is mine, he would bear rule, and I
Desire the like, onely in sympathy.

Of Lawlesse.

Lawlesse the worst times liketh best, why ist ?
Because then *Lawlesse* may doe what he list.

A rich Curre.

Dru dares good men deprave because hee's rich,
Whether more fool or knave, I know not which.

On a Youth married to an Old Woman.

A smooth-fac'd youth, what wedded to an old
Decrepit shrew ! (such is the power of gold)
Thy fortune I dare tell ; perchance thou'lt have
At supper dainties, but in bed a grave.

On a Fly in a glasse.

A fly out of his glasse a guest did take,
E're with the liquor he his thirst would slake ;

When he had drunk his fill, again the fly
Into the glasse he put, and said, though I
Love not flyes in my drink, yet others may,
Whose humour I nor like, nor will gain-say.

On Collimus.

If that *Collimus* any thing do lend,
Or dog, or horse, or hawk unto his friend,
He to endear the borrowers love the more,
Saith he ne'r lent it any one before,
Nor would to any but to him : His wife
Having observ'd these speeches all her life,
Behinde him forks her fingers, and doth cry,
To none but you, I'de do this courtesie.

To Loquax.

Loquax, to hold thy tongue would do thee wrong,
For thou wouldst be no man but for thy tongue.

Good wits jump.

Against a post a scholar chanc'd to strike
At unawares his head; like will to like :
Good wits will jump (quoth he:) if that be true,
The title of a block-head is his due.

On Womens Masks.

It seems that masks do women much disgrace,
Sith when they wear them they do hide their face.

Of Sawcy the Intruder.

Sawcy, though uninvited, is so rude,
As into every comp'ny to intrude;
But he's no fit companion for any,
Who alwayes makes the number one too many.

Vpon a pair of Tongs.

The burnt child dreads the fire; if this be true,
Who first invented tongs its fury knew.

Lawyers and Souldiers.

If Lawyers had for *Term*, a tearm of warre,
Souldiers would be as rich as lawyers are;
But here's the difference 'tween guns and gowns,
These take good angels, th'other take crack't crowns.

On Momus.

Momus can call another fool, but he
Can never make his brain and wit agree.

Woman.

A *woman* is a book, and often found
To prove far better in the sheets then bound:
No marvail then, why men take such delight
Above all things to *study in the night.*

Clytus cunning.

Clytus the barber doth occasion fly,
Because 'tis bald, and he gains nought thereby.

Rich promises.

Lords promise soon, but to perform are long,
Then would their purse-strings were ty'd to their tongue.

On Comptulus.

I wonder'd *Comptulus*, how thy long hair,
In comely curles should show so debonair,
And every hair in order be, when as
Thou couldst not trim it by a looking glasse,
Nor any barber did thy tresses pleat ;
'Tis strange ; but *Monsieur* I conceive the feat ;
When you your hair do kemb, you off it take,
And order't as you please for fashion sake.

On Gellius.

In building of his house, *Gellius* hath spent
All his revenues and his ancient rent,
Ask not a reason, why *Gellius* is poor,
His greater house hath turn'd him out of door.

To Ponticus.

At supper time will *Pontus* visit me,
I'd rather have his room then company ;
But if him, from me I can no ways fright,
I'd have him visit me each fasting night.

Balbus.

Balbus a verse on *Venus* boy doth scan,
But ere 'twas finish'd *Cupid's* grown a man.

On a Pot-Poet.

What lofty verses *Cælus* writes? it is
But when his head with wine oppressed is :
So when great drops of rain fall from the skies
In standing pools, huge bubbles will arise.

On Onellus.

Thou never supp'st abroad, *Onellus*, true,
For at my home I'm sure to meet with you.

Of professed Atheists.

If even devils themselves believe and tremble,
Atheists profest methinks should but dissemble.

To Termagant.

My *Termagant*, as I have ought to save,
I neither cal'd thee fool, nor knave :
That which I cal'd thee is a thing well known.
A trifle not worth thinking on :
What I suppose thy self wilt easily grant,
I cal'd thee cuckold, *Termagant*.

On a Vertuous Talker.

If vertue's alwayes in thy mouth, how can
It e're have time to reach thy heart, fond man?

To Severus.

Beleeve *Severus*, that in these my rimes
I tax no person but the common crimes.

Vpon Pigs devouring a bed of Penny-royall,
commonly called Organs.

A good wife once a bed of organs set,
The pigs came in and eat up every whit,
The good man said, wife you your garden may
Hogs Norton call, here pigs on organs play.

On Gubs.

Gubs calls his children kitlins : and wo'd bound
(Some say) for joy to see those kitlins dround.

On a Fortune-teller.

The influence of th'stars are known to thee,
By whom thou canst each future fortune see :
Yet sith thy wife doth thee a cuckold make,
Tis strange they do not that to thee partake.

To sweet sir Out-side.

Th'expence in odours, is a foolish sin,
Except thou couldst sweeten thy corps within.

On a Gallant.

A glittering gallant, from a prancing steed,
Alighting down desir'd a boy with speed
To hold his horse a while, he made reply,
Can one man hold him fast ? 'twas answer'd, I :
If then one man can hold him sir, you may
Do it your self, quoth he, and slunk away.

To Eras-mus.

That thou art a man each of thy learn'd works shows,
But yet thy name tels us *thou wast a mouse.*

On Bunce.

Money thou ow'st me; prethee fix a day
For payment promis'd, though thou never pay:
Let it be dooms-day; nay, take longer scope;
Nay when th'art honest, let me have some hope.

On an empty House.

Lollus by night awak'd heard theeves about
His house, and searching narrowly throughout
To find some pillage there, he said, you may
By night, but I can find nought here by day.

A trim Barber.

Neat Barber trim, I must commend thy care,
Which dost all things exactly to a haire.

On a bragging Coward.

Corsus in camp, when as his mates betook
Themselves to dine, encourag'd them and spoke,
Have a good stomach lads, this night we shall
In heaven at supper keep a festivall.
But battail join'd he fled away in hast,
And said, I had forgot, this night I fast.

On a great Nose.

Thy nose no man can wipe, *Proclus*, unless
He have a hand as big as *Hercules* :
When thou dost sneeze the sound thou dost not hear
Thy nose is so far distant from thine ear.

On an unequall pair.

Fair *Phillis* is to churlish *Priscus* wed,
As stronger wine with waters mingled ;
Priscus his love to *Phillis* more doth glow
With fervency then fire ; hers cold as snow :
'Tis well, for if their flames alike did burn,
One house would be too hot to serve their turn

In Quintum.

Quintus is burnt, and may thereof be glad,
For being poor he hath a good pretence
At every church to crave benevolence,
For one that had by fire lost all he had.

On a changeable Rayment.

Know you why *Lollus* changeth every day,
His perriwig, his face, and his array ?
'Tis not because his comings in are much,
Or 'cause hee'l swill it with the roaring Dutch ;
But 'cause the sergeants (who a writ have had
Long since against him) should not know the lad.

On Guesse.

Guesse cuts his shooes, and limping goes about
To have men think he's troubled with the gout,
But 'tis no gout (believe it) but hard beere,
Whose acrimonious humour bites him here.

On Stale-Batch.

For all night-sins with other wives unknown
Batch now doth daily penance in his own.

To sir Guilty.

Guilty, be wise; and though thou knowest the crimes
Be thine I tax; yet do not own my rimes;
'Twere madnesse in thee to betray thy fame,
And person to the world, ere I thy name.

Veritas subverta.

Luke that a man on hors-back met but late,
Would simply seem thus to equívocate,
And strong maintain 'gainst them, contend who dare,
'Twas meerly, but a taylor and a mare.

On Hugh.

Hugh should have gone to Oxford th'other day,
But turn'd at Tiburn, and so lost his way.

On a Painted Madam.

Men say y'are fair; and fair ye are, 'tis true,
But (hark!) we praise the painter now, not you.

On Barossa.

Barossa boasts his pedigree, although
He knows no letter of the Christ-crosse row,
His house is ancient, and his gentry great,
For what more ancient e're was heard of yet
Then is the family of fools? how than
Dare you not call *Barossa* gentleman?

Experto credendum.

How durst *Capritius* call his wedlock whore,
But that he speaks it *plusquam per narratum*.
Nam ipse teste: what require you more,
Unlesse youl'd have it *magis approbatum?*

On Jack Cut-purse.

Jack Cut-purse is, and hath been patient long,
For hee's content to pocket up much wrong.

On Afer.

Afer hath sold his land and bought a horse,
Whereon he pranceth to the royall Burse,
To be on hors-back he delights; wilt know?
'Cause then his company he'd higher show:
But happy chance tall *Afer* in his pride,
Mounts a gunnelly and on foot doth ride.

On Charismus.

Thou hast compos'd a book, which neither age,
Nor future time shall hurt through all their rage;

For how can future times or age invade,
That work which perished as soon as made?

Facilis descensus averni.

The way to hell is easie, th'other day,
A blind man thither quickly found the way.

Age and Youth.

Admire not youth, despise not age, although
Some young are grave, most old men children grow.

On Orus.

Orus sold wine, and then tobacco, now
He aqua-vitæ doth his friends allow.
What e're he had was sold to save his life,
And now turn'd pander, he doth sell his wife.

On Sneape.

Sneape has a face so brittle, that it breaks
Forth into blushes, whensoere he speaks.

On Acerra.

Tobacco hurts the brain physitians say,
Doth dull the wit, and memory decay,
Yet fear not thou Acerra, for 'twill ne're
Hurt thee so much by use, as by thy feare.

Empta nostra.

Madam La Foy wears not those locks for nought,
Ask at the shop else, where the same she bought.

On Briso.

Who private lives, lives well, no wonder then,
You doe absent you from the sight of men,
For out of doors you ne'r by day appear,
What, is a sergeant such a huge bug-bear ? *

A Foolish Querie.

How rich a man is, all desire to know;
But none inquires if good he be or no.

On the King of Swedens Picture.

Who but the half of this neat picture drew,
That it could ne're be fully done, well knew.

B. J. answer to a Thief bidding him stand.

Fly villain hence, or by thy coat of steel,
I'le make thy heart my brazen bullet feel,
And send that thrice as theevish soule of thine
To hell, to wear the devils valentine.

Thiefs reply.

Art thou great *Ben?* or the revived ghost
Of famous *Shakespeare?* or some drunken host?
Who being tipsie with thy muddy beer,
Dost think thy rimes shall daunt my soule with fear?
Nay know base slave, that I am one of those
Can take a purse as well in verse as prose;
And when th' art dead write this upon thy herse,
Here lyes a poet that was rob'd in verse.

* The fourth line in ed. 1641 runs thus :
Since last you lost i'th pillory your eare.

Nothing new.

Nothing is new : we walk were others went ;
There's no vice now but has his president.

On Cupid.

Cupid hath by his sly and subtill art,
A certain arrow shot, and pierc'd my heart ;
What shall I doe to be reveng'd on love ?
There is but one way, and that one I'll prove ;
I'le steale his arrows, and will head them new
With womens hearts, and then they'l ne'r fly true.

A Tobacconist.

All dainty meats I doe defie,
Which feed men fat as swine,
He is a frugall man indeed
That on a leaf can dine.
He needs no napkin for his hands,
His fingers ends to wipe,
That keeps his kitchin in a box,
And roast-meat in a pipe.

Feeble standing.

Mat being drunken, much his anger wreaks
On's wife ; but stands to nothing that he speaks.

Long and Lazie.

That was the proverb. Let my mistriss be
Lazie to others ; but be-long to me.

On the Tobaconist.

If mans flesh be like swines, as it is said
The metamorphosis is sooner made :
Then full fac'd *Gnatho* no tobacco take,
Smoaking your corps, lest bacon you do make.

Another.

Tom I commend thee above all I know,
That sold'st thy cushion for a pipe of To——
For now 'tis like if e're thou study more,
Thou'lt sit to't harder then thou didst before.

On Button the grave-maker.

Ye powers above and heavenly poles,
Are graves become but *Button*-holes ?

On long hair.

Lucas long hair down to his shoulders wears,
And why ? he dares not cut it for his ears.

To a stale Lady.

Thy wrinkles are no more, nor less,
Then beautie turn'd to sowerness.

A Crab is restorative.

The crab of the wood
Is sawce very good,
  For the crab of the foaming sea ;
But the wood of a crab
Is sawce for a drab
  That will not her husband obey.

Alius altior.

Would you with *Cajus* offer now confer
In such familiar sort as heretofore?
And not observe he's grown an officer,
That looks for adoration ten times more?
Tut! what of pedegree, or *turpe domo.*
Tis not so now ye see, *nam ecce homo.*

Sorte tua contentus.

If adverse fortune bring to passe,
And will that thou an asse must be;
Then be an asse, and live an asse,
For out of question wise is he
    That undergoes with humble mind,
    The state that chance hath him assign'd.

On a pretender to Prophecy.

Ninety two years the world as yet shall stand,
If it do stand or fall at your command;
But say, why plac'd you not the worlds end nigher
Lest ere you dy'd you might be prov'd a lyer?

Mart. lib. 8. Epigr. 69.

Old poets onely thou dost praise,
    And none but dead ones magnifie;
Pardon *Vocerta*, thee to please,
    I am not yet in mind to die.

On a Gamester.

For hundred-thousands *Matho* playes;
    Olus what's that to thee?

Not thou by means thereof, I trow,
   But *Matho* poor shall be.

Parcus profusus.

Old doting *Claudus* that rich miser known,
Made drunk one night, and jumping but with *Joan*
Was forc't not only to discharge the shot,
But keep the bastard which the gull ne'r got.

On Fr. Drake.

Sir *Drake*, whom well the worlds end knew,
   Which thou didst compasse round,
And whom both poles of heaven once saw,
   Which north and south do bound,
The stars above would make thee known,
   If men here silent were ;
The sun himselfe cannot forget,
   his fellow traveller.

B. J. approbation of a copy of verses.

One of the witty sort of gentlemen,
That held society with learned *Ben*——
Shew'd him some verses of a tragick sense ;
Which did his ear much curious violence ;
But after *Ben* had been a kinde partaker
Of the sad lines, he needs must know the maker ;
What unjust man he was, that spent his time,
And banish'd reason to advance his rime :
Nay gentle *Ben*, replyes the gentleman,
I see I must support the poet than ;

Although those humble strains are not so fit
For to please you, hee's held a pretty wit;
Is he held so? (sayes *Ben*) so may a goos,
Had I the holding,. I would let him loos.

Vt pluma persona.

Why wears *Laurentius* such a lofty feather?
Because he's proud and foolish both together.

Gain and Gettings.

When other gain much by the present cast,
The coblers getting time, is at the last.

Domina prædominans.

Ill may *Radulphus* boast of rule or riches,
That lets his wife rule him, and wear the breeches.

On Doll.

Doll she so soone began the wanton trade;
She ne'r remembers that she was a mayde.

To a Nose and Teeth very long.

Gape 'gainst the sun, and by thy teeth and nose
'Tis easie to perceive how the day goes.

On a Welshman and an Englishman.

There was a time a difference began,
Between a Welshman and an Englishman,
And thus it was; the Englishman would stand
Against all argument, that this our land

Was freest of her fruits : there is a place,
Quoth he, whose ground so fruitfull is of grasse,
But throw a staffe in't but this night, you shall
Not see't the morrow, 'twould be cover'd all.
The Welshman cry'd, 'tis true it might lye under
The o'r-grown grass, which is with us no wonder :
For turn your horse into our fruitfull ground,
And before morning come, he shan't be found.

On Pride.

Why Pride to others doth her selfe prefer,
The reason's clear, she's heir to *Lucifer*.

On Skrew.

Skrew lives by·shifts ; yet swears by no small oaths ;
For all his shifts, he cannot shift his cloathes.

O Mores.

Now *vertu's* hid with *follies* jugling mist,
And hee's no man that is no humorist.

To Teltale.

Thy glowing ears, to hot contention bent,
Are not unlike red herrings broyl'd in lent.

Sperando pariens.

Hodg hir'd him such a house, at such a rent,
As might 'gainst marriage, much his state augment ;
But lingring fates did so his hopes prevent,
As *Hodg* perforce must fly, for all was spent.

On a Souldier.

The souldier fights well, and with good regard,
But when he's lame, he lies at an ill ward.

Vivens mortuis.

What makes young *Brutus* beare so high his head,
And on the sudden gallant it so brave?
Pray understand sir; 's father's newly dead,
Who hath so long been wish'd for laid in's grave.

A secret necessity.

What makes *F. G.* wear still one pair of hose?
Ask *Banks* the broker; he the businesse knows.

On Garret and Chambers.

Garret and his friend *Chambers* having done
Their city businesse, walkt to *Paddington*,
And coming neer the fatall place, where men,
I mean offenders, ne'r return agen,
Looking on Tyburn in a merriment,
Sayes *Chambers*, here's a pretty tenement
Had it a Garret: *Garret* hearing that,
Replyes, friend *Chambers* I do wonder at
Your simple censure, and could mock you for it,
There must be Chambers, e'r there be a Garret.

Dubium indubitatum.

Say *Parnels* children prove not one like th'other;
The best is yet, she's sure th'ad both one mother.

On Linnit.

Linnit plays rarely on the lute, we know;
And sweetly sings, but yet his breath sayes no.

On Vsuring Gripe.

Gripe feels no lameness of his knotty gout,
His moneys travell for him in and out.
And though the soundest legs goe every day,
He toyls to be at hell as soon as they.

A phrase in Poetry.

Fairer then that word faire, why so she must,
Or be as black as *Timothies* toasted crust.

A Witt-all.

Jeppa thy wit will ne'r endure a touch,
Thou knowst so little, and dost speak so much.

Ad Lectorem.

Is't possible that thou my book hast bought,
That said'st 'twas nothing worth? why was it nought;
Read it agen, perchance thy wit was dull,
Thou may'st finde something at the second pull:
Indeed at first thou nought didst understand;
For shame get something at the second hand.

On Skinns.

Skinns he din'd well to day; how do you think?
His nayles they were his meat, his reume the drink.

Suum cuique pulchrum.

Posthumus not the last of many more,
Asks why I write in such an idle vain,
Seeing there are of epigrams such store ;
O give me leave to tell thee once again,
  That epigrams are fitted to the season,
  Of such as best know how to make rime reason.

Certa dissimulans.

Monsieur Piero's wife trades all in French,
And coyly simpring cryes, *Pardona moy :*
As who should think, she's sure no common wench
But a most true dissembler, *par ma foy.*

In magnis voluisse sat est.

In matters great to will it doth suffice :
I blush to hear how loud this proverb lyes,
For they that ow great sums by bond or bill,
Can never cancell them with meer good will.

As proud as witlesse Dracus.

Dracus his head is highly by him born,
And so by straws are empty heads of corn.

Saltem videretur.

A Welshman and an Englishman disputed,
Which of their lands maintain'd the greatest state ;
The Englishman the Welshman quite confuted,
Yet would the Welshman nought his brags abate,

Ten cooks, quoth he, in *Wales* one wedding fees,
Truth, quoth the other, each man tosts his cheese.

Knowing and not knowing.

Cosmus by custome taunts each man,
And yet can nought of reason scan,
How can that be, when who knows least
Knows he should wise be, that would jest :
Then thus no further I allow,
That *Cosmus* knows, but knows not how.

Stupid Binus.

Sith time flyes fast away, his safest flight
Binus prevents with dreaming day and night.

Postrema pessima.

Cacus in's cunning ne'r so prov'd o'r-reacht
As now at last, who must be halter-stretcht.

On his Mistris.

My love and I for kisses play'd,
She would keep stakes, I was content,
And when I won she would be paid ;
This made me ask her what she meant,
Saith she, since you are in this wrangling vain,
Take you your kisses, and give me mine again.

On a proud Maid.

She that will eat her breakfast in her bed,
And spend the morn in dressing of her head,

And sit at dinner like a maiden-bride,
And talk of nothing all day but of pride;
God in mercy may do much to save her,
But what a case is he in that shall have her?

Tempus edax rerum.

Time eateth all things, could the poets say,
The times are chang'd, our times drink all away.

Facies ignota.

Why should not *Rubin* rich apparell wear,
That's left more money then an asse can bear?
Can any guesse him by his outward guise,
But that he may be generous and wise?

On a coy Woman.

She seems not won, yet won she is at length;
In loves war, women use but halfe their strength.

On bed keeping.

Bradus the smith hath often sworn and sed,
That no disease should make him keep his bed;
His reason was, I oft have heard him tell it,
He wanted money, therefore he would sell it.

On a man stealing a Candle from a Lanthorn.

One walking in the street, a winter night,
Climb'd to a lanthorn, thought t'have stole the light,
But taken in the manner and descri'd
By one o'th'servants, who look'd and cry'd,

Whose there: what d'you? who doth our lanthorn
    handle?
Nothing, said he, but onely snuffe the candle.

On Fraternus.

Fraternus' opinions show his reason weak,
He held the nose was made for man to speak.

Little and loud.

Little you are: for womens sake be proud;
For my sake next, (though little) be not loud.

On a French Fencer, that challenged Church an English Fencer.

The fencing Gaules in pride and gallant vaunt,
Challeng'd the English at the fencing skill,
The fencer *Church*, or the *Church* militant,
His errors still reprov'd and knock'd him still;
But sith our *Church* him disciplin'd so sore,
He (rank recusant) comes to Church no more.

On Gella.

Gella is light, and like a candle wasteth,
Even to the snuffe, that stinketh more it lasteth.

On I. Lipsius who bequeathed his Gown to the V. Mary.

A dying Latinist of great renown,
Unto the Virgin *Mary* gave his gown;
And was not this false Latine so to joyn
With female gender, the case masculine?

On two striving together.

Two falling out, into a ditch they fell,
Their falling out was ill; but in, was well.

A Lawyers Will.

A lawyer being sick and extreame ill,
Was moved by his friends to make his will,
Which soon he did, gave all the wealth he had
To frantick persons, lunatick and mad;
And to his friends this reason did reveale;
(That they might see, with equity hee'd deal)
From mad mens hands I did my wealth receive,
Therefore that wealth to mad mens hands I leave.

Youth and Age.

Age is deformed, youth unkinde,
We scorn their bodies, they our minde.

Somnus decipiens.

Dod sweetly dreamt this other night had found
In gold and silver ne'r an hundred pound,
But waking felt he was with fleas sore bitten,
And further smelt he had his shirt be——

To a Shoomaker.

What boots it thee to follow such a trade,
That's alwayes under foot and underlaid?

Death.

The lives of men seem in two seas to swim,
Death comes to young folks, and old go to him.

Quos ego, &c.
Rufus in rage the pots flings down the stairs,
And threats to pull the drawer by the ears,
For giving such attendance : Slave (sayes he)
Where's thine observance ? Ha ! must such as we
Be no more waited on ? Go, bring to pay,
And keep my rapier till I come this way.

A Disparity.
Children fondly blab truth,
  and fools their brothers ;
Women have learn'd more wisdome
  of their mothers.

To Maledict.
Thou speakest ill, not to give men their dues,
But speakest ill, because thou canst not chuse.

On Newter Ned.
Newter convict of publick wrongs to men,
Takes private beatings, and begins agen ;
Two kinds of valour he doth chew at once,
Active in's brains, and passive in his bones.

Interpone tuis &c.
Not mirth, nor care alone, but interwreath'd
Care gets mirths stomach, mirth makes care long
  breath'd.

Ignotus sibi.

Fastidius finds it *Nimis ultra posse*,
How to distinguish of *Teipsum nosce:*
I do not marvell much it should be so,
For why the coxcomb, will himselfe not know.

On Craw.

Craw cracks in sirrop, and do's stinking say,
Who can hold that (my friends) that will away.

Pot Poet.

Poet and pot differ but in a letter,
Which makes the poet love the pot the better.

Content.

Content is all we aim at with our store;
If that be had with little, what needs more?

Fast and loose.

Paphus was marry'd all in hast,
  And now to rack doth run;
So knitting of himselfe too fast,
  He hath himselfe undone.

Tortus.

Tortus accus'd to lye, to fawn, to flatter,
Said he but set a good face on the matter;
Then sure he borrow'd it, for 'tis well known,
Tortus ne're wore a good face of his own.

On Raspe.

Raspe plays at nine holes; and 'tis known he gets
Many a teaster by his game, and bets;
But of his gettings there's but little signe;
When one hole wasts more then he gets by nine.

Impar impares odit.

Sotus hates wise men, for himselfe is none,
And fools he hates, because himselfe is one.

Similis doctrina libello.

Crœsus of all things loveth not to buy
So many books of such diversity :
Your almanack (says he) yeeld's all the sence
Of time's past, profit, and experience.

On Tullus.

Tullus who was a taylor by profession,
Is late turn'd lawyer, and of large possession.
So who before did cut but countrey freese,
Now cuts the countrey in excessive fees.

Vt parta perdita.

Marcellus proves a man of double means,
First rais'd by drunkards, then undone by queans.

On Jack and Jill.

Since *Jack* and *Jill* both wicked be;
It seems a wonder unto me,
That they no better do agree.

On Women.

Woman's the centre, and the lines be men,
The circles, love; how do they differ then ? ·
Circles draw many lines into the center,
But love gives leave to only one to enter.

. On Womans love.

A womans love is like a Syrian flow'r,
That buds, and·spreads, and withers in an hour.

On Cook a Cuckold.

A young Cook marry'd upon Sunday last,
And he grew old e'r Tuesday night was past.

. Nomine, non re.

Grace I confess it, hath a comely face,
Good hand and foot as answerable to it :
But what's all.this except she had more grace ?
Oh you will say, 'tis want that makes her do it.
True, want of grace indeed, the more her shame :
Gracelesse by nature, only *Grace* by name.

A Monsieur Naso, vero le.

Naso let none drink in his glasse but he,
Think you 'tis pride? 'tis courtesie.

A Butcher marrying a Tanners Daughter.

A fitter match then this could not have bin,
For now the flesh is married to the skin. ·

A Widow.

He which for's wife a widow doth obtain,
Doth like to those that buy clothes in *Long-lane*,
One coat's not fit, another's too too old,
Their faults I know not, but th'are manifold.

On a Farmer Knighted.

In my conceit Sir *John*, you were to blame,
To make a quiet good-wife, a mad-dame.

On Pallas and Bacchus Birth.

Pallas the off-spring of *Joves* brain,
Bacchus out of his thigh was ta'en :
He breaks his brain that learning wins,
When he that's drunk breaks but his shins.

On an old man doting upon a yong Wench.

A rich old man loving a fair young lasse,
Out of his breeches his spectacles drew,
Wherewith he writ a note how rich he was ;
All which (quoth he) sweet heart I'l give to you.
    Excuse me sir (quoth she) for all your riches,
    I'l marry none that wears his eyes in's breeches.

On a Welshman.

The way to make a Welshman think on blisse,
And dayly say his prayers on his knees,
Is to perswade him that most certain 'tis,
The moon is made of nothing but green cheese ;
Then he'l desire of *Jove* no greater boon,
Then to be plac'd in heaven to eat the moon.

On Lungs.

Lungs (as some say) ne'r sits him down to eat,
But that his breath doth fly-blow all his meat.

As many dayes in the year, so many Veins in man.

That every thing we doe might vain appear,
We have a vein for each day in the year.

To a friend on the losse of his Mistresse.

If thou the best of women didst forgo,
Weigh if thou found'st her, or didst make her so:
If she was found, know there is more then one;
If made, the workman lives though she be gone.

On a Whore.

Rosa is faire, but not a proper woman;
Can any woman proper be that's common?

Æqualis consensus.

Cæcus and's choyce, for change no time defers,
Both separate, yet consenting each together,
He maids for his turn takes, the men for hers,
And so they jump, though seldome joyn together.

On a Welshman.

A Welshman late coming into an inn,
Asked the maid what meat there was within;
Cow-heels she answer'd, and a breast of mutton;
But quoth the Welsh-man, since I am no glutton;
Either of both shall serve; to night the breast,
The heels i'th morning, then light meat is best;

At night he took the brest, and did not pay,
I'th morning took his heels, and run away.

On Men and Women.

Ill thrives that haplesse family that shows
A cock thats silent, and a hen that crows:
I know not which lives more unnaturall lives,
Obeying husbands, or commanding wives.

On Linus.

Linus told me of verses that he made,
Riding to *London* on a trotting jade;
I should have known, had he conceal'd the case,
Even by his verses of his horses pace.

Sauce for Sorrows.

Although our sufferings meet with no relief,
An equall mind is the best sauce for grief.

On a little diminutive Band.

What is the reason of God-dam-me's band,
    Inch-deep, and that his fashion doth not alter?
God-dam-me saves a labour, understand,
    In pulling't off when he puts on the halter.

On fine apparell.

Some that their wives may neat and cleanly go,
Do all their substance upon them bestow:
But who a gold-finch, fain would make his wife,
Makes her perhaps a wagtail all her life.

Vpon Conscience.

Many men this present age dispraise,
And think men have small conscience now adays;
But sure, I'l lay no such fault unto their charge,
I rather think their conscience is too large.

Dicta prædicta.

Buttus breaks jests on any thing that's spoken,
Provided alwayes, they before are broken.

On Vmber.

Vmber was painting of a lyon fierce,
And working it, by chance from *Vmbers* erse
Flew out a crack, so mighty, that the fart,
(as *Vmber* swears) did make his lyon start.

In Cornutum.

Cornutus call'd his wife both whore and slut,
Quoth she, you'l never your brawling but—
But what quoth he? quoth she, the post or door,
For you have horns to butt, if I'm a whore.

A witty passage.

An old man sitting at a Christmasse feast,
By eating brawne occasioned a jest;
For whilst his tongue and gums chased about,
For want of pales the chased bore broke out;
And light perchance upon a handsome lasse,
That neer him at the table placed was;

Which when she spy'd, she pluck'd out of her sleeve
A pin, and did it to the old man give;
Saying, sith your brawn out of your mouth doth slip,
Sir take this pin, and therewith close your lip;
And bursting into laughter, strain'd so much,
As with that strain her back-part spake low-dutch
Which th'old man hearing, did the pin restore,
And bad her therewith close her postern door.

On Cob.

Cob clouts his shooes, and as the story tels,
His thumb-nayls par'd afford him sparables.

Omnia pariter.

Ralph reads a line or two, and then cryes mew;
Deeming all else according to those few;
Thou might'st have thought and prov'd a wiser lad,
(As *Joan* her fooding bought) some good, some bad.

A new marryed Bride.

The first of all our sex came from the side of man,
I' thither am return'd from whence I came.

On a Pudding.

The end of all, and in the end,
  the praise of all depends.
A pudding merits double praise,
  because it hath two ends.

Answer.

A pudding hath two ends ; you lye my brother,
For it begins at one, and ends at th'other.

Si nihil attuleris, ibis, &c.

Planus, an honest swaine, but moneylesse,
Besought a lawyer to be good unto him,
Who either (*gratis*) must his cause redresse,
Or promise what he never meant to do him.
Being asked why he carelesse lingred it ?
Made this reply, *Ex nihilo nihil fit.*

On Maids.

Most maids resemble *Eve* now in their lives,
Who are no sooner women, then th'are wives ;
As *Eve* knew no man, e'r fruit wrought her wo ;
So these have fruit oft e'r their husbands know.

Vt cecidit surgit.

Now *Martha* married is, shee'l brave it out,
Though ne'r so needy known to all about ;
And reason good, she rise once in her life,
That fell so oft before she was a wife.

On a man whose choyce was to be hang'd or marryed.

M. Lo here's the bride, and there's the tree,
     Take which of these best liketh thee.
R. The choyce is bad on either part,
     The woman's worst, drive on the cart.

Women.

Were women as little as they are good,
A pescod would make them a gown and a hood.

On a Louse.

A louse no reason hath to deal so ill,
With them of whom she hath so much her will;
She hath no tongue to speak ought in their praise,
But to backbite them finds a tongue alwayes.

A Courtier and a Scholler meeting.

A courtier proud walking along the street,
Hap'ned by chance a scholler for to meet:
The courtier said (minding nought more then place)
Unto the scholler (meeting face to face)
To take the wall, base men I'l not permit;
The scholler said, I will, and gave him it.

Cede majoribus.

I took the wall, one rudely thrust me by,
And told me the high-way did open ly,
I thank'd him that he would me so much grace,
To take the worse and leave the better place;
For if by owners we esteem of things,
The wall's the subjects, but the way the kings.

On Betty.

Sound teeth has *Betty,* pure as pearl and small,
With mellow lips, and luscious therewithall.

A Rule for Courtiers.

He that will thrive in court, must oft become,
Against his will, both blind, and deaf, and dumb.

Why women wear a fall.

A question 'tis, why women wear a fall;
The truth on't is, to pride they're given all,
And pride, the proverb sayes, will have a fall.

Foras expertus.

Priscus hath been a traveller, for why?
He will so strangely swagger, swear and lye.

To a painted Whore.

Whosoever saith thou sellest all, doth jest,
Thou buy'st thy beauty, that sells all the rest.

Detur quod meritum.

A courtier kind in speech, curst in condition,
Finding his faults could be no longer hidden,
Came to his friend to clear his bad suspition,
And fearing least he should be more then chidden,
Fell to flatt'ring and most base submission,
Vowing to kisse his foot if he were bidden.
  My foot said he? nay that were too submisse;
  You three foot higher, well deserve to kisse.

Non lubens loquitur.

Gluto at meals is never heard to talk,
For which the more his chaps and chin do walk,

When every one that sits about the bord,
Makes sport to ask, what *Gluto*, ne'r a word?
He forc'd to answer being very loath,
Is almost choak'd, speaking and eating both.

On Philos.

If *Philos*, none but those are dead doe praise,
I would I might displease him all his dayes.

The Promise-breaker.

Ventus doth promise much, but still doth break,
So all his promises are great and weak:
Like bubbles in the water (round and light)
Swelling so great that they are broke out-right.

Change.

What now we like, anon we disapprove;
The new successor drives away old love.

On a passing Bell.

This dolefull musick of impartiall death,
Who danceth after, danceth out of breath.

Nummos & demona jungit.

Bat bids you swell with envy till you burst,
So he be rich, and may his coffers fill,
Bringing the example of the fox that's curst
And threatning folks who have least power to kill;
  For why 'tis known, his trade can never fall,
  That hath already got the devill and all.

Nil gratum ratione carens.

Paulus a pamphlet doth in prose present
Unto his lord (the fruits of idle time)
Who far more carelesse, then therewith content,
Wisheth it were converted into rime:
Which done, and brought him at another season,
Said, now 'tis rime, before nor rime nor reason.

Non cessat perdere lusor.

Ask Ficus how his luck at dicing goes:
Like to the tide (quoth he) it ebbs and flows,
Then I suppose his chance cannot be good,
For all men know 'tis longer ebbe than flood.

Womens policy.

To weep oft, still to flatter, sometime spin,
Are properties women excell men in.

Volucrem sic decipit auceps.

Hidrus the horse-courser (that cunning mate)
Doth with the buyers thus equivocate;
Claps on his hand, and prays he may not thrive,
If that his gelding be not under five. ☞

Perdat qui caveat emptor.

Nor lesse meant Promus when that vow he made
Then to give o'r his cousening tapsters trade,
Who check'd for short and frothy measure, swore
He never would from henceforth fill pot more.

On Death.

How base hath sin made man, to fear a thing
Which men call *Mors?* which yet hath lost all sting,
And is but a privation as we know,
Nay is no word if we exempt the O :
Then let good men the fear of it defie,
All is but O, when they shall come to dye.

To Mr. Ben Johnson, demanding the reason why he call'd his plays works.

Pray tell me *Ben*, where doth the mystery lurk,
What others call a play, you call a work.

Thus answer'd by a friend in Ben Johnsons defence.

The authors friend thus for the author sayes,
Bens playes are works, when others works are plays.

On Crambo a lousie shifter.

By want of shift, since lice at first are bred,
And after by the same increast and fed ;
Crambo I muse how you have lice so many,
Since all men know you shift as much as any.

Ad Aristarchum.

Be not agriev'd, my humorous lines afford
Of looser language here and there a word :
Who undertakes to sweep a common sink,
I cannot blame him, though his broom do stink.

In Aulum.

Aulus gives naught, men say, though much he crave,
Yet I can tell to whom the pox he gave.

On covetous persons.

Patrons are latrons, then by this
   Th'are worst of greedy people,
Whose cognizance a wolfs head is,
   And in his mouth a steeple.

On a Dyer.

Who hath time hath life, that he denies,
This man hath both, yet still he dies.

Non verbera, sed verba.

Two schollars late appointed for the field;
Must, which was weakest to the other yield;
The quarrell first began about a word,
Which now should be decided by the sword:
But e'r they drew, there fell that alteration,
As they grew friends again by disputation.

Love and Liberty.

Love he that will; it best likes me
To have my neck from loves yoke free.

To a neat Reader.

Thou say'st my verses are rude, ragged, ruffe,
Not like some others rimes, smooth dainty stuffe;

Epigrams are like satyrs, rough without,
Like chesnuts sweet, take thou the kernel out.

Of Letting.

In bed a young man with his old wife lay,
O wife, quoth he, I've let a thing to day,
By which I fear, I am a loser much :
His wife replyes, youths bargains still are such ;
So turning from him angry at her heart,
She unawares let out a thundring ——:
O wife, quoth he, no loser am I now,
A marv'lous saver I am made by you ;
Young men that old wives have may never sell,
Because old wives, quoth he, let things so well.

Sublata causa &c.

Why studies *Silvester* no more the laws,
'Tis thought *Duck-lane* has tane away the cause.

Sapiat qui dives, oportet.

'Tis known how well I live, sayes *Romeo*,
And whom I list, I'le love, or. will despise :
Indeed it's reason good it should be so :
For they that wealthy are, must needs be wise :
　But this were ill if so it come to passe,
　That for your wealth you must be beg'd an asse.

In Dossum.

Dosse riding forth,. the wind was very big,
And strained court'sie with his perriwig,

Leaving his sconce behind so voyd of haire,
As *Esops* crow might break her oyster there;
Fool he to think his hair could tarry fast,
When *Boreas* tears forrests with a blast.

Post dulcia, finis amarus.

Jenkin a Welshman, that had suits in law,
Journying to *London*, chanc'd to steal a cow;
For which (pox on her luck as ne'r mon saw)
Was burnt within the fist and know not how :
Being ask'd if well the laws with him did stand,
Hur have hur now (quoth *Jenkin*) in hur hand.

Feminæ ludificantur viros.

Kind *Katharine* to her husband kist these words,
Mine own sweet *Will*, how dearly do I love thee!
If true (quoth *Will*) the world no such affords.
And that it's true, I durst his warrant be;
  For ne'r heard I of woman good or ill,
  But alwayes loved best, her owne sweet will.

Ad Tusserum.

Tusser, they tell me when thou wert alive,
Thou teaching thrift, thy self couldst never thrive;
So like the whetstone many men are wont
To sharpen others when themselves are blunt.

Præstat videri quam esse.

Clitus with clients is well customed,
That hath the lawes but little studied;

No matter *Clitus,* so they bring their fees,
How ill the case and thy advice agrees.

Tunc tua res agitur.

A jealous merchant that a sailor met,
Ask'd him the reason why he meant to marry,
Knowing what ill their absence might beget,
That still at sea, constrained are to tarry?
Sir (quoth the saylor) think you that so strange?
'Tis done the time whiles you but walke th'exchange.

On Skoles.

Skoles stinks so deadly, that his breeches loath
His dampish buttocks furthermore to cloath:
Cloyd they are up with arse; but hope, and blast
Will whirle about, and blow them thence at last.

A Conference.

A Dane, a Spaniard, a Polonian,
My self a Swisse, with an Hungarian,
At supper met, discoursed each with other,
Drank, laught, yet none that understood another.

In Marcum.

Marcus is not an hypocrite, and why?
He flyes all good, to fly hypocrisy.

Quod non verba suadeant?

Sextus halfe sav'd his credit with a jest,
  That at a reckoning this devise had got,

When he should come to draw amongst the rest,
   And saw each man had coyn, himself had not ;
His empty pocket feels, and 'gins to say,
In sadness sirs, here's not a crosse to pay.

Stupid Binus.

Sith time flyes fast away, his safest flight
Binus prevents with dreaming day and night.

In divites.

Rich men their wealth as children rattles keep,
When play'd a while with't then they fall asleep.

In Fannium.

What fury's this? his foe whilst *Fannius* flyes,
He kils himself, for fear of death he dyes.

On a vaunting Poetaster.

Cecilius boasts his verses worthy be
To be ingraven on a cypresse tree ;
A cypresse wreath befits them well, 'tis true ;
For they are near their death and crave but due.

In divites iracundos.

Rich friends 'gainst poor to anger still are prone :
It is not well but profitably done.

Durum telum necessitas.

Coquus with hunger pennilesse constrain'd
To call for meat and wine three shillings cost,

Had suddenly this project entertain'd,
In stead of what's to pay, to call mine host;
Who being come entreateth him discusse,
What price the law alots for shedding blood:
Whereto mine host directly answers thus;
'Twas alwayes forty pence he understood:
So then, quoth *Coquus*, to requite your pains,
Pray break my head, and give me what remains.

To an Vpstart.

Thy old friends thou forgotst having got wealth:
No marvaile, for thou hast forgot thy selfe.

Ambition.

In wayes to greatnesse, think on this,
That slippery all ambition is.

Suum cuique.

A strange contention being lately had,
Which kind of musick was the sweet'st and best,
Some praise the sprightly sound; and some the sad,
Some lik't the viols; and among the rest,
  Some in the bag-pipes commendation spoke,
  Quoth one stood by, give me a pipe of smoke.

In Prodigum.

Each age of men new fashions doth invent;
Things which are old, young men do not esteem:
What pleasd our fathers, doth not us content:
What flourish'd then, we out of fashion deem:

And that's the cause as I do understand,
Why *Prodigus* did sell his fathers land.

In Medicum.

When *Mingo* cryes, how do you sir? 'tis thought
He patients wanteth; and his practice's naught:
Wherefore of late, now every one he meeteth,
With [I am glad to see you well] he greeteth:
But who'l believe him now, when all can tell,
The world goes ill with him, when all are well?

On Zelot.

Is *Zelot* pure? he is: yet see he wears
The signe of *Circumcision* in his ears.

Crispati crines plumæ dant calcar amori.

Why is young *Annas* thus with feathers dight?
And on his shoulder wears a dangling lock?
The one foretels hee'l sooner fly then fight,
The other shows hee's wrapt in's mothers smock.
  But wherefore wears he such a jingling spur?
  O know, he deals with jades that will not stir.

On Boung-Bob.

Bob, thou, nor souldier, theef, nor fencer art,
Yet by thy weapon liv'st, th'ast one good part.

On Glaucus.

Glaucus a man, a womans hair doth wear,
But yet he wears the same com'b out behind:

So men the wallet of their faults do bear,
For if before him, he that fault should find :
I think foul shame would his fair face invade,
To see a man so like a woman made.

On Crab.

Crab faces gowns with sundry furres; 'tis known,
He keeps the fox-furre for to face his own.

Dolo intimus.

Nor hauk, nor hound, nor horse, those letters *hhh*,
But ach its self, 'tis *Brutus* bones attaches.

Of Batardus.

Batardus needs would know his horoscope,
To see if he were born to scape the rope :
The *Magus* said, ere thou mine answer have,
I must the name of both thy parents crave :
That said, *Batardus* could not speak but spit ;
For on his fathers name he could not hit :
And out of doors at last he stept with shame,
To ask his mother for his fathers name.

Consuetudo lex.

Two wooers for a wench were each at strife,
Which should enjoy her to his wedded wife,
Quoth th'one, she's mine, because I first her saw ;
She's mine, quoth th'other, by pye-corner law :
Where sticking once a prick on what you buy,
It's then your own, which no man must deny.

On Womens denial.

Women, although they ne're so goodly make it,
Their fashion is but to say no, and take it.

In Battum.

Battus affirm'd no poet ever writ,
Before that love inspir'd his dull-head wit:
And that himself in love had wit no more,
Then one stark mad, though somewhat wise before.

On Marriage.

Wedding and hanging the destinies dispatch,
But hanging seems to some the better match.

Vidua aurata.

Gallus hath got a widow wondrous old,
The reason is he woo'd her for her gold:
Knowing her maids are young and serve for hire,
Which is as much as Gallus doth desire.

In Dol prægnantem.

Dol learning Propria quæ maribus without book,
Like Nomen crescentis genitivo doth look.

Timidos fortuna repellit.

When Miles the serving-man my lady kist,
She knew him not (though scarcely could resist)
For this (quoth he) my master bid me say;—
How's that (quoth she) and frowning flings away:

Vext to the heart, she took her marke amisse,
And that she should a serving creature kisse.
Why thus it is when fools must make it known,
They come on others businesse, not their own.

Against a certain —

For mad men Bedlam, Bridewell for a knave,
Choose whether of those two th'adst rather have.

Loves progresse.

Loves first approach, delights sweet song doth sing :
But in departure, she woes sting doth bring.

On old Scylla.

Scylla is toothlesse, yet, when she was young,
She had both teeth enough, and too much tongue.
What shall I then of toothlesse Scylla say,
But that her tongue hath worn her teeth away ?

On Gallants Cloaks.

Without, plain cloaks ; within, plusht : but I doubt
The wearer's worst within, and best without.

On Banks the Vsurer.

Banks feels no lamenesse on his knotty gout,
His money travels for him in and out :
And though the soundest legs go every day,
He toils to be at hell as soon as they.

Pæcunia prævalens.

Tell *Tom* of *Plato's* worth or *Aristotles;*
Hang't give him wealth enough; let wit stop bottles.

On the same.

Tom vow'd to beat his boy against the wall,
And as he struck, he forthwith caught a fall:
The boy deriding, said, I do aver,
Y'have done a thing, you cannot stand to sir.

On Debt.

To be indebted is a shame men say,
Then 'tis confessing of a shame to pay.

A forsworn Maid.

Rosa being false and perjur'd, once a friend
Bid me contented be, and mark her end:
But yet I care not, let my friend go fiddle;
Let him mark her end, I'le mark her middle.

Adversity.

Love is maintain'd by wealth, when all is spent,
Adversity then breeds the discontent.

On Soranzo.

Soranzo's broad brim hat I oft compare
To the vast compasse of the heavenly sphere:
His head, the earth's globe, fixed under it;
Whose center is, his wondrous little wit.

To a great Guest.

With other friends I bid you to my feast,
Though coming late, yet are you not the least.

In Cottam.

Cotta when he hath din'd saith, God be praisd,
Yet never praiseth God for meat or drink :
Sith *Cotta* speaketh, and not practiseth,
He speaketh surely what he doth not think.

De Corde & Lingua.

The tongue was once a servant to the heart,
And what it gave she freely did impart :
But now hypocrisie is grown so strong,
She makes the heart a servant to the tongue.

On Rumpe.

Rump is a turn spit, yet he seldome can
Steale a swolne sop out of the dripping-pan.

On Poverty.

If thou be poor, thou shalt be ever so,
None now do wealth, but on the rich bestow.

In Ebriosum.

Fie man (saith she) but I tell Mistrisse *Anne*,
Her drunken husband is no drunken man.
For those wits which are overcome with drink,
Are voyd of reason, and are beasts I think.

Wills error.

Will sayes his wife's so fat, she scarce can go,
But she as nimbly answers, Faith sir no :
Alas good *Will*, thou art mistaken quite,
For all men know, that she is wondrous light.

On Rome.

Hate & debate, *Rome* through the world hath spread,
Yet *Roma, amor* is, if backward read :
Then is't not strange, *Rome* hate should foster ? no,
For out of backward love all hate doth grow ?

On Tuck.

At post and paire, or slam, *Tom Tuck* would play
This Christmasse, but his want therewith, says nay.

Something no savour.

All things have savour, though some but small ;
Nay, a box on th'ear, hath no smell at all.

Art, Fortune, and Ignorance.

When Fortune fell asleep, and hate did blind her,
Art, Fortune lost ; and Ignorance did find her :
Sith when, dull Ignorance with Fortunes store,
Hath been inrich'd, and Art hath still been poor.

On Bibens.

Bibens to shew his liberality,
Made *Lusus* drunk ; (a noble quality,

And much esteem'd) which *Bibens* fain would prove
To be the signe of his familiar love :
Lusus beware, thou'lt finde him in the end,
Familiar devil, no familiar friend.

On Tobacco.

Things which are common, common men do use,
The better sort do common things refuse :
Yet countries-cloth-breech, & court-velvet-hose,
Puffe both alike tobacco through the nose.

On Cupid.

Cupid no wonder was not cloth'd of old,
For love though naked, seldome e'r is cold.

On Ebrio.

See where *Don Ebrio,* like a Dutchman goes,
Yet drunk with English ale, one would suppose
That he would shoulder down each door & wall,
But they must stand, or he, poor fool must fall.

On Love.

Love hath two divers wings, as lovers say :
Thou following him, with one he flyes away;
With th'other, if thou fly he follows thee :
Therefore the last, love, onely use for me.

On the same.

Love, as 'tis said, doth work with such strange tools,
That he can make fools wise-men, wise-men fools,

Then happy I, for being nor fool, nor wise,
Love with his toyes and tools I shall despise.

On a Wanton.

Some the word *Wanton* fetch, though with small skill,
From those that want one to effect their will
If so, I think that wantons there are none,
For till the world want men, can they want none.

Ingluviem sequitur fames.

Curio would feed upon the daintiest fare,
That with the court or country might compare:
For what lets *Curio* that he need to care,
To frolick freely with the proud'st that dare:
But this excesse was such in all things rare,
As he prov'd bankrupt e'er he was aware.

On Maulsters.

Such *Maulsters* as ill measure sell for gain,
Are not meer knaves, but also knaves in grain.

In Corbum.

Corbus will not, perswade him all I can,
The world should take him for a gentleman:
His reason's this, because men should not deem,
That he is such as he doth never seem.

On Priscus Mistresse.

Priscus commends his mistris for a girle,
Whose lips be rubies, and whose teeth are pearle:

Th'had need prove so, or else it will be found,
He payes too dear; they cost him many a pound.

On Women.

Women think wo—men far more constant be,
Than we—men, and the letter O we see,
In wo—men, not in we—men, as they say,
Figures earths constant orbe; we—men say nay :
It means the moon, which proves (none think it strange)
Women are constant, & most true in change.

On Souldiers.

Nor faith, nor conscience common souldiers carry,
Best pay, is right; their hands are mercenary.

Drusius and Furio.

Furio would fight with Drusius in the field,
Because the straw, stout Drusius would not yield,
On which their mistriss trod; they both did meet;
Drusius in field fell dead at Furio's feet;
One had the straw, but with it this Greek letter Π
The other lost it, pray who had the better ?

On Cupid.

Love is a boy, and subject to the rod
Some say, but lovers say he is a god :
I think that love is neither god nor boy,
But a mad brains imaginary toy.

On Candidus.

When I am sick, not else, thou com'st to see me,
Would fortune from both torments still would free me.

On a Puritan.

From impure mouths, now many bear the name
Of puritan, yet merit not the same.
This one shall onely be my puritan
That is a knave, yet seems an honest man.

Ostendit hedera vinum.

A scoffing mate, that past along Cheap-side,
Incontinent a gallant lasse espide;
Whose tempting breasts (as to the sale laid out)
Incites this youngster thus to 'gin to flout.
Lady (quoth he) is this flesh to be sould?
No lord (quoth she) for silver nor for gold,
But wherefore ask you? (and there made a stop?
To buy (quoth he) if not shut up your shop.

Quantum mutatus ab illo!

Pedes grown proud makes men admire thereat,
Whose baser breeding, should they think not beare it,
Nay, he on cock-horse rides, how like you that?
Tut! Pedes proverb is, Win gold and weare it.
  But Pedes you have seen them rise in hast,
    That through their pride have broke their neck at
        last.

Vpon Lavina.

Lavina brought to bed, her husband looks
To know's childs fortune throughout his books,
His neighbours think h'had need search backward rather,
And learn for certain who had been the father.

Report and Error.

Error by error, tales by tales, great grow;
As snow-balls do, by rowling to and fro.

In Superbum.

Rustick Superbus fine new cloaths hath got,
Of taffata and velvet, fair in sight;
The shew of which hath so bewitcht the sot,
That he thinks gentleman to be his right:
    But he's deceiv'd, for true that is of old,
    An ape's an ape, though he wear cloth of gold.

No truth in Wine.

Truth is in wine, but none can finde it there,
For in your taverns, men will lye and sweare.

On Infidus.

Infidus was so free of oaths last day,
That he would swear, what e'r he thought to say:
But now such is his chance, whereat he's griev'd,
The more he swears, the lesse he is believ'd.

On Celsus.

Celsus doth love himselfe, Celsus is wise,
For now no rivall e'r can claim his prize.

On Christmasse Ivy.

At Christmasse men do alwayes ivy get,
And in each corner of the house is set :
But why do they, then, use that *Bacchus* weed ?
Because they mean, then *Bacchus*-like to feed.

Adversity.

Adversity hurts none, but onely such
Whom whitest fortune dandled has too much.

On Bacchus.

Pot-lifting *Bacchus* to the earth did bend
His knee to drink a health unto his friend :
And there he did so long in liquor pour,
That he lay quite sick-drunk upon the floor.
Judge, was there not a drunkards kindnesse shown,
To drink his friend a health, and lose his own ?

Of a fat man.

Hee's rich, that hath great in-comes by the year :
Then that great belly'd man is rich, I'l swear :
For sure his belly ne'r so big had bin,
Had he not daily had great comings in.

A wished Cramp.

Some have the cramp in legs, and hands, 'tis told,
I wish't in my wifes tongue, when she doth scold.

Vindicta vim sequitur.

Kitt being kick'd and spurr'd, pursues the law,
That doom'd the dammage at twice forty.pence.

Which, when the party which had wrong'd him saw;
Thought 'twas too great a fine for such offence.
  Why then, quoth *Kitt*, if I too much request,
  Thou maist at any time lick out the rest.

On Flaccus.

Flaccus being young, they said he was a gull;
Of his simplicity each mouth was full:
And pitying him, they'd say, the foolish lad
Would surely be deceived, of all he had.
His youth is past, now may they turne him loose;
For why? the gull is grown to be a goose.

Per plumas anser.

See how young *Rufus* walks in green each day,
As if he ne'r was youthful until now:
E're Christmass next, his green goose will be gray,
And those high burnish'd plumes in's cap will bow:
  But you do wrong him, since his purse is full,
  To call him goose, that is so young a gull.

Of Jenkin.

Jenkin is a rude clown, go tell him so;
What need I tell, what he himself doth know?
Perhaps he doth not, then he is a sot;
For tell me, what knows he that knows it not?

On Trigg.

Trigg having turn'd his sute he struts in state,
And tells the world he's now regenerate.

K 2

To Fortune.

Poets say Fortune's blind, and cannot see,
And therefore to be born withall, if she
Sometimes drop gifts on undeserving wights:
But sure they are deceiv'd; she hath her sight,
   Else could it not at all times so fall out,
   That fools should have, and wise men go without.

On Briscus.

I pray you give Sir *Briscus* leave to speak,
The gander loves to hear himself to creak.

On an English Ape.

Would you believe, when you this Monsieur see,
That his whole body should speak *French*, not he?
That he untravell'd should be *French* so much,
As *French* men in his company should seem *Dutch?*
Or hung some *Monsieurs* picture on the wall;
By which his *damme* conceiv'd him, cloaths and all?
No, 'tis the new *French* taylors motion, made
Dayly to walk th'Exchange, and help the trade.

Possessions.

Those possessions short liv'd are
Into the which we come by warre.

Nulla dies sine linea.

By ever learning, *Solon* waxed old,
For time he knew, was better far than gold:

Fortune would give him gold which would decay,
But fortune cannot give him yesterday.

In Cornutum.

One told his wife a hearts-head he had bought,
To hang his hat upon, and home it brought :
To whom his frugall wife, What needs that care ?
I hope, sweet-heart, your head your hat can beare.

On More-dew.

More-dew the mercer, with a kind salute,
Would needs intreat my custome for a suite :
Here sir, quoth he, for sattins, velvets call,
What e'r you please, I'l take your word for all.
I thank'd, took, gave my word ; say than,
Am I at all indebted to this man ?

Pari jugo dulcis tractus.

When *Cæcus* had bin wedded now three dayes,
And all his neighbours bad God give him joy,
This strange conclusion with his wife assayes,
Why till her marriage day she prov'd so coy :
Fore God (saith he) 'twas well thou didst not yeeld
For doubtless then my purpose was to leave thee.
Oh sir (quoth she) I once was so beguild,
And thought the next man should not so deceive me.
Now fie upon't (quoth he) thou breedst my wo.
Why man (quoth she) I speak but *quid pro quo.*

On Sims marriage.

Six moneths, quoth *Sim*, a suiter, and not sped ?
I in a sev'n night did both woo and wed.
Who green fruit loves, must take long pains to shake;
Thine was some down-fall, I dare undertake.

Vpon Sis.

Sis brags sh'hath beauty, and will prove the same ;
As how ? as thus sir ; 'tis her puppies name.

On Clym.

Clym cals his wife, and reckoning all his neighbors,
Just halfe of them are cuckolds, he avers.
Nay fie, quoth she, I would they heard you speak ;
You of your self, it seems, no reckoning make.

On Gut.

Science puffs up, says *Gut*, when either pease
Make him thus swell, or windy cabbages.

On Womens faults.

We men in many faults abound,
But two in women can be found :
The worst that from their sex proceeds ;
Is naught in words, and naught in deeds.

To a Muck-worm.

Content great riches is, to make which true,
Your heir would be content to bury you.

On Law.

Our civill law doth seem a royall thing,
It hath more titles then the Spanish king:
But yet the common-law quite puts it down,
In getting, like the pope, so many a crown.

In Coam.

A nor Ω will *Coa* espy,
Till she ascend up to the corner'd Π.

Maids Nay's.

Maides nay's are nothing, they are shie
But to desire what they denie.

De Ore.

Os of *O*, a mouth, *Scaliger* doth make;
And from this letter, mouth his name doth take:
And I had been of *Scaligers* belief, .
But that I look'd in *O*, and saw no teeth.

In Hugonem.

Though praise, and please, doth *Hugo* never none,
Yet praise, and please, doth *Hugo* ever one;
For praise, and please, doth *Hugo* himself alone.

On Severus.

Severus is extreame in eloquence,
For he creates rare phrase, but rarer sense:
Unto his serving-man, *alias* his boy,
He utters speech exceeding quaint and coy;

Diminutive, and my defective slave,
My pleasures pleasure is, that I must have
My corps coverture, and immediately,
T'insconce my person from frigility.
His man believes all's Welsh his master spoke,
Till he rails English; Rogue go fetch my cloke.

On Julias weeping.

She by the river sate, and sitting there,
She wept, and made it deeper by a tear.

On a Gallant.

What gallant's that, whose oaths fly through mine ears?
How like a lord of *Pluto's* court he swears!
How Dutch-man like he swallows down his drink!
How sweet he takes tobacco till he stink!
How lofty sprighted, he disdains a boor!
How faithfull hearted he is to a ——!
How cock-tail proud he doth himself advance!
How rare his spurrs do ring the morrice-dance!
Now I protest by Mistriss *Susans* fan,
He and his boy will make a proper man.

On Vertue, Milla's Maid.

Saith *Aristotle*, *Vertue* ought to be
Communicative of her self, and free;
And hath not *Vertue*, *Milla's* maid, been so?
Who's grown hereby, as big as she can go.

On Corydon.

An home-spun peasant with his urine-glasse,
The doctor ask'd what country-man he was.
Quoth *Corydon*, with making legs full low,
Your worship, that, shall by my water know.

On a Spanish Souldier.

A Spanish souldier, sick unto the death,
His pistoll to's physitian did bequeath.
Who did demand, what should the reason be,
'Bove other things to give him that; (quoth he)
This with your practice joyned, you may kill,
Sir, all alive, and have the world at will.

Vpon the Asse.

The asse a courtier on a time would bee,
And travail'd forain nations for to see;
But home returned, fashion he could none,
His main and tail were onely larger grown.

On Hypocrisie.

As venison in a poor mans kitchin's rare;
So hypocrites and usurers in heaven are.

Dæmonum certamen.

A broker and an usurer contended,
Which in's profession was the most befriended;
And for experience more to have it tryde,
A scrivener must the difference decide:
   To whom (quoth he) you like the fox and cub,
   One shall be *Mammon*, th'other *Belzebub*.

On Love.

Love's of it self too sweet: the best of all
Is; when loves honey has a dash of gall.

On Man and Woman.

When man and woman dyes, as poets sung;
His heart's the last that stirs, of hers, the tongue.

On Fabullus.

I ask'd *Fabullus*, why he had no wife?
(Quoth he) because I'd live a quiet life.

On Furnus.

Furnus takes pains, he need not without doubt,
O yes, he labors much, How? with the gout.

Quid non ebrietas.

Rubin reports, his mistriss is a punk:
Which being told her, was no whit dismaid,
For sure as death (quoth she the villains drunk)
And in that taking, knows not what he said.
   'Twas well excus'd, but oft it comes to passe,
   That true we finde, *In vino veritas*.

No Paines, no Gaines.

If little labour, little are our gaines,
Mans fortunes are according to his paines.

Infirmis animosus.

Pontus by no means from his coyn departs,
Z'foot, will you have of men more than their hearts?

A culina ad curiam.

Lixa, that long a serving-groom hath been,
Will now no more the man be known or seen:
And reason good, he hath the place resign'd;
Witness his cloak, throughout with velvet lin'd.
Which by a paradox comes thus to passe;
The greasie gull is turn'd a gallant asse.

Frustra vocaveris heri.

Dick had but two words to maintain him ever,
And that was Stand, and after stand Deliver.
But *Dick's* in Newgate, and he fears shall never
Be blest again with that sweet word, Deliver.

Magnis non est morandum.

See how *Silenus* walks accomplished,
With due performance of his fathers page:
Looks back of purpose to be honoured,
And on each slight occasion 'gins to rage;
    You, villain, dog! where hath your stay been such?
    Quoth he, the broker would not lend so much.

Puduit sua damna referre.

Such ill success had *Dick* at dice last night,
As he was forc'd, next day, play least in sight:
But if you love him, make thereof no speeches,
He lost his rapier, cloak, and velvet breeches.

Ad Lectorem.

Reader, thou seest how pale these papers look,
While they fear thy hard censure on my book.

Nimis docuit consuetudo.

Old *Fucus* board is oft replenished,
But naught thereof must be diminished,
Unlesse some worthlesse upper-dish or twain;
The rest for service still again remain.
His man that us'd to bring them in for show,
Leaving a dish upon the bench below,
Was by his master (much offended) blam'd,
Which he, as brief, with answer quickly fram'd;
T'hath been so often brought afore this day,
As now ch'ad thoft it self had known the way.

Poculo junguntur amici.

A health, saith *Lucas*, to his loves bright ey;
Which not to pledge, were much indignity;
You cannot do him greater courtesie,
Than to be drunk, and damn'd for company.

Nullum stimulum ignaris.

Cæcus awake, was told the sun appear'd,
Which had the darknesse of the morning clear'd:
But *Cæcus* sluggish, thereto makes reply,
The sunne hath further far to go than I.

In Richardum.

At three go-downs *Dick* doffs me off a pot,
The English gutter's Latine for his throat.

Non penna, sed usus.

Cajus accounts himselfe accurst of men,
Onely because his lady loves him not:

Who, till he taught her, could not hold her pen,
And yet hath since, another tutor got.
   Cajus it seems, thy skill she did but cheapen,
   And means to try him at another weapon.

An absolute Gallant.

If you will see true valour here display'd,
Heare *Poly-phemus*, and be not afraid.
D'ye see me wrong'd, and will ye thus restrain me?
Sir let me go, for by these hilts I'll brain ye.
Shall a base patch with appearance wrong me?
I'll kill the villain, pray do not prolong me,
Call my tobacco putrified stuffe?
Tell me it stinks? say it is drosse I snuffe?
Sirrah! what are you? why sir, what would you?
I am a prentice, and will knock you too:
O are you so? I cry you mercy then,
I am to fight with none but gentlemen.

To Momus.

Momus thou say'st my verses are but toyes:
'Tis true, yet truth is often spoke by boyes.

In Dolentem.

Dolens doth shew his purse, and tell you this,
It is more horrid then a pest-house is;
For in a pest-house many mortals enter,
But in his purse one angell dares not venter.

Abditio perditio.

From *Mall* but merry, men but mirth derive,
For *trix* 'is makes her prove demonstrative.

On a Gallant.

Sirrah, come hither, boy, take view of me,
My lady I am purpos'd to go see;
What doth my feather flourish with a grace?
And this my curled hair become my face?
How decent doth my doublet's form appear?
I would I had my sute in Long-lane here.
Do not my spurs pronounce a silver sound?
Is not my hose-circumference profound?
Sir, these be well, but there is one thing ill,
Your taylor with a sheet of paper-bill,
Vow's hee'l be paid, and sergeants he hath fee'd,
Which wait your comming forth to do the deed.
Boy God-a-mercy, let my lady stay,
I'll see no counter for her sake to day.

In Sextum.

Sextus six pockets wears, two for his uses,
The other foure to pocket up abuses.

A Stammerer.

Balbus with other men would angry be,
Because they could not speak as well as he;
For others speak but with their mouth he knows,
But *Balbus* speaks both through the mouth and nose.

On himself.

I dislikt but even now;
Now I love I know not how.
Was I idle, and that while
Was I fir'd with a smile?
Ile to work, or play, and then
I shall quite dislike agen.

Tom's fortune.

Tom tel's he's robb'd, and counting all his losses,
Concludes, all's gone, the world is full of crosses:
If all be gone, Tom take this comfort then,
Th'art certain never to have crosse agen

Opus & Vsus.

Opus for need consum'd his wealth apace,
And ne'r would cease untill he was undone;
His brother Vsus liv'd in better case
Than Opus did, although the eldest son.
  'Tis strange it should be so, yet here was it,
  Opus had all the land, Vsus the wit.

A good Wife.

A batchelor would have a wife were wise,
Fair, rich, and young, a maiden for his bed—
Nor proud, nor churlish, but of faultlesse size;
A country houswife in the city bred.
  But he's a fool, and long in vain hath staid;
  He should bespeak her, there's none ready made.

Anger.

Wrongs if neglected, vanish in short time ;
But heard with anger, we confesse the crime.

Vpon Gellia.

When *Gellia* went to school, and was a girle ;
Her teeth for whiteness might compare with pearle
But after she the taste of sweet meats knew,
They turn'd all opals, to a perfect blew ;
Now *Gellia* takes tobacco, what should let,
But last they should converted be to jet ?

On an unconstant Mistresse.

I dare not much say when I thee commend,
Lest thou be changed e'r my praises end.

In Lesbiam.

Why should I love thee *Lesbia ?* I no reason see :
Then out of reason, *Lesbia,* I love thee.

In Paulinum.

Paul by day wrongs me, yet he daily swears,
He wisheth me as well as to his soul :
I know his drift to damn that he nought cares,
To please his body ; therefore good friend *Paul,*
If thy kind nature will afford me grace,
Hereafter love me in thy body's place.

On Zeno.

Zeno would fain th'old widow *Egle* have ;
Trust me he's wise, for she is rich and brave :

But *Zeno, Zeno,* she will none of you ;
In my mind she's the wiser of the two.

Of a Drunkard.

Cinna one time most wonderfully swore,
That whilst he breath'd he would drink no more.
But since I know his meaning, for I think
He meant he would not breath whilst he did drink.

To Cotta.

Be not wroth *Cotta,* that I not salute thee,
I us'd it whilst I worthy did repute thee ;
Now thou art made a painted saint, and I,
Cotta, will not commit idolatry.

To Women.

Ye that have beauty, and withall no pitty,
Are like a prick-song lesson without ditty.

On Creta.

Creta doth love her husband wondrous well,
It needs no proof, for every one can tell :
So strong's her love, that if I not mistake, ·
It doth extend to others for his sake.

On Priscus.

Why still doth *Priscus* strive to have the wall ?
Because he's often drunk and fears to fall.

On Rufus.

At all, quoth *Rufus*, lay you what you dare,
I'l throw at all, and 'twere a peck of gold;
No life lies on't, then coyn I'l never spare;
Why *Rufus*, that's the cause of all that's sold?
  For with frank gamesters it doth oft befall,
  They throw at all, till thrown quite out of all.

On Tobacco.

Tobacco is a weed of so great pow'r,
That it (like earth) doth all it feeds, devour.

Vpon Nasuto.

When at the table once I did averre,
Well-taken discords best did please the ear,
And would be judg'd by any quirister,
Were in the chappel, *Pauls*, or *Westminster;*
Nasuto sitting at the nether end,
(First having drunk and cough'd) quoth he my friend,
  If that were true, my wife and I, I fear,
  Should soon be sent to some cathedral quire.

Nec vultus indicat virum.

Dick in a raging deep discourtesy,
Calls an atturny meer necessity:
The more knave he; admit he had no law,
Must he be flouted at by every daw?

On Furius.

Furius a lover was, and had loving fits,
He lov'd so madly that he lost his wits;

Yet he lost nought, yet grant I, he was mad,
How could he lose that which he never had ?

Fools·Fortune.

Fools have great fortune, but yet not all,
For some are great fools, whose fortune's small.

Tace sed age.

Little or nothing said, soon mended is,
But they that nothing do, do most amisse.

On Count-surly.

Count-surly will no scholler entertain :
Or any wiser than himself ; how so ?
The reason is, when fools are in his train,
His wit amongst them, makes a goodly show.

On Women.

When man lay dead-like, woman took her life,
From a crook't embleme of her nuptiall strife ;
And hence (as bones would be at rest) her ease
She loves so well, and is so hard to please.

Verses.

Who will not honour noble numbers, when
Verses out-live the bravest deeds of men ?

Poor Irus.

Irus using to lye upon the ground,
One morning under him a feather found,

Have I all night here lien so hard (quoth he)
Having but one poor feather under me : ·
  I wonder much then how they take their ease,
  That night by night, lie on a bed of these.

Merry Doll.

I blame not lusty *Doll*, that strives so much,
To keep her light heart free from sorrows touch ;
Shee'l dance and sing a hem boyes, hey all six,
She's steel to th'baek, all mirth, all *meretrix*.

Heaven and Hell.

If heaven's call'd the place where angels dwell,
My purse wants angels, pray call that hell.

Like question like answer.

A young beginner walking through Cheapside,
A house shut up he presently espy'd
And read the bill, which o'r the door was set,
Which said, the house and shop was to be let ;
That known, he ask'd a young man presently,
Which at the next door stood demurely ;
  May not this shop be let alone ? quoth he,
  Yes, you may let't alone for ought I see.

On deaf Joan.

She prates to others, yet can nothing heare,
Just like a sounding jugge that wants an eare.

Of an ill Wife.

Priscus was weeping when his wife did dye,
Yet he was then in better case than I :
I should be merry, and should think to thrive,
Had I but his dead wife for mine alive.

Meum & Tuum.

Megge lets her husband boast of rule and riches,
But she rules all the roast, and wears the breeches.

Deaths trade.

Death is a fisherman, the world we see
His fish-pond is, and we the fishes be.
He sometimes, angler-like, doth with us play,
And slily takes us one by one away;
Diseases are the murthering-hooks, which he
Doth catch us with, the bait mortality,
Which we poor silly fish devour, til strook,
At last too late we feel the bitter hook.
At other times he brings his net, and then
At once sweeps up whole cities ful of men,
Drawing up thousands at a draught, and saves
Onely some few, to make the others graves :
His net some raging pestilence ; now he
Is not so kind as other fishers be ;
For if they take one of the smaller frye,
They throw him in again, he shall not dye :
  But death is sure to kill all he can get,
  And all is fish with him that comes to net.

On Bice.

Bice laughs when no man speaks, and doth protest
It is his own breech there that breaks the jest.

Valiant in drink.

Who onely in his cups will fight, is like
A clock that must be oil'd wel ere it strike.

Master and Scholler.

A *pedant* ask'd a *puny* ripe and bold,
In an hard frost, the Latine word for *cold:*
I'l tell you out of hand (quoth he) for lo,
I have it at my fingers ends, you know.

Gasters great belly.

Gaster did seem to me to want his eyes,
For he could neither see his legs nor thighs;
But yet it was not so; he had his sight,
Onely his belly hanged in his light.

Drunken Dick.

When *Dick* for want of drunken mates grows sick,
Then with himself to work goes faithfull *Dick.*
The buttery dore t'himself he shutteth close
That done, then goes the pot straight wayes to's nose:
A health (quoth noble *Dick*) each hogs-head than
Must seeming pledge this honest faithfull man :
But straight from kindness *Dick* to humors grows,
And then to th'barrels he his valour shows,

Throwing about the cups, the pots, the glasses,
And rails at the tuns, calling them drunken asses :
   Ne'r ceasing this same faithfull coyl to keep,
   Till under th'hogs-head *Dick* fals fast asleep.

In Sextinum.

A pretty block *Sextinus* names his hat,
So much the fitter for his head by that.

Sine Sanguine.

Ralph challeng'd *Robin*, time and place appointed,
Their parents heard on't, O how they lamented !
But good luck was, they soon were freed of fear,
The one ne'r meant, the other came not there.

On humane Bodies.

Our bodies are like shooes, which off we cast,
Physick their cobler is, and death the last.

On Trencherman.

Tom shifts the trenchers, yet he never can,
Endure that luke-warm name of servingman ;
Serve or not serve, let *Tom* do what he can,
He is a serving, who's a *Trencher-man*.

A Toothlesse-Pratler.

Nature the teeth doth as an hedge ordain,
The nimble frisking tongue for to contain :
No marvel then since that the hedge is out,
If *Fuscus* tongue walketh so fast about.

A musicall Lady.

A lady fairer far than fortunate,
(In dancing) thus o'r-shot her self of late,
The musick not in tune, pleasd not her mind,
For which she with the fidlers fault did find;
Fidlers (quoth she) your fiddles tune for shame,
But as she was a speaking of the same,
To mend the consort, let she did a (F.)
Whereas the fidling knaves thus did her greet,
Madam your pipe's in tune, it plays most sweet;
Strike up, qd. they, (but then the knaves did smile)
And as you pipe, wee'l dance another while.
 At which, away the blushing lady flings,
 But as she goes, her former note she sings.

In Laurettam.

Lauretta is laid o'r, how Ile not say,
And yet I think two manner of wayes I may,
Doubly layd o'r, videlicet, her face,
Laid o'r with colours, and her coat with lace.

On Macer.

You call my verses toy's, th'are so, 'tis true,
Yet they are better then ought comes from you.

. Briskap the Gallant.

Though thou hast little judgement in thy head,
More than to dresse thee, drink and go to bed;
Yet may'st thou take the wall, and th'way shalt lead,
Sith logick wills that simple things precede.

Necessity hath no Law.

Florus did beat his cook, and 'gan to sweare,
Because his meat was rotten roasted there.
Peace good sir (quoth the cook) need hath no law,
'Tis rotten roasted, 'cause 'twas rotten raw.

In Carentium.

Carentius might have wedded where he woo'd,
But he was poor, his means was nothing good,
'Twas but for lack of living that he lost her;
For why? no penny now, no *Pater Noster*.

On Harpax.

Harpax gave to the poor all by his will,
Because his heir should not faign'd tears distill.

To a Barber.

Tonsorius onely lives by cutting haire,
And yet he brags that kings to him sit bare:
Me thinks he should not brag and boast of it,
For he must stand to beggars while they sit.

Vpon Grandtorto.

The morrow after just Saint *Georges* day,
Grandtorto piteous drunk, sate in a ditch,
His hands by's side, his gelding stray'd away,
His scarlet hose, and doublet very rich;
    With mud and mire all beastly raid, and by
    His feather with his close-stool-hat did ly.

We ask'd the reason of his sitting there,
Zounds 'cause I am King *Solomon* (quoth he)
And in my throne; then for the love we beare,
(Replyed my selfe) unto your majesty,
Wee'l pull you out, and henceforth wish your grace
Would speak your proverbs in a warmer place.

The Fencer and Physick Doctor.

Lie thus (the fencer cryes) thus must you guard,
Thus must you slip, thus point, thus pass, thus ward,
And if you kill him sir, this trick learn then
With this same trick you may kill many men.
A doctor standing by, cryes, Fencing fool,
Both you and he to me may come to school,
　　Thou dost but prate : my deeds shall show my skill,
　　Where thou hurt'st one, an hundred I do kill.

In Lusiam.

Lusia who scorns all others imitations,
Cannot abide to be out-gone in fashions :
She sayes she cannot have a hat or ruffe,
A gown, a peticoat, a band, or cuffe.
But that these citizens (whom she doth hate)
Will get into't, at ne'r so dear a rate :
But *Lusia* now doth such a fashion wear,
Whose hair is curl'd, and costs her somwhat dear :
That there's no citizen, what e'r she be,
Can be transform'd so like an owl as she.

Kisses.

Give the food that satisfies a guest:
Kisses are but dry banquets to a feast.

A Civilian.

A lusty old grown-grave gray-headed sire,
Stole to a wench, to quench his lusts desire;
She ask'd him what profession he might be?
I am a civil lawyer, girle, (quoth he)
A civil lawyer sir! you make me muse,
Your talk's too broad for civil men to use;
   If civil lawyers are such bawdy men,
    Oh what (quoth she) are other lawyers then?

Rainaldo, and Rainer.

Rainaldo meeting Rainer in the street,
Deep in his debt, he doth thus Rainer greet,
You know some money is betwixt us two,
That well-nigh now these ten years hath been due;
Quoth Rainer (looking down unto his feet)
I' faith and we will part it, if I see't:
   But as I live Rainaldo I find none,
    As fain as you, I would you had your own.

Spinus his choyce.

Spinus would wed, but he would have a wench
That hath all tongues, Italian, Spanish, French,
But I disswade him; for if she hath any,
She hath enough, if two, she hath too too many.

Backbiters.

When *Codrus* catches fleas, what e'r he ailes,
He kils them with his teeth, not his nails;
Saying, that man by man may blamelesse go,
If every one would use backbiters so.

In Salonus.

Oft in the night *Salonus* is inclin'd,
To rise and pisse, and doth as oft break wind:
If's urinall be glasse, as 'tis no doubt,
I wonder it so many cracks holds out.

In Leonatum.

The filthiest, the fowlest, deformedst lasse,
That is, will be, I think or ever was,
Leonatus loves; wherewith should she him draw,
Except as she's like jet, he be like straw?

Nosce teipsum.

Walking and meeting one not long ago,
I ask't who 'twas, he said he did not know:
I said, I know thee; so said he, I you,
But he that knows himselfe I never knew.

An old Silvium.

Silvius by simony a living got,
And he liv'd well upon it; pray why not?
For he the poor did pill, the rich did lurch,
And so became a pillar of the church.

On Perfumes.

They that smell least, smell best : which intimates,
They smell like beasts that smell like civet cats.

Arcades ambo.

Jack and Dick both with one woman dealt
So long till she the pains of woman felt :
Now Dick he thinks to put a trick on Jack
And Jack again to hang it on Dicks back :
Which got the child, it seems a double case,
It hath so like (they say) Jacks nose, Dicks face.
But by both marks my judgement should be quick,
Et vitulo tu dignus Jack & Dick.

On Punchin.

Give me a reason why men call
Punchin a dry plant-animall.
Because as plants by water grow,
Punchin by beer and ale spreads so.

Ne fide colori.

When Bassa walks abroad she paints her face,
And then she would be seen in every place,
For then your gallants who so e'r they are,
Under a colour will account her faire.

In Flavium.

When Flavius once would needs praise tin,
His brain could bring no reason in ;

But what his belly did bethink,
Platters for meat, and pots for drink.

Ad Quintum.

Thy lawfull wife, fair *Lelia* needs must be,
For she was forc'd by law to marry thee.

In virtutem.

Vertue we praise, but practice not her good,
(Athenian-like) we act not what we know ;
So many men do talk of *Robin-Hood,*
Who never yet shot arrow in his bow.

A good wits diet.

That which upholds our tottering walls of flesh,
Is food : and that which doth our wits refresh,
Is wholsome study : for like longer fare,
Be solid arts, but sweet meats poems are.

On Womens tongue.

Things that be bitter, bitterer than gall,
Physitians say, are alwayes physicall.
Then womens tongues, if into powder beaten,
And in a potion, or a pill be eaten,
Nothing more bitter is. I therefore muse,
That womens tongues in physick they ne'r use :
There's many men who live unquiet lives,
Would spare that bitter member of their wives.
Then prove them doctor, use them in a pill ;
Things oft help sick men, that do sound men kill.

A proper comparison.

As there are three blue beans in a blue bladder,
As there are thrice three rounds in a long ladder,
As there are three nooks in a corner'd cap,
And three corners and one in a map,
  Even so like all these,
  There are three universities.

Of Death.

He that fears death, or mourns it in the just,
Shews of the resurrection little trust.

Woman.

Woman was once a rib, (as truth hath said)
Else sith her tongue runs wide from every point,
I should have dream'd her substance had bin made
Of *Adams* whirle-bone, when t'was out of joynt.

Pepertit, &c.

Nels husband said, she brought him nought but toys,
But yet (without his help) she brings him boys.

Insipiens.

Two friends discoursing that together stood,
The one enquiring if the other could
Tell whether such a man were wise?
He answer'd no, but he is otherwise.

Romes wifelesse Clergy.

Long did I wonder, and I wonder'd much,
Rome should her clergy that contentment grudge

As to debar them of their proper due;
What, doth she all with continence indue?
O no; they find a womans lips so dainty,
They'l tye themselves from one, 'cause they'l have twenty.

On Eves Apples.

Eve for thy fruit thou gav'st too dear a price,
What? for an apple give a paradise?
If now adayes of fruit such gaines were made,
A coster-monger were a devilish trade.

Will the perfumer met me in the street,
I stood amaz'd, he ask'd me what I meant;
In faith, said I, your gloves are very sweet,
And yet your breath doth cast a stronger sent.

Beauty.

Beauty's no other but a lovely grace,
Of lively colours, flowing from the face.

On Poetical Blinks.

He nine wayes looks, and needs must learned be,
That all the Muses at one view can see.

A Conceit.

As *Sextus* once was opening of a nut,
With a sharpe knife his finger deeply cut,
What signe is this, quoth he, can any tell?
'Tis sign, quoth one, y'have cut your finger well.

Not so, saith he, for now my finger's sore,
And I am sure that it was well before.

Women.

Howsoe'r they be, thus do they seem to me,
They be and seem not, seem what least they be.

Mutuans Dissimulans.

Dick crafty borrows to no other end,
But that he will not ought to others lend,
That else might ask him : 'tis some wisdome *Dick*
How ere, accounted but a knavish trick.

Writing.

When words we want, love teacheth to indite ;
And what we blush to speak, she bids us write.

A cure for Impatience.

Who would be patient, wait he at the pool,
For bull-heads, or for block-heads in the school.

Satisfaction.

For all our works, a recompence is sure :
'Tis sweet to think on what was hard t'endure.

To Mistriss mutable.

Love runs within your veins, as it were mixt
With quick-silver, but would be wisely fixt :
For though you may for beauty bear the bell,
Yet ever to ring changes sounds not well.

On a Mad-man.

One ask'd a mad-man, if a wife he had ?
A wife! quoth he, I never was so mad.

To Scilla.

If it be true that promise be a debt,
Then *Scilla* will her freedom hardly get ;
For if she hath vow'd her service to so many,
She'l neither pay them all, nor part from any.
Yet she to satisfie her debts, desires
To yeeld her body, as the law requires.

Nescis, quid serus vesper vehat.

Lyncus deviseth as he lyes in bed,
What new apparrell he were best to make him :
So many fashions flow within his head,
As much he fears the taylor will mistake him :
  But he mistook him not, that by the way
  Did for his old suit lay him up that day.

To Ficus.

Ficus hath lost his nose, but knows not how,
And that seems strange to ev'ry one that knows it :
Me thinks I see it written in his brow,
How, wherefore, and the cause that he did loose it.
  To tell you true, *Ficus,* I thus suppose,
  'Twas some French caniball bit off your nose.

On a painted Curtezan.

Whosoever saith thou sellest all, doth jest,
Thou buy'st thy beauty, that sels all the rest.

Of Arnaldo.

Arnaldo free from fault, demands his wife,
Why he is burthen'd with her wicked life?
Quoth she, good husband do not now repent,
I far more burthens bear, yet am content.

Labor improbus omnia vincit.

Glogo will needs be knighted for his lands,
Got by the labour of his fathers hands,
And hopes to prove a gentleman of note,
For he hath bought himself a painted coat.

Quis nisi mentis inops—

Ware proffer'd stinks; yet stay good proverb, stay,
Thou art deceiv'd, as clients best can say;
Who proferring trebble fees, for single care,
It's well accepted, gold it is such ware.

On a friend indeed.

A reall friend a cannon cannot batter;
With nom'nal friends, a squib's a perilous matter.

On an Italian Proverb.

Three women met upon the market day,
Do make a market, (they do use to say
In *Italy*) and why? their tongues do walk
As loud, as if an hundred men did talk.
One hearing this, swore had his wife been there
And made a fourth, there might have been a faire.

Mans ingresse and egresse.

Nature, which head-long into life did throng us,
With our feet forwards to our grave doth bring us.
What is lesse ours, than this our borrow'd breath?
We stumble into life, we go to death.

On bad Debtors.

Bad debtors are good lyars; for they say,
I'l pay you without faile, on such a day;
Come is the day, to come the debt is still,
So still they lye, though stand in debt they will.
But *Fulcus* hath so oft ly'd in this wise,
That now he lyes in *Ludgate* for his lyes.

On a Justasse.

A *Justice* walking o'r the frozen Thames,
The ice about him round, began to crack;
He said to's man, here is some danger, *James*,
I pray thee help me over on thy back.

Genitoris nesciens.

Tom asks no fathers blessing, if you note him,
And wiser he, unlesse he knew who got him.

To a sleeping Talker.

In sleep thou talk'st un-forethought mysteries,
And utter'st un-foreseen things, with close eyes.
How wel wouldst thou discourse if thou wert dead
Since sleep, deaths image, such fine talk hath bred?

Omne simile non est idem.

Together as we walk'd, a friend of mine
Mistook a painted madam for a signe,
That in a window stood; but I acquainted,
Told him it was no wooden sign was painted,
But Madam *Meretrix :* yea, true, said he,
Yet 'tis a little signe of modesty.

Tandem manifestum.

Katharine that hid those candles out of sight,
May well conceive they'l come at length to light.

Qui ebrius laudat temperantiam.

Severus likes not these unseason'd lines
Of rude absurdities, times foul abuse,
To all posterities, and their assignes,
That might have been (saith he) to better use.
What senslesse gull, but reason may convince,
Or jade so dull, but being kick'd will wince?

Quantum mutatus ab illo.

Would any deem *Manasses* now the man,
That whilome was not worth a wooden kan :
Doubtlesse the dunce in something doth surpasse,
Yet his red nose is still the same it was.

On wisdome and vertue.

Wise-men are wiser than good-men, what then?
'Tis better to be wiser than wise men.

On Ducus.

Ducus keeps house, and it with reason stands,
That he keep house, hath sold away his lands.

Mysus and Mopsa.

Mysus and *Mopsa* hardly could agree,
Striving about superiority:
The text which saith that man and wife are one,
Was the chief argument they stood upon:
She held, they both one woman should become;
He held, they should be man, and both but one.
So they contended daily, but the strife
Could not be ended, till both were one wife.

On Photinus.

I met *Photinus* at the B—— court,
Cited (as he said) by a knave relator:
I ask'd him, wherefore? he in a laughing sort,
Told me it was but for a childish matter.
How e're he laught it out, he lied not;
Indeed 'twas childish, for the child he got.

On Castorites.

See, see, what love is now betwixt each fist,
Since *Castriotes* had a scabby wrist:
How kindly they, by clawing one another,
As if the left hand were the right hands brother!

New Rhetorique.

Good arguments without coyn, will not stick;
To pay, and not to say, 's best rhetorick.

To some kinde Readers.

This book of mine I liken to a glasse,
Wherein the fool may look and laugh his fill:
  He having done with't readers, as ye passe,
Here take and use it, as long as you will.

Est mihi Divi parens.

Owinus wondreth, since he came from *Wales*,
What the description of this isle might be;
That ne'r had seen but mountains, hils, and dales,
Yet would he stand and boast on's pedegree.
  From Rice ap *Richard*, sprung from *Dick* a Cow,
  Be cot, was right good gentleman, law ye now?

Principia sordida.

Bassus hath lands good store, and leases farms,
Whose mother, milk-pails bore, e'r he bore arms.

On Thirsites.

Although *Thirsites* have a filthy face,
And staring eyes, and little outward grace:
Yet this he hath, to make amends for all,
Nature her selfe, is not more naturall.

On Zoilus.

If souldiers may obtain four terms of war,
Muskets should be the pleaders, pikes the bar;
For black bags, bandeliers, jackets for gowns,
Angels for fees, we'll take no more crackt crowns.

On a long beard.

Thy beard is long, better it would thée fit,
To have a shorter beard, and longer wit.

On my selfe.

Who seeks to please all men each way,
　And not himselfe offend;
He may begin to work to day,
　But God knows when hee'l end.

Nimium ne crede colori.

Battas believed for a simple truth,
That yonder guilt-spur spruce and velvet youth,
Was some great personage, or worthy weight,
Untill one told him he was but a knight.
A knaight (quoth *Battas*) vaith I chud a zworne,
A hod not bin lass then zome gen-man borne.

Silens simplex.

Will would seem wise, and many words let passe,
Speaking but little 'cause he's such an ——

To the mis-interpreter.

Cease gaul'd back guilt, these inscious lines to mince,
The world wil know y'are rub'd if once ye wince;
They hem within their seeming critique wall,
Particularly none; generally all:
'Mongst which if you have chanc'd to catch a prick
Cry we-hy if you will, but do not kick.

To Mary Meare.

Meare, since unmixt, unmary'd, and a *maid;*
Then you to be a *Mearmaid* may be said :
A mearmaid's flesh above, and fish below,
And so may you be too, for ought I know.

Ad Rinaldum amic.

See, see, *Rinaldus!* prethee who is that,
That wears yon great green feather in his hat,
Like to some tilter ? sure it is some knight,
Whose wits being green, his head must needs be light.

On himselfe.

Mirth pleaseth some, to others 'tis offence,
Some commend plain conceit, some profound sence;
Some wish a witty jest, some dislike that,
And most would have themselves, they know not what.
Then he that would please all, and himself too,
Takes more in hand then he is like to do.

Fingers end.

Philomathes once studying to indite,
Nibled his fingers, and his nailes did bite :
By this I know not what he did intend,
Unlesse his wit lay at his fingers end.

Sapia qui vendit oportet.

Janus doth jesting, use equivocation,
Which he alludes as doubtfull words of art,
To hide the colour of his occupation,
But to the devil he bears an honest heart.

Clamans Asinus.

Who says *Tom Tipstaffe* is no man of calling?
Can any cryer at sessions be more bawling?

Vpon Dunmo.

I *Dunmo* ask'd as we at supper sate,
How long he had liv'd in the married state,
Sir, just (quoth *Dunmo*) with my wife I met
In the great plague time, I remember yet,
And sighing, as he would have burst in twain,
Said, now almost the thirtieth of her raign.

Vpon Tom Tolthams Nose.

The radiant colour of *Tom Toltham's* nose,
Puts down the lilly, and obscures the rose;
Had I a jewell of such precious hew,
I would present it to some monarch's view,
No subject should possesse such jems as those,
Ergo, the king must have *Tom Toltham's* nose.

Domina prædominans.

Ill may *Rodolphos* boast of rule or riches,
That lets his wife rule him, and wear the breeches.

Titus the Gallant.

Brave *Titus* three years in the town hath been,
Yet not the lyons, nor the tombs hath seen;
I cannot tell the cause without a smile,
He hath bin in the Counter all this while.

In Lalum.

Lalus which loves to hear himself discourse,
  Talks to himself as if he frantick were,
And though himself might no where hear a worse,
  Yet he no other but himself will heare;
    Stop not his mouth if he be troublesome,
    But stop his ears, and then the man is dumbe.

To Criticus.

Criticus about to kisse a mayden throng,
He hapned first on one whose nose was long;
He flouting, said, I fain would kisse you sweet,
But that I fear our lips will never meet,
Your nose stands out so far; the maiden dy'd
Her cheeks with crimson, but soon thus reply'd,
  Pray sir, then kisse me in that place where I
  To hinder you, have neither nose nor eye.

Profundo Scientia.

Sal can by silence, deep profundity,
Force you cry, fough! Jeronimo go by.

On two by Sea.

Two youngsters going by sea, th'one
That ne'r before had been the sea upon,
Casts up; and as he heaves, he bo doth cry;
O said the other, sir, y'are sick, ye'll dy.
No (says the sea-sick) though my stomack's loose,
You see, I can cry bo unto a goose.

Aurum volat ocius Euro.

Monsieur *Flemingo* fraught with angels store,
Would see fair *London*, never seen before :
Where lodging with his mistress but one night,
Had (ere he parted) put them all to flight.

To Pontilianus.

Dogs on their masters fawn and leap,
  And wag their tails apace ;
So, though the flatt'rer want a taile,
  His tongue supplies the place.

Instabilis stans.

Mat being drunken, much his anger wreaks
On's wife ; but stands to nothing that he speaks.

On some Lawyers.

Law serves to keep disordered men in aw,
But *aw* preserves orders, and keeps the law,
Were *aw* away *l[aw]yers* would lyars be,
For *lucre;* which they have and *hold in fee.*

Health.

Even from my heart, much *health I wish,*
  No *health I'l wash* with drink,
Health wish'd, not wash'd, in words, not wine,
  To be the best I think.

Case is altered.

Tom Case (some do report) was lately haltered ;
If this be true, why then the case is altered.

Quæ placuit Domino nupta est Ancilla sodali.

Madam *Rugosa* knows not where to find,
One chamber-maid of ten to please her mind.
But yet my lord so likes their comely carriage,
As he prefers them to his men in marriage.

Plagis mitior.

Katharine that grew so curst, and fit for no man,
With beating soon became a gentle-woman.

Priscus.

When *Priscus* raisd from low to high estate,
Rode through the street in pompous *jollity;*
Cajus his poor familiar friend of late,
Bespake him thus, Sir, now you know not me;
Tis likely friend (quoth *Priscus*) to be so,
For at this time my self I do not know.

Anger soon appeased.

When *John Cornutus* doth his wife reprove,
For being false and faithlesse in her love,
His wife to smooth those wrinkles in his brow,
Doth stop his mouth with, *John come kisse me now.*

A foole for Company.

Fatuus will drink with no such asse,
That lets his jests (unapprehended) passe:
Or if he jest with such of shallow brain,
He laughs himselfe to make his jests more plain.
Thus *Fatuus* doth jest and play the sany,
To laugh at's self, hee's fool if there be any.

In Cineam.

When *Cineas* comes amongst his friends in mourning,
He slily notes, who first his cap doth move;
Him he salutes, the rest so grimly scorning,
As if for ever he had lost his love;
I knowing how the *humor* it did fit
Of the fond gull to be saluted first,
Catch at my cap, but move it not a whit,
Which he perceiving, seems with spight to burst.
But *Cineas*, why expect you more of me
Then I of you? I am as good a man,
And better too by many a quality:
For vault, and dance, and fence, and rime I can:
You keep a whore at your own charge, men tell me,
Indeed friend *Cineas*, therein you excell me.

On Captain Sharke.

One ask'd a friend where Captain *Shark* did lye,
Why sir (quoth he) at Algate, at the Pye;
Away, quoth th'other, he lies not there I know't,
No, sayes the other, then he lies in's throat.

A witty Answer.

A lean, yet fat recusant being confin'd
Unto a justice house, whose wife was great,
(Not great with child, but hugely great with meat)
At supper thus began to grope his mind,
To *hoc est corpus* what say you? she sed;
Marry (quoth he) I say it is well fed.

Gossips discourse.

When *Gillian* and her gossips all are met,
And in the match of gossiping down set,
And plain mass-parson cutting bread for th'table
To tell how fast they talk, my tongue's not able;
One tels strange news, th'other godsworbet cries,
The third shakes her head, alack replies,
She on her hens, this on her ducks do talk,
On thousand things at once their tongues do walk.
  So long as cocks can tread, and hens will lay,
  Gill, and Gills gossips will have words to say.

Capax incapabilis.

Produs in's office seems a simple scribe,
Yet hath he cunning learnt to take a bribe.

A Parson and a Thief.

A lusty parson riding on the way,
Was by a thief commanded for to stay;
The parson drew his sword, for well he durst,
And quickly put his foe unto the worst.
Sir (quoth the thief) I by your habit see
You are a church-man, and debate should flee,
You know 'tis written in the sacred word,
Jesus to *Peter* said, *Put up thy sword:*
True (quoth the parson) but withall then hear,
Saint *Peter* first had cut off *Malchus* ear.

Similes habent labra lactucas.

Dick swash (or swaggering *Dick*) through *Fleetstreet*
With *Sis* and *Brettice* waiting at his heels: (reeles,

To one that would have tane the wall, he swore,
Zounds, dost.not see my punck and paramour?

A Souldiers jest.

One told a souldier sitting at the board,
(And silent) that he had an edgelesse sword;
Who straight reply'd, Sir, I will do my best,
To break your pate, though I ne'r break a jest.

Good Advice.

One to a serving-man this counsell sent,
To get a master that's intelligent;
Then if of him no wages he could get,
Yet he would understand he's in his debt.

Theeves.

Two theeves by night began a lock to pick,
One in the house awake, thus answer'd quick,
Why, how now? what a stir you there do keep?
Goe, come again, we are not yet asleep.

Asse.

He that loves glasse without a G.
Leave out L. and what is he?

Enecat amplexu nimio, sic simia fœtum.

Call *Davus* knave, he straight-way draws his sword,
And makes you prove as much, or eat your word.
But if you call him honest rogue, or Jew,
He huggs you then for.giving him his due.

To Festus.

Festus th'art old, and yet wouldst mary'd be:
Ere thou do so, this counsel take of me:
Look into Lillies Grammar, there thou'lt find,
Cornu a horn, a word still undeclin'd.

A Gentleman and his Physitian.

A gentleman not richest in discretion,
Was alwayes sending for his own physitian.
And on a time, he needs would of him know,
What was the cause his pulse did go so slow?
Why (quoth the doctor) thus it comes to passe,
T'must needs go slow, which goes upon an asse.

On Saint George.

To save a maid Saint George a dragon slue,
Which was a noble act, if all be true;
Some say there are no dragons; and 'tis said
There's no Saint George; pray Jove there be a maid.

Similis cum simili.

Tom went to the market, where Tom met with Tom,
Tom asked Tom, what Tom? how far'st thou Tom?
Who Tom, I Tom? Is Tom (quoth Tom) you Tom;
Well God a mercy Tom; how do you Tom?
Faith ne'r so well (quoth Tom) since Tom was Tom:
And thus was the greeting past 'twixt Tom and Tom.

Ebrius oblitus.

Fucus was fox'd last night, but 'tis conceal'd,
And would not for his office 'twere reveal'd.

Dulce quod utile.

An honest vicar riding by the way,
Not knowing better how to spend the day,
Did sing unto himself some certain psalms;
A blind man hearing him, strait begg'd his alms;
To whom (quoth he) with coyn I cannot part,
But God thee blesse, good man with all my heart.
O, said the blind man, greater is my losse,
When such as you do blesse without a crosse.

In Dacum.

Dacus with some good colour and pretence,
Tearms his wifes beauty silent eloquence;
For she doth lay more colours on her face,
Then ever Tully us'd his speech to grace.

In Sillam.

Though I were blind, or though I never saw him,
Yet if I should Silla but talking hear;
For a right roaring gallant I should know him,
For of a whore he talks, and still doth swear.

Varietas iniquitas.

Mat will not marry: true, 'cause ty'd to none,
He may have wenches new, when th'old are gone.

Good sawce.

I went to sup with Cinna th'other night,
And to say true (for give the devil his right)
Though scant of meat we could a morsell get,
Yet there with store of passing sawce we met,

You ask what sawce, where pittance was so small?
This, is not hunger the best sawce of all.!'

To a Lawyer.

To go to law, I have no maw,
  Although my suite be sure,
For I shall lack suits to my back,
  Ere I my suit procure.

Semel insanivimus.

Bedlam fate bless thee, thou wantst nought but wit,
And having gotten that, we'r freed from it;
Bridewell, I cannot any way dispraise thee,
For thou dost feed the poor, and jerk the lazie.
Newgate, of thee I cannot much complain;
For once a moneth, thou freest men out of pain;
But from the *Counters,* goodnesse it self defend us?
To *Bedlam, Bridewell,* or to *Newgate* send us,
For there in time, wit, work, or law sets free;
But here wit, work, nor law gets liberty.

Of himselfe.

Some men there be, which say of me,
  That I am not a *poet ;*
They say well, why? I do not lye,
  I write the truth; I know it.

Vpon Annes marriage with a Lawyer.

Anne is an angel, what if so she be?
What is an angel, but a lawyers fee?

Ænigma.

The Devil, men say, in Devonshire dy'd of late,
But Devonshire lately liv'd in rich estate,
Till *Rich* his toys did Devonshire so bewitch,
As Devonshire dy'd, and left the Devil Rich.

On Cupid.

Why feign they *Cupid* robbed of his sight?
Can he whose seat is in the eye, want light?

An Answer.

Experience shew, and reason doth decree
That he who sits in's own light cannot see.

Lucus journey.

Lucus hath travel'd with an hundred pound,
Was rob'd and left well beaten, and fast bound:
But when to share their prize, they had begun,
No miracle was wrought, yet he undon.

Of Nature.

Nature did well in giving poor men wit,
That fools well monifi'd may pay for it.

Vilescit dives avarus.

Rufus is wondrous rich, but what of that?
He lives obscurely, like a water-rat.

Visum ignotum.

That *Crambo's* wife's with child, her belly shews it:
But who was't got it? pray ask those that know it.

Vpon Marriage.

Marriage as old men note, hath lik'ned bin
  Unto a publick fast, or common rout,
Where those that are without would fain get in,
  And those that are within would fain get out.

On Annas a News-monger.

Annas hath long ears for all news to passe:
His ears must needs be long, for he's an asse.

Sir John.

Now good Sir John (the beggar cries) I pray
Bestow your worship's alms on me to day,
Relieve my wants (quoth he) I am your brother,
We born are, one to help and ayd another;
My brother (qd. Sir John) poor wretched wight,
Why, thou mistakest me, I am a knight;
I know't, quoth he, but hark you kind Sir John,
There's many a knight kin to the beggar man.

Conjectus.

Conjectus says hee'l plainly prove,
Anothers child he ought to love,
More than his parents; which is strange,
And yet 'tis true; for I protest,
He ought to love his wife the best.

Aulus.

Some (speaking in their own renown)
Say that this book was not exactly done;

I care not much, like banquets let my books,
Rather be pleasing to the guests than cooks.

On envy.

Why say some, wealth brings envy, since 'tis known
Poor men have backbiters fifteen for one?

Errantes errare licet.

Pandorus spends the day by telling news,
Of such his travels as will make you muse:
Nay sir believe it, hee'l discourse at large,
How should he else be fed at others charge?

To a Drunkard.

Much pratling causeth greatest thirstinesse?
Thy wife talks more then thou, why drinks she lesse.

On Pru.

Pru give me leave to laugh, why shouldst thou buy
Ceruse, and stibium, and mercury,
And sleiking oyles, the best that may be got,
When thy whole face Pru is not worth a groat?

To Momus.

Leave for shame, Momus, leave to bark and cry,
My actions give thy slanderous tongue the lye.

To Roba.

Th'art fair, 'tis true; and pretty too, I know it;
And well bred (Roba) for thy manners show it;

But whilst thou mak'st self-praise thy onely care,
Th'art neither pretty, nor well bred, nor faire.

On Gallo.

Gallo's a pretty man, hath pretty hair,
A pretty hat, and cloke as one need wear;
Gallo's a gallant, and as gallants use,
Can court his mistress, with a sprightly muse:
Gallo's a dunce, for I supply his wit,
Which he makes nonsence by his reading it,
And 'tis no wonder, as all wise-men know,
For pretty gallants to be dunces now.

Pudor est sua damna referre.

Peter hath lost his purse, but will conceale it,
Least she that stole it, to his shame reveale it.

Wheele-greace.

Men th'axletree do greaze, that they not screak,
But lawyers must be greaz'd to make them speak.

Who best friend.

A louse I say, for when a man's distrest,
And others fall off, she sticks the surest.

O times and manners!

Why thus do men, manners and times accuse,
When men themselves, manners and times abuse?
W'are bad in them, they worse by us do grow,
Yet we complain that help to make them so.

Carpe.

Of all our modern writers, *Carpe* likes none,
He loves th'old poets that are dead and gone:
Pardon me honest *Carpe*, I would not be
Laid in my grave a while yet, to please thee.

Non nunquam jactat egenus.

Jack is a gentleman I must confesse,
For there's no womans taylor can be lesse.

On Terpin.

Terpin sips wine, and gluts down meat; I think,
My *Terpin* drinks his meat, and eats his drink.

To Phaulo.

As often (*Phaulo*) as thou dost amisse,
Thou hast no more excuse for it, but this,
It was against thy will; why, be it so,
Against thy will thou shalt be punisht to.

Little, nothing, too much, enough.

The poor have *little*, beggars *none*,
The rich *too much*, *enough* not one.

On Spurco of Oxford.

Spurco from chandler, started alderman,
And trust me now most elder-like he can
Behave himself: he ne'r appears in town,
But in his beaver, and his great fur'd gown:
His ruffe is set, his head set in his ruffe;
His reverend trunks become him well enough;

He wears a hoop ring on his thumb; he has
Of gravidud a dose full in his face:
And trick'd and trim'd, thus bravely he supposes
Himself another man; but men have noses;
And they that have so, maugre *Spurco's* skill,
Through all his robes may smell the chandler still.

On the same.

Spurco made candles once, 'tis true enough,
Yet when I told him so, he tookt in snuffe.

To Damon.

What cause, what confidence draws thee to town?
Oxford can yeeld thee nothing, get thee down;
Thou canst not turn rogue for thy private ends,
Thou canst not play the baud to please thy friends.
Thou hat'st to sell thy breath at any price,
Or flatter great ones to their prejudice.
Whence wilt thou live? (unhappy wretch!) I am
A trusty friend, thou say'st, an honest man.
That's nothing, *Damon*, set thy wits to school,
Not to be knave here, is to be a fool.

Compotatio.

Tasso, Torquato, Trew-wit, Manlius,
Brave merry Greeks all, and ingenious:
Let us be mad a while: come here thou squire
Of pints and pottles, pile us up a fire:
Then bring some sack up, quick you canniball,
Some cleanly sack to wash our brains withall:

There is I am sure, no other Thespian spring,
No other Helicon to bathe us in.
Troul then your sack about boyes, never faile,
Commending dull men to their stands of ale.
Tinkers wind off whole pottles in a breath,
I hate such puddle coxcombs worse than death :
But we true brats of *Bacchus*, as our use is,
With lusty wines will sacrifice to th'Muses.

Conscientia testis.

What makes *Antonia* deem himself undone,
Being question'd since his office first begun :
But that a conscience tells him *quæ sumuntur*
Tam male parta, male dilabuntur?

On Terpin.

Listen who list, my *Terpins* nose I sing,
And much I labour to expresse the thing :
For when he snorts, it is his trumpet shrill ;
It is his conduit, for 'tis running still ;
It is his drag, his eele-spear in the brook ;
His spade, his mattock, and his pruning hook :
'Tis a convenient staple for a wall,
A handsome wedge to cleave his wood withall :
'Twill make a good ship-anchor when he lacks,
It is his gimlet, and his twibill axe.
Regard not then, what man thy nose abuses ;
Thy nose is proper *Terpin* for most uses.

On Ned.

Have not I friends (quoth *Ned*) I dare to say,
I have not supt at home this twelve months day :
And very true it is, for sherking *Ned*,
At home (poor man) goes supperlesse to bed.

Pecunia prævalens.

Hand off, sir sauce-box! think you Mistris *Phips*
Allows such lobs as you to touch her lips ?
But then 'tis question'd further ; if you bring her
Some *legem pone*, that's another thing sir.

On Love.

Where love begins, there dead they first desire :
A spark neglected, makes a mighty fire.

A. Herculean taske.

To curb the courage and *wives tongue* keep under,
May well be call'd *Hercules* thirteenth wonder.

On Coritia.

Coritia, when all her table's set
With manchet, sauches, and good wholsome meat,
She still gives brown bread to her son and heir,
And tells the little boy 'twill make him fair.
If so (my love) if it be true you say,
You never ate brown bread *Coritia*.

On Drammato.

Drammato makes new playes great store ; and yet
'Tis plain, *Drammato* has not too much wit :

He strives too, to be pleasant, and brings in
Mimicks, and fools, to make the people grin,
I know not what the rest think, but I say,
Drammato's the best fool in every play.

Taming of a Shrew.

Wouldst tame thy wife : first tame her tongue,
Who thus his wife comes o'r shall overcome.

Liberty.

If he be well which hath what he can wish,
Why then do men for stinging serpents fish !
True liberty 'mongst vertues bears the bell ;
He may live as he will, which may live well.

Drammato.

Of all *Drammato's* playes that ere I see,
Nothing could ever make me laugh but he.

On Galba.

Galba she sayes, she never tasted man ;
Galba will lye, beleeve it, now and than.

To the Reader.

Such tenour I have kept here all along,
As none (I hope) can challenge me with wrong.
I injure not the least, I give no blow
To any person ; he that knows not how
To scourge mans vice, unlesse he tax his name,
Makes a base libel of an epigram.

On Formidando.

Stout *Formidando* walks imperiously,
With tragick *Bilbo* girt upon his thigh;
His roping locks, his buffe becomes him well,
And to say sooth, he looks right terrible;
He swayes the town before him, and will slay
Whatever man he be that dares gain-say:
But *Formidando* pawn'd his coat last night,
And *Formidando's* out of money quite;
Nor oaths will passe, nor credit from henceforth,
For one poor penny, or a penny-worth:
Starv'd creditors begin to gape; and how
To quit himself he scarcely knows; that now
Stout *Formidando* who was wont to daunt
Whole thousands, trembles at a pursivant.

The German-Dutch.

Death's not to be: so *Seneca* doth think:
But Dutchmen say 'tis death to cease to drink.

Death.

What death is, dost thou ask of me?
Till dead I do not know;
Come to me when thou hear'st I'm dead,
Then what 'tis I shall show.

On Carp and Manilla.

Manilla would with *Carp* be maried,
   Manilla's wise I trow:
But *Carp* by no means will *Manilla* wed;
   Carp's the wiser of the two.

On Carp.

These are my verses which *Carp* reads; 'tis known;
But when *Carp* makes them non-sense, th'are his own.

To Phaulos.

Thou art offended (*Phaulos*) as I hear,
Because I sometimes call thee whoremaster;
My nature's blunt, and so will ever be;
I call a spade a spade, pray pardon me.

To Coracine.

What *Crispulus* is that in a new gown,
All trim'd with loops and buttons up and down?
That leans there on his arm in private chat
With thy young wife, what *Crispulus* is that?
He's proctor of a court, thou say'st, and does
Some businesse of my wives: thou brainlesse goose!
He does no businesse of thy wives, not he,
He does thy businesse (*Coracine*) for thee.

On Pru.

Pru praises her complexion, nay swears
She dares compare with any of her years;
And very true it is, that *Prudence* sayes,
I saw not better sold these many dayes.

The Parret.

If lawful't be, of things t'invent the name;
With pratling *Parret*, *prater* is the same.

To Maronilla.

My *Maronilla*, I could easily spare
Thy hands and arms, thy shoulders and fraught haire,
I could well spare thy feet, thy legs and thighs,
Thy tongue and teeth, thy lips, cheeks, forehead, eyes:
And not to reckon each part severall,
My *Maronilla* I could spare thee all.

Study.

Some men grow mad by studying much to know;
But who grows mad by studying good to grow?

To Lionell.

Lionell shows his honourable scars,
And labours to invite me to the wars:
But I will not by no means *Lionell;*
I do not love to live ill, and drink well.

On Pumilio a Dwarfe.

Pumilio lying in despaire
Of further life, said, take no care
To make a tomb for me, good folks,
I will be buried in a box.

Sharpe sauce.

Kisses and favours are sweet things,
But those have thornes, and these have stings.

On Drad-nought.

Drad-nought was for his many riots laid
Ith'Counter lately, now he's wondrous staid.

On Phaulos and Gellia.

Phaulos he visits, *Gellia* she's sick:
I am no wizard, yet I know their trick.

To his Friend.

I will not be a foe to any,
Nor be familiar with too many;
And twice I will not love my friend,
But whom I love, I'l love to th'end.

Maried Folke.

Man love thy wife; thy husband, wife obay:
Wives are our heart, we should be head alway.

On Pru and Galla.

Why are *Pru's* teeth so white, and *Galla's* black?
  The reason is soon known:
Pru buyes new teeth as often as she lacks,
  But *Galla* wears her owne.

On Bombo.

When *Bombo* preaches (and that's thrice a year)
Nothing but wit sounds wisely in his ear.
His fustain phrases make a noise; each strain
And swelling rapture fills his mouth again:
He's parcell-states-man, parcell-priest, and so
If you observe, he's parcel-poet to.
Bombo thy fetches, and thy fangles may
Become a stage perhaps, but us'd this way,
Th'are base, and impious: let me prevail,
Talk till thy strong lines choak thee; if they fail,

Commence at Tyburn in a cart, sweet poet,
And there a strong line will for certain do it.

On Lulls.

Lulls swears he is all heart, but you'l suppose
By his probassis, that he is all nose.

On Pæto.

Implore the Muses, and their two top'd hill,
Still to supply fresh matter to thy quill:
Crave *Phœbus* aid, call *Homer* with the throng
Of all the bardes, learn'd *Manes*, to thy song.
I dare not (*Pæto*) be so bold, as do it,
Nor seem so like what I am not; a poet.
My page invokes no deities: here love,
And indignation the best Muses prove.

On the same.

My *Pæto* thinks he sings melodious,
And like a swan: alas he's but a goose.

On Plutus.

Plutus, rich *Plutus* would have me bestow
Some new-years gift, as other neighbours do.
Why I will send thee what thou want'st my friend;
Nothing thou want'st, and nothing I will send.

To Phocion.

Thou buy'st up all that thou canst light upon,
This is the way to sell all *Phocion*.

To Lividus.

Do not raile basely, do not swell with spight,
Do not scoffe (*Lividus*) at what I write :
For ridden, trust me, I can hardly pace,
Nor bear thee gently like a patient asse;
But trot amain, and if thou chance to kick,
I shall wince too, and gall thee to the quick.
Flinging full fast till I have thrown thee off,
Till I have shook thy snaffle from thy mouth ;
And then in triumph (*Lividus*) look to't,
I spurn thy pride and follies under foot.

On his Verses.

He's blind with love that likes them ev'ry one,
And he is blind with envy, that likes none.

Truth.

Truth is best found out by the time and eyes ;
Falshood wins credit by uncertainties.

Time.

Time all consumes, both us and every thing,
We time consume; thus, both one song do sing.

To Bombo.

Most men condemn thee *Bombo*, when they hear
Thy high and mighty sermons, but I swear
Thou preachest movingly; and well I may;
Thou preachest all thy auditors away.

On Plutus.

Rich *Plutus* needs would buy a fool, and paid
Fifty good pounds : but after triall made,
Perceiving him an understanding man,
Plutus would have his money back again.

To Linus.

Thou wast my debtor when I lent the coin,
Pay me mine own, and then I will be thine.

Leven.

Love is a leven, and a loving kiss
The *leven* of a loving sweet-heart is.

To Phaulos.

Thou ask'st me whom I think best man to be,
He's the best (*Phaulos*) that is least like thee.

To Claudius and Linus.

Ungodly *Claudius*, to be good,
  Wants nothing but a will :
Lewd *Linus*, also wanteth nought
  But power to be ill.

Hot-waters.

Our trickling tears expresse our private love,
Love causeth tears, strange ! fire should water prove.

On Grotto.

Talk but of death, *Grotto* begins to rage,
And sweat, and swear, and yet he's blind with age.

Fie on thee *Grotto*, what a coil you keep?
Thy windows they are shut, 'tis time to sleep.

On Boreman.

Boreman takes tole, cheats, flatters, lyes, yet *Boreman*
For all the devill helps, will be a poor man.

On Crab.

Crab being caught, and in the serjeants power,
For shame and anger look'd both red and sower.

On Fargo.

Fargo by his wit and pleasing tongue,
Hath won a wench that's wondrous fair & young;
The match (he saith) is halfe concluded, he
Indeed is wondrous willing; but not she.

On Richard.

Dick being drunk, in bed thought on his sin,
And that lewd course of life he lived in,
Yet long hereof for thirst, *Dick* could not think,
But, drawer, cryes, now for thy smallest drink.

To Spruce.

Spruce wears a comb about him, alwayes he
To prune and smooth his polisht haire:
The cock's ne'r too without his comb you see,
Spruce 'tis a *coxcomb* then you weare.

On this wise age.

The wise men were but seaven : now we scarce know
So many fools, the world so wise doth grow.

On Profuso.

Unstayd *Profuso* hath run thorough all,
Almost the story of the *Prodigall*,
Yet swears, he never with the hoggs did dine,
That's true, for none durst trust him with their swine.

On a fire in a Town.

One night through all the streets the men did cry,
Fire, fire ! at which I wak't and wondred by ;
Not that dry wood should burn, but because all
Did cry *fire*, when for water they should call.

To either Vniversity.

Indulgent *mother*, and kind *aunt*, no where
Throughout all *Europe* find I such a paire ;
From whose fair breasts those milky rivers run,
That thousands feed, else thousands were undone.
Oh were it not that some are wean'd too young,
And some do suck (like *Essex* calves) too long.

On Monsieur Congee.

A proper handsome courtly man indeed,
And well set out with cloaths, can for a need
Discourse with legs, and quarter congees, and
Talk halfe an houre with help of foot and hand ;
But when I view'd this *Monsieur* clean throughout,
I found that he was onely man without.

y person is ano   t,
I now but act the epigrammatist.

On Physitians.

Physitians are most miserable men,
   that cannot be deny'd:
For they are never truly well, but when
   most men are ill beside.

On Puff.

Puff quarrels in his cups, and then will fight,
Is beaten sober; troth he is served right.

To Flash.

Flash when thou'rt drunk, then in thy own conceit
Thou'rt valiant, wise, great, honest, rich, discreet.
Troth Flash be alwayes drunk! for well I know
When you are sober you are nothing so.

Wittily wicked.

Good wine (they say) makes vinegar most tart,
Thou, the more witty, the more wicked art.

A Doctor and his Patient.

A doctor told his patient Omphida;
The grief she felt was a sciatica:
Which she not perfect how to nominate,
Mistaking cryes, O my certificate!

On Monsieur Powder-wig.

Oh doe but mark yon crisped sir you meet!
How like a pageant he doth walk the street?
See how his perfum'd head is powdered ore:
Twu'd stink else, for it wanted salt before.

To Rash.

Rash swear not! think not 'cause you swear that I
Believe you, no : he that will swear will lye.

Drunk-bounty.

I'l tell you why the drunk so lavish are,
They have too much, nay more then they can bear.

To Gut.

Gut eats and drinks, doth nothing else but swill,
His teeth do grind, his mouth's the water-mill.

To Simple.

Simple, you know I gave you good advice;
Little to say, that men might think you wise;
If you'l proclaim your selfe a fool you may;
I onely tell you now what others say.

On Quaff.

To quench his sorrows Quaff drinks very free,
Sorrow is dry, he sayes, and so is he.

To Tom Coriat.

Of all the Toms that ever yet were nam'd,
Was never Tom like as Tom Coriat fam'd.

Tom Thumb is dumb, untill the pudding creep,
In which he was intomb'd, then out doth peep.
Tom Fool may go to school, but ne'r be taught
Speak Greek, with which our *Tom* his tongue is fraught.
Tom Asse may passe, but for all his long ears,
No such rich jewels as our *Tom* he wears.
Tom Tell-troth is but froth, but truth to tell,
Of all *Toms*, this *Tom*, bears away the bell.

To a fat Vsurer.

Fat folks we say by nature are most free :
You and your purse are fat, and yet I see
Your hand and that still shut, the reason's this ;
In costive flesh thy *leane* soule buried is.

On Brisk.

Brisk brag'd of's ready wit ; I tempting him
But for one distick, did propound this theam
Nothing : It cannot be, he wondring said
That out of nothing ought shu'd ere be made.
Dul *Brisk* thou ne'r couldst tune *Apollo's* lyre :
A pure steeld-wit, will strike *Mercuriall* fire
Out of the flintiest subject : but thy head
Is all compos'd of softer mettle, *lead*.

Semel insanivimus omncs.

Thus have I waded through a worthlesse task,
Whereto I trust there's no exception ta'n,
For meant to none, I answer such as ask,
'Tis like apparrell made in *Birchen-lane;*

If any please to suit themselves and wear it,
The blame's not mine, but theirs that needs will bear it.

On Sullen.

Sullen will eat no meat, but peevishly
Replies, I care not, nor I will not, I :
Troth I commend his abstinence, 'tis great,
When having such a stomach hee'l not eat.

To Bankes.

When *Spendall* asks to borrow, you reply,
You know not when hee'l pay you; troth nor I.

To Boldface.

Boldface, I wonder at thy impudence,
That dar'st affirme things so against all sence :
For shame ben't impudent and foolish too !
And think all men are fooles 'cause you are so.

Of this Booke.

Part of the work remaines; one part is past :
And here my ship rides having anchor cast.

On Bearill.

Bearill because his wife is somewhat ill,
Uncertain in her health, indifferent still ;
He turns her out of doores without reply ;
Wondring at which I askt the reason why ?
In sicknesse and in health, sayes he, I'm bound
Onely to keep her, either weak or sound ;

But now shee's neither, he replies; you'l see,
Shee'l quickly now or mend or end, sayes he.

On Bib.

Wisdome doth teach us silence, now *Bib* is
With drink made speechless, is he not then wise.

On Silly.

Silly by chance did loose his diary
Of wit, which he had got in company:
No marl he now so mute and pensive sits,
How can he choose, since he hath lost his wits.

Ad sesquipidales poetastros.

Hence *Brauron*'s god to *Tauriminion*,
And you levaltoring corybants be gon;
Fly thundering bronsterops to *Hippocrene*,
And *Mauros* to nymph-nursing *Mytelene*;
Grisly *Megæra*'s necromantique spell
Depart to black nights *Acherontick* cell:
Avaunt transformed *Epidaurian*,
Unto th'antipod isles of Traproban,
Away *Cyllenius* plumy-pinnion'd god,
With thy peace making wand, snake-charming rod;
And all the rest not daring look upon
Vranus blood-born brood, and fell *Typhon*;
Chimera's victor great *Bellerophon*,
Thou vanquisher of Spanish *Geryon*.
Stout *Asdruball* Sicilian lord of yore,
Thou that destroy'dst the *Caledonian* bore,

Couragious conqueror of Cretes *Minotaure,*
Thou pride of *Mermeno's* cloudy *Semitaure.*
Perseus whose marble stone transforming shield,
Enforc'd the whale, *Andromeda* to yeeld,
You *Argonautes* that scour'd *Syndromades,*
And pass'd the quick-sands of *Symplegades,*
Help *Demogorgon,* king of heaven and earth,
Chaos, Lucina, at *Litigiums* birth,
The world with childe looks for delivery
Of *Canibals,* or *Poetophagy.*
A devilish brood from *Ericthonius,*
From *Iphidemia, Nox,* and *Erebus,*
Chide *Pegasus* for op'ning *Helicon,*
And poets damn to *Pyry-Phlegeton;*
Or make this monstrous birth abortive be,
Or else I will shake hands with poetry.

———*Nihil hic nisi carmina desunt.*

Marmora Mæonii vincunt monumenta libelli;
Vivitur ingenio, cætera mortis erunt.

The Muses works stone monuments out-last;
'Tis wit keeps life, all else death will down cast.

Epitaphs.

On a leacherous Warrener.

BEHOLD here lyes a scalded pate quite bare,
In catching conies, who lost many a hare.

On a faire Damosell.

Life is the road to death, and death heavens gate must be,
Heaven is the throne of Christ, and Christ is life to me.

On Prince Henry.

In natur's law 'tis a plaine case to dye,
No cunning lawyer can demurre on that;
    For cruell death and destiny
    Serve all men with a latitat.
So princely Henry; when his case was try'd,
Confess'd the action, paid the debt, and dy'd.

On Queene Anne.

Thee to invite the great God sent his star,
Whose friends and kinsmen mightie princes are,
For though they run the race of men and dye,
Death serves but to refine their majesty.
So did the queen from hence her court remove,
And left the earth to be enthron'd above.
Thus is she chang'd, not dead, no good prince dyes
But like the day-star, onely sets to rise.

On an onely child.

Here lyes the fathers hope, the mothers joy,
Though they seeme haplesse, happy was the boy,
Who of this life, the long and tedious race
Hath travell'd out in lesse then 2 moneths space.
Oh happie soule, to whom such grace was given,
To make so short a voyage backe to heaven,
As here a name and christendome t'obtaine
And to his maker then returne againe.

On Edmund Spencer, poet laureat.

He was, and is (see then where lyes the odds)
Once god of poets, poet now to th' gods,
And though his time of life be gone about,
The life of his lines never shall weare out.

On Master Stone.

Here worthy of a better chest,
A pretious stone inclos'd doth rest,

Whom nature had so rarely wrought
That Pallas it admir'd, and thought
No greater jewell than to weare
Still such a diamond in her eare:
But sicknesse did it from her wring,
And placed it in Libitina's ring,
Who changed natures worke anew
And death's pale image in it drew.
Pitty that paine had not been sav'd,
So good a stone to be engrav'd.

On a Tobacconist.

Loe here I lye, roll'd up like th' Indian weede,
My pipes I have pack'd up, for breath I neede.
Man's breath's a vapour, he himselfe is grasse
My breath, but of a weede, the vapour was.
When I shal turne to earth, good friends! beware
Least it evap'rate, and infect the ayre.

On M. Pricke.

Vpon the fifth day of November
Christ's colledge lost a privie member:
Cupid and death did both their arrowes nicke,
Cupid shot short, but death did hit the pricke.
Women lament, and maidens make great mones,
Because the pricke is laid beneath the stones.

On Prince Henry.

Loe where he shineth yonder
A fixed starre in heaven,

Whose motion thence coms under
  None of the planets seven :
If that the moone should tender
  The sunne her love and marry,
They both could not engender
  So bright a starre as Harry.

On Richard Burbage a famous Actour.
—————— Exit Burbage.

On a Printer whose Wife was lame.
Sleepe *William*, sleepe, she that thine eyes did close,
Makes lame iambiques for thee as shee goes.

On an Infant unborne, the Mother dying in travell.

The father digg'd a pit, and in it left
Part of himselfe interr'd, that soone bereft
The mother of the gift, she gave, life ; so
Both now are buried in one tombe of woe.
'Tis strange the mother should a being give,
And not have liberty to make it live.
'Twas strange, that the child blindfold espi'd
So quick and neere away to parricide ;
Yet both are justly question'd, child and mother
Are guilty of the killing of each other.
Not with an ill intent, both did desire
Preserves for life, and not a funerall fire ;
And yet they needs must dye, and 'was thought best
To keep the infant in the mother's chest ;

It had both life and death from her, the wombe
In which it was begot, became the tombe;
There was some marble sav'd, because in her
The wombe that bare it, was a sepulcher,
Whose epitaphs are these, here lies a child that shal
Be free from all sins but originall.
Here lies a pittied mother that did dye
Onely to beare her poore child companie.

On M. Washington, page to the Prince.

Knew'st thou whose these ashes were;
  Reader thou would'st weeping sweare,
The rash fate err'd here, as appeares,
  Counting his vertues for his yeeres,
  His goodnesse made them so o're seene,
  Which shew'd him threescore; at eighteene.

Enquire not his disease or paine!
  He dy'd of nothing else but spayne,
Where the worst calenture he feeles,
  Are Jesuits, and Alguaziles,
  Where he is not allow'd to have,
  (Unlesse he steal't) a quiet grave.

He needs no other epitaph or stone
  But this, here lyes lov'd *Washington*,
Write this in teares, in that loose dust,
  And every greiv'd beholder must,
  When he weighs him, and knowes his yeeres,
  Renew the letters with his teares.

On the death of Mary, Countesse of Pembroke.

Under-neath this sable hearse,
Lies the subject of all verse.
Sidneys sister Pembrookes mother,
Death e're thou hast kill'd another,
  Faire and learned good as shee,
  Time shall throw a dart at thee.
Marble pillers let none raise
To her name for after dayes.
Some kind woman borne as shee,
Reading this as *Niobe*,
  Shall turne marble and become,
  Both thy mourner and thy tombe.

On the King of Sweden's death.

'Tis sin to praise or weepe; oh let me vent
My passion ouely in astonishment.
Who sheads a teare for thee (brave Swead thus slain)
His eyes do penance for his weaker braine;
And yet those eyes themselves deserve this doome,
Which thus mistake a trophie for a tombe.
Or else thy foes may weepe, as then they did
As when thou dyest, but all their teares were blood.
O what a tempest, what a sea was forc't,
Of tribute, groanes and teares, to waft one ghost.
No way but death they had to flie thy face:
Thou quit's thy body to pursue thy chase.
But who pretends thy praise in best expression,
Indites his judgment of confest presumption.

Bold tongue, touch not that head, that heart, that hand
Which brought on's knees (whē he did tip-to stand)
The pride of Austria, back't what all but heaven.
Himselfe of all, but of himselfe bereven.
Thus having plum'd th'imperiall bird alone,
Upon those eagle wings to heaven he's flowne:
Why should he stay on earth, the game is done;
Others can part the stake that hee hath wonne,
'Tis low ambition, underneath his story,
To ayme at any crowne, but that of glory.
   Then cannon play, his body's sacrific'd,
   He is not cannon'd, no he's canoniz'd.

On a Lyer.

Good passenger! here lies one here,
That living did lie every where.

On a Dyer.

He lives with God none can deny,
That while he liv'd to th'world did dy.

On a Jugler.

Death came to see thy tricks, and cut in twain
Thy thread; why did'st not make it whole again?

On Mr. Fish.

Worms bait for *Fish*, but here is a great change.
Fish bait for worms, is not that very strange?

On a Child.

A child and dead? alas! how could it come?
Surely thy thred of life was but a thrum.

On Mr. Do.

Do is my name, and here I lie,
My grammar tels me *Do fit Di*.

On Taylor a Sergeant, kill'd by a Horse.

A taylor is a theef, a sergeant is worse,
Who here lyes dead, god-a-mercy horse.

On Mr. Thomas Best.

With happy starres he sure is blest,
Where s'ere he goes, that still is *Best*.

On Robin.

Round *Robin's* gone, and this grave doth inclose
The pudding of his doublet and his hose.

On Bell the Tinker.

Bell though thou dy'dst decrepit, lame forlorn,
Thou was't a man of mettle, I'll be sworn.

On proud Tygeras.

Proud and foolish, so it came to passe,
He liv'd a *Tyger*, and he dy'd an Asse.

On John Cofferer.

Here lyes *John Cofferer*, and takes his rest,
Now he hath chang'd a coffer for a chest.

On blind and deaf Dick Freeman.

Here lyes *Dick Freeman,*
That could not hear nor see man.

On a Miller.

Death without warning was as bold as brief,
When he killed two in one, miller and theef.

On a Lady.

Here lyes one dead under this marble stone,
Who when she liv'd, lay under more than one.

On a Wrestler.

Death to the wrestler gave a pretty fall,
Tript up his heels, and took no hold at all.

On John Death.

Here's *Death* interred, that liv'd by bread,
Then all should live, now *Death* is dead.

On an Infant.

The reeling world turn'd poet, made a play;
I came to see't, dislik'd it, went my way.

On a little but very ingenious youth.

Grim Death perceiving, he had far outran
The elder youths; mistooke him for a man.

On a Lady dying quickly after her Husband.

He first deceased, she a little try'd
To live without him, lik'd it not, and dy'd.

On Mr. Stone.

Jerusalems curse is not fulfill'd in mee,
For here a stone upon a stone you see.

On Mr. Strange.

Here lies one *Strange*, no Pagan, Turk, nor Jew,
It's strange, but not so strange as it is true.

A Fart's Epitaph.

Reader, it was born, and cry'd,
Crack'd so, smelt so, and so dy'd.

On Mr. Anguish a Scholler.

Some do for anguish weep, for anger I,
That ignorance should live, and art should die.

On a lovely young youth.

From thy quick death; conclude we must,
The fairest flowers are gather'd first.

On Mr. Thomas Allen.

No epitaphs need make the just man fam'd,
The good are prais'd when they are onely nam'd.

On a Lady.

Finis and *Bonum* are converted, so
That every good thing to an end must go.

On a pious Benefactor.

The poor, the world, the heavens, and the grave,
His alms, his praise, his soul, and body have.

On a Poet in prison.

Though I in prison here do lye,
My Muse shall live although I dye.

On a poor Poet.

Here lies the poet buried in the night,
Whose purse, men know it, was exceeding light.

A man and his wife.

Viator siste, eoce miraculum!
Vir & uxor hic non ligitant.

On a Pauls-walker.

Defessus sum ambulando.

On a Scrivener.

May all men by these presents testifie,
A lurching scrivener here fast bound doth lie.

On one that cheated his Father.

Here lies a man, who in a span
Of life, beyond his father ran.

On a Cut-purse.

Death hath that cutpurse seiz'd on at Alhallows,
Who by good hap hath so escap'd the gallows.

On a young great Wit.

Great wits are dangerous, for then,
It seems, they seldome come to men.

On an Vsurer.

That all those goods and riches scrap'd together,
Should with himself depart, and knows not whither.

On a Captain.

Who late in wars did dread no foes in field,
Now free of scars his life in peace doth yeeld.

On a Potter.

He that on clay his chiefest trust repos'd,
Is now in clay, instead of dust repos'd.

On a Merchant.

Who from accounts and reck'nings ne'r could rest,
At length hath summ'd up his *quietus est*.

On a young man newly maried, dyed.

The world and thou art quickly gon about,
That but now entring in, art entred out.

On John Friend.

How ere he fail'd in's life, 'tis like *Jack Friend*,
Was no mans foe but's own, and there's an end.

On Christopher Fowler.

Let all say what they can, 'tis known *Kit Fowler*,
Was held an honest man, though no good bowler.

On Dorathy Rich.

Here resteth young *Doll Rich*, that dainty drab,
Who troubled long with itch, dy'd of the scab.

On Ralph.

Ralph bids adue to pleasures good or ill,
But tells you true, 'tis much against his will.

On Walter Moone.

Here lies Wat Moone, that great tobacconist,
Who dy'd too soon for lack of had I wist.

On Jo. Cooling a Player-foole.

Death hath too soon remov'd from us Jo. Cooling,
That was so well belov'd, and liv'd by fooling.

On a Welshman.

Who living least, espy'd his life should leese,
By meere methegglin dy'd, and tosted cheese.

On Jo. Long.

Here sleep J. Long, who liv'd till New-years-tide,
Full fourscore strong, but then fell sick and dy'd.

On Stephen Spooner.

Death hath time borrow'd of our neighbour Spooner
Whose wife much sorrow'd that he di'd no sooner.

On a Lawyer.

God works wonders now and than,
Here lies a lawyer dy'd an honest man.

On a Water-man.

Here sleeps Will. Slater, why? by deaths command,
Hath left the water to possesse the land.

On Sir Francis Drake.

England his heart, his corps the waters have,
And that which rais'd his fame, became his grave.

On a Gallant.

Who cloth of tissue wore, here flat doth lye,
Having no issue more than that in's thigh.

On John Garret.

Gone is John Garret, who to all mens thinking,
For love to claret kill'd himselfe with drinking.

On notable Ned.

Cause of the good nought must be said but good,
'Tis well for Ned that nought be understood.

On a Taylor who dy'd of the stitch.

Here lies a taylour in this ditch,
Who liv'd and dyed by the stitch.

On a travelling Beggar.

Here lies a vagrant person whom our laws
(Of late grown strict) denied passage, 'cause
He wandring thus, therefore return he must,
From whence at first he hither came, to dust.

On a Mason.

So long the mason wrought on others wals,
That his own house of clay to ruine fals:
No wonder spitefull death wrought his annoy,
He us'd to build, and death seeks to destroy.

On a Schoolmaster.

The grammar school, a long time taught I have,
Yet all my skill could not decline the grave,
But yet I hope it one day will be shown
In no case save the ablative alone.

On Prince Henry.

I have no vein in verse, but if I could
Distill on every word a pearl, I would.
Our sorrows pearls drop, not from pens, but eyes,
Whilst other Muses write, mine onely cryes.

On the death of Mr. Newcomin of Clare-hall in Cambridge.

Weep ye Clarenses, weep all about,
For *New-com-in* is new gone out ;
Weep not Clarenses, weep not at all,
He's gone but from Clare to Trinity-hal.

On Hobson the Carrier.

Hobson (what's out of sight, is out of mind)
Is gone and left his letters here behind,
He that with so much paper us'd to meet
Is now, alas! content to take one sheet.

Another.

He that such carriage store, was wont to have,
Is carried now himselfe unto his grave :
O strange! he that in life ne'r made but one,
Six carriers makes, now he is dead and gone.

Another.

Here *Hobson* lyes, prest with a heavy load,
Who now is gone the old and common road; .
The waggon he so lov'd, so lov'd to ride,
That he was drawing on whilst that he dy'd.

Another.

Hobson's not dead, but *Charls* the northern swain
Hath sent for him to draw his lightsome wain.

On a Footman.

This nimble footman ran away from Death,
And here he rested being out of breath;
Here Death him over-took, made him his slave,
And sent him on an errand to the grave.

Justus Lipsius.

Some have high mountains of Parian stone,
And some in brasse carve their inscription,
Some have their tombs of costly marbles rear'd;
But in our tears onely are they interr'd.

On a Child.

Like birds of prey,
Death snatcht away,
  This harmlesse dove,
Whose soule so pure
Is now secure
  In heaven above.

On a rich Gentleman.

Of woods and plains, and hills and vales,
Of fields, of meads, of parks, and pales;
  Of all I had, this I possesse;
  I need no more, I have no lesse.

On a Child.

That flesh is grasse
Its grace a flower,
Read ere you passe
Whom worms.devoure.

On a Lock-Smith.

A zealous lock-smith dy'd of late,
Who by this time's at heaven gate,
The reason why he will not knock,
Is 'cause he means to pick the lock.

On a Collier.

Here lies the collier *Jenkin Dashes*,
By whom Death nothing gain'd he swore,
For living he was dust and ashes,
And being dead he is no more.

On Dick Pinner.

Here lyes *Dick Pinner*, O ungentle Death!
Why didst thou rob *Dick Pinner* of his breath?
For living, he by scraping of a pin,
Made better dust than thou hast made of him.

On a Sack-sucker.

Good reader blesse thee, be assur'd,
The spirit of sack lyes here immur'd :
Who havockt all he could come by
For sack, and here quite sack'd doth ly.

On a Child.

Into this world as stranger to an inne,
This child came guest-wise, where when it had bin
A while, and found nought worthy of his stay,
He onely broke his fast, and went away.

On a Candle.

Here lyes the chandlers chiefest joy,
Here lyes the schollers pale-fac'd boy ;
Having nought else but skin and bone
Dy'd of a deep consumption.

On T. H. the Pannier-man of the Temple.

Here lyes *Tom Hacket* this marble under,
Who often made the cloysters thunder ;
He had a horn, and when he blew it,
Call'd many a cuckold that never knew it.

On a young Infant.

The life of man,
Is but a span,
The common saying is ;
But Death did pinch
His to an inch,
Ere he could say, what's this ?

Yet he hath gain'd, not lost, thereby
Changing time for eternity.

On Mr. Calfes death.

Heaven of his soul take charge, for he,
Of all his dayes liv'd but the halfe;
Who might have grown to be an oxe,
But dyed (as you see) a *Calfe*.

On Bolus.

If gentlenesse could tame the fates, or wit
Delude them, *Bolus* had not dyed yet;
But one that death o'r-rules in judgement sits,
And sayes our sins are stronger then our wits.

On a Clown.

Softly tread this earth upon,
For here lyes our *Corydon:*
Who through care to save his sheep
Watch'd too much, oh let him sleep!

On a Child.

As carefull nurses on their beds do lay
Their babes, which would too long the wantons play,
So to prevent my youths ensuing crimes,
Nature my nurse laid me to bed betimes.

On a Musitian.

Be not offended at our sad complaint,
You quire of angels, that have gain'd a saint;

Where all perfection met in skill and voyce,
We mourn our losse, but yet commend your choyce.

On a Gardener.

Could he forget his death that every houre
Was emblem'd to it, by the fading flower?
Should he not mind his end? yes, sure he must,
That still was conversant 'mongst beds of dust.

On a Drunkard.

Bibax the drunkard, while he liv'd would say,
The more I drink, the more methinks I may;
But see how death hath proved his saying just,
For he hath drunk himselfe as dry as dust.

On a Child.

Tread softly passenger, for here doth lye,
A dainty jewell of sweet infancy:
A harmlesse babe, that onely came and cry'd
In baptism to be wash'd from sin, and dy'd.

Another.

In this marble casket lyes
A matchlesse jewell of rich prize,
Whom nature in the worlds disdain
But shew'd, and put it up again.

On Mr. Sands.

Who would live in others breath?
Fame deceives the dead mans trust,

When our names do change by death,
Sands I was, and now am dust.

On Mr. Goad.

Go adde this verse, to *Goad's* herse,
For *Goad* is gone, but whither?
Goad himselfe is gone to God,
'Twas deaths goad drove him thither.

On Monday.

Hallowed be the Sabbath
And farewell all worldly pelf;
The week begins on Tuesday,
For *Munday* hath hang'd himself.

On a Child.

Here a pretty baby lyes
Sung asleep with lullabies:
Pray be silent, and not stir
Th'easie earth that covers her.

On a Matron.

Here lies a wife was chast, a mother blest;
A modest matron, all these in one chest:
Sarah unto her mate, *Mary* to God,
Martha to men, whilst here she had aboad.

In Latine thus.

Vxor casta, Parens felix, Matrona pudica,
Sara viro, mundo Martha, Maria Deo.

On a Souldier.

When I was young, in wars I shed my blood,
Both for my king, and for my countries good :
In elder years, my care was chief to be
Souldier to him that shed his blood for me.

On Mr. Dumbelow, that dyed of the winde Challicke.

Dead is *Dick Dumbelow*
Would you the reason know ?
Could his *tail* have but spoken,
His stout heart had not broken.

On Mr. Kitchins death.

Kitchin lyes here (for so his name I found)
I see Death keeps his *Kitchin* under ground.
And the poor worms (that flesh of late did eat
Devour their *Kitchin* now for want of meat.

On Isabella a Curtezan.

He who would write an epitaph,
Whereby to make fair *Is'bell* laugh,
Must get upon her, and write well,
Here underneath lies *Isabell.*

On a vertuous Wife.

In brief, to speak thy praise, let this suffice,
Thou wert a wife most loving, modest, wise,
Of children carefull, to thy neighbours kind,
A worthy mistresse, and of liberall mind.

On Mr. Christopher Lawson.

Death did not kill unjustly this good man,
But death, in death, by death did shew his power,
His pious deeds and thoughts to heaven fore-ran,
There to prepare his soul a blessed bower.

On a Welshman.

Here lyes puryed under these stones,
Shon ap Williams, ap Shinkin, ap Shones,
Her was porn in *Whales,* her was kill'd in *France,*
Her went to Cot by a very mis-shance.

La ye now.

On Mr. Carter, burnt by the great powder-mischance in Finsbury.

Here lies an honest *Carter* (yet no clown)
Unladen of his cares, his end the crown,
Vanish'd from hence, even in a cloud of smoke,
A blown-up citizen, and yet not broke.

On a Lady dying in Childbed.

Born at the first to bring another forth,
She leaves tne world, to leave the world her worth :
Thus phœnix-like, as she was born to bleed,
Dying her selfe, renews it in her seed.

On a Faulconer.

Death with her talons having seiz'd this prey,
After a tedious flight, truss'd him away :

Q 2

We mark'd him, here he fell, whence he shall rise
At call, till then unretriv'd here he lyes.

On Joan Truman who had an issue in her legge.

Here lyes crafty *Joan,* deny it who can,
Who liv'd a false maid, and dy'd a *Truman,*
And this trick she had, to make up her cunning,
Whilst one leg stood still, the other was running.

On a youth.

Now thou hast heaven for merit, but 'tis strange,
Morality should envy at thy change:
God thought us unfit for such as thee,
And made thee consort of eternity,
We grieve not then that thou to heaven art taken,
But that thou hast thy friends so soon forsaken.

On Prince Henry.

Did he dye young? O no, it could not be,
For I know few that liv'd so long as he,
Till God and all men lov'd him; then behold,
The man that lives so long, must needs be old.

On — born before his time.

Griev'd at the world and times, this early bloom
Look'd round, and sigh'd, and stole into his tomb,
His fall was like his birth, too quick; this rose
Made hast to spread, and the same hast to close:
Here lyes his dust, but his best tomb's fled hence,
For marble cannot last like innocence.

On a very fat man.

Under this pebble stone;
Here fast sleepeth one,
  And that is not two;
Yet was without doubt
Far bigger about,
  Then both I, and you;
His kidneys encreast
So much, that his wast
  Was hooped all round:
But his girdle death cuts,
And down fell his guts,
'Bouts heels to the ground.

On John Newter.

Reader, *John Newter* who erst plaid
The Jack on both sides, here is laid
Who like the herb *John* indifferent
Was not for king or parliament,
Yet fast and loose he could not play
With death, he took him at a bay;
What side his soul hath taken now
God or devil? we hardly know:
But this is certain, since he dy'd
He hath been mist of neither side.

On Hocas Pocas.

Here *Hocas* lyes with his tricks and his knocks,
Whom death hath made sure as his juglers box:

Who many hath cozen'd by his leiger-demain.
Is presto convey'd and here underlain :
Thus *Hocas* he's here, and here he is not,
While death plaid the *Hocas*, and brought him to th'pot.

On a Child of two years old, being born and dying in July.

Here is laid a *July* flowre
With surviving tears bedew'd,
Not despairing of that houre
When her spring shall be renew'd ;
  Ere she had her summer seen,
  She was gather'd fresh and green.

On a Cobler.

Death at a coblers door oft made a stand,
And alwayes found him on the mending hand ;
At last came death in very foul weather,
And ript the sole from the upper leather :
Death put a trick upon him, and what was't ?
The cobler call'd for's awle, death brought his last.

On a young Gentlewoman.

Nature in this small volume was about
To perfect what in woman was left out :
Yet carefull least a piece so well begun,
Should want preservatives when she had done :
Ere she could finish what she undertook,
Threw dust upon it, and shut up the book.

On a Scholler.

Forbear friend t'unclaspe this book,
Only in the forefront look,
For in it have errours bin,
Which made the author call it in :
   Yet know this, 't shall have more worth,
   At the second coming forth.

On a young Woman.

The body which within this earth is laid,
Twice six weeks knew a wife, a saint, a maid ;
Fair maid, chast wife, pure saint, yet 'tis not strange
She was a woman, therefore pleasd to change :
And now shees dead, some woman doth remain,
For still she hopes once to be chang'd again.

On Brawne.

Here *Brawne* the quondam begger lyes,
   Who counted by his tale,
Full sixscore winters in his life ;
   Such vertue is in ale.
Ale was his meat, ale was his drink,
   Ale did him long reprive,
And could he still have drunk his ale,
   He had been still alive.

On a Candle.

Here lyes (I wot) a little star
That did belong to *Jupiter,*

Which from him *Prometheus* stole,
And with it a fire-coale.
Or this is that I mean to handle,
Here doth lye a farthing candle,
That was lov'd well, having its light,
But loosing that, now bids good night.

On M. R.

Who soonest dyes, lives long enough;
Our life is but a blast or puffe.
I did resist and strive with death,
But soone he put me out of breath;
He of my life thought to bereave me,
But I did yield onely to breath me.
O'r him I shall in triumph sing,
Thy conquest grave, *where is thy sting?*

On a Child.

Here she lyes a pretty bud,
Lately made of flesh and blood:
Who, as soon, fell fast asleep,
As her little eyes did peep;
Give her strewings; but not stir
The earth that lightly covers her.

On an Inne-keeper.

It is not I that dye, I doe but leave an inn,
Where harbour'd was with me, all filthy kind of sin;
It is not I that dye, I doe but now begin
Into eternall joy by faith to enter in.

Why weep you then my friends, my parents, and my kin?
Lament ye when I loose, but weep not when I win.

On a cobler.

Come hither, read my gentle friend,
And here behold a coblers end.
Longer in length his life had gone,
But that he had no last so long;
O mighty death, whose dart can kill
The man that made him souls at will.

On M. Aire.

Under this stone of marble faire,
Lies th'body intomb'd of *Gervaise Aire*.
He dy'd not of an ague fit,
Nor surfeited of too much wit,
Me thinks this was a wondrous death,
That *Aire* should dye for want of *breath*.

On Mr. Rice M.

Who can doubt (*Rice*) to what eternall place
Thy soul is fled, that did but know thy face?
Whose body was so light it might have gone
To heaven without a resurrection;
Indeed thou wert all type, thy limbs were signes,
Thy arteries but mathematick lines;
As if two souls had made the compound good,
Which both should live by faith, and none by blood.

On Thomas Jones.

Here for the nonce
Came *Thomas Jonce*
  In St. *Jileses* church to lye.
None welsh before,
None Welshman more
  Till *Shon Clerk* dye.
Ile tole the bell,
Ile ring his knell,
He dyed well,
He's saved from hell:
And so farewell
  Tom Jonce.

On a young Man.

Surpriz'd by grief and sicknesse here I lye,
Stopt in my middle age, and soon made dead,
Yet doe not grudge at God, if soon thou dye,
But know he trebles favours on thy head.
  Who for thy morning work equals thy pay,
  With those that have endur'd the heat oth'day.

On the two Littletons that were drowned at Oxford. 1636.

Here lye we (reader, canst thou not admire?)
Who both at once by water dy'd and fire,
For whilst our bodyes perish'd in the deep,
Our soules in love burnt, so we fell asleep;
Let this be then our epitaph: Here lyes
Two, yet but one, one for the other dyes.

On a Butler.

That death should thus from hence our butler catch,
Into my mind it cannot quickly sink;
Sure death came thirsty to the buttry-hatch,
When he (that busi'd was) deny'd him drink.
Tut! 'twas not so, 'tis like he gave him liquor,
And death made drunk, him made away the quicker;
Yet let not others grieve too much in mind
(The butler's gone) the keys are left behind.

On M. Cook.

To God, his country, and the poor he had,
A zealous soul, free heart, and lib'rall mind.
His wife, his children, and his kindred sad,
Lack of his love, his care and kindnesse find:
    Yet are their sorrows asswag'd with the thought
    He hath attain'd the happinesse he sought.

On a Porter.

At length by works of wondrous fate,
Here lyes the porter of Winchester-gate:
If gone to heav'n, as much I feare:
He can be but a porter there:
He fear'd not hell so much for's sin,
As for th'great rapping and oft coming in.

Vpon one who dyed in Prison.

Reader, I liv'd, enquire no more,
Lest a spy enter in at doore;

Such are the times, a dead man dare
Not trust nor credit common aire.
But dye and lye entombed here,
By me, I'l whisper in thine ear
Such things as onely dust to dust
(And without witnesse) may entrust.

On Waddam Colledge Butler.

Man's life is like a new tunn'd cask they say,
The formost draught, is oft times cast away;
Such are our younger years, the following still
Are more and more inclining unto ill;
Such is our manhood, untill age at length,
Doth sowre its sweetnes, and doth stop its strength:
Then death prescribing to each thing its bounds,
Takes what is left, and turns it all to grounds.

On a Horse.

Here lies a horse, who dyed but
To make his master go on foot.
A miracle should it be so:
The dead to make the lame to go;
Yet fate would have it, that the same
Should make him goe, that made him lame.

On an old Man a Residenciary.

Tread, sirs, as lightly as you can
Upon the grave of this old man.
Twice forty (bating but one yeare,
And thrice three weeks) he lived here.

Whom gentle fate translated hence
To a more happy residence.
Yet, reader let me tell thee this,
(Which from his ghost a promise is)
If here ye will some few tears shed,
He'l never haunt ye now he's dead.

On a Maid.

Here she lyes (in bed spice)
Fair as *Eve* in Paradise.
For her beauty it was such
Poets co'd not praise too much.
Virgins come, and in a ring
Her supreamest *requiem* sing;
Then depart, but see ye tread
Lightly, lightly ore the dead.

On Husband and Wife.

To these, whom death again did wed,
This grav's the second marriage-bed.
For though the hand of fate could force,
'Twixt soule and body a divorce;
It could not sever man and wife,
Because they both liv'd but one life;
Peace, good reader, doe not weep,
Peace, the lovers are asleep :
They (sweet turtles) folded lye,
In the last knot that love could tye.
Let them sleep, let them sleep on,
Till this stormy night be gone.

And th'eternall morrow dawne,
Then the curtaines will be drawne,
And they waken with that light,
Whose day shall never sleep in night.

On Aretyne.

Here biting *Aretyne* lyes buried,
With gall more bitter, never man was fed.
The living nor the dead to carp he spar'd,
Nor yet for any king or *Cæsar* car'd:
Onely on God to raile he had forgot,
His answer was, indeed I know him not.

On William Coale an Alehouse-keeper, at Coaton near Cambridge.

Doth *William Coale* lye here? henceforth be stale,
Be strong and laugh on us thou *Coaton* ale:
Living indeed, he with his violent hand
Never left grasping thee, while he could stand.
But death at last, hath with his fiery flashes
Burnt up the *Coale*, and turn'd it into ashes.

On one Andrew Leigh, who was vext with a shrewd wife.

Here lyes *Leigh*, who vext with a shrewd wife,
To gain his quiet, parted with his life;
But see the spight! she that had alwayes crost
Him living, dyes, and means to hunt his ghost.
But she may faile, for *Andrew* out of doubt
Will cause his brother *Peter* shut her out.

In quendam.

Stay mortall, stay, remove not from this tomb,
Before thou hast considered well thy doome;
My bow stands ready bent, and couldst it see,
Mine arrow's drawn to th'head, and aims at thee:
Prepare yet wandring ghost, take home this line;
The grave that next is open'd may be thine.

On a vertuous youth.

Reader, let a stone thee tell
That in this body there did dwell
A soule, as heavenly, rich, and good,
As e'r could live in flesh and blood:
And therefore heav'n that held it deare,
Did let it stay the lease while here,
Whose corps here sacred ashes makes;
Thus heav'n and earth have parted stakes.

On a Cock-master.

Farewell stout Hot-spur, now the battel's done,
In which thou'rt foil'd, and death hath overcome,
Having o'r-match'd thy strength that made thee stoop
She quickly forc'd thee on the pit to droop:
From whence thou art not able rise or stir;
For death is now become the vanquisher.

On a Mathematician.

Loe, in small closure of this earthly bed,
Rests he, that heavens vast motions measured,

Who having known both of the land and sky,
More than fram'd *Archimed*, or *Ptolomy*,
Would further presse, and like a *Palmer* went,
With *Jacobs* staffe, beyond the firmament.

On a Taylor.

Jack Snip the taylor's dead, 'tis now too late
To brawle or wrangle with the cruel fate,
Yet sure 'twas hardly done to clip his thred,
Before he gave them leave, in his own bed.
He dy'd at forty just; poor shred of base
Mortality! who pities not his case?
Of a whole ell of cloth, he would not take
Above a nail at most, for conscience sake:
But of his span of life, I dare to say,
Death stole not much lesse than one half away;
And coward-like, just when he was not well,
With his own bodkin (pitiful to tell)
He board a hole through him, that all his men
And prentises could not stitch up agen.

On his Mistris Death.

Unjustly we complain of fate,
For shortning our unhappy dayes,
When death doth nothing but translate,
And print us in a better phrase.
Yet who can chuse but weep? not I:
That beauty of such excellence
And more vertue than could dye,
By deaths rude hand is vanish'd hence.

Sleep blest creature in thine urn,
My sighs, my teares shall not awake thee.
I but stay untill my turn ;
And then, O then! I'l overtake thee.

On Hobson the Carrier.

If constellations which in heaven are fixt,
Give life by influence to bodies mixt,
And every sign peculiar right doth claime
Of that to which it propagates a name ;
Then I conjure, *Charles* the great northern star
Whistled up *Hobson* for to drive his car.
He is not dead, but left his mansion here,
Has left the Bull, and flitted to the Beare.
Me thinks I see how *Charons* fingers itches,
But he's deceiv'd he cannot have his riches.

Another on Hobson.

Whom seek ye sirs? old *Hobson* ? fie upon
Your tardinesse, the carrier is gon,
Why stare you so? nay, you deserve to faile,
Alas, her's nought, but his old rotten maile.
He went a good-while since, no question store
Are glad, who vext he would not goe before :
And some are griev'd hee's gone so soone away,
.The Lord knows why he did no longer stay.
How could he please you all? I'm sure of this,
He linger'd soundly, howsoe'r you misse ;
But gone he is, nor was he surely well
At his departure, as mischance befell :

For he is gone in such unwonted kind,
As ne'r before, his goods all left behind.

Old Hobsons Epitaph.

Here *Hobson* lyes among his many betters,
A man unlearned, yet a man of letters;
His carriage was well known, oft hath he gone
In embassy 'twixt father and the sonne:
There's few in *Cambridge*, to his praise be it spoken,
But may remember him by some good token.
From whence he rid to *London* day by day,
Till death benighting him, he lost his way:
His team was of the best, nor would he have
Been mir'd in any way, but in the grave.
Nor is't a wonder, that he thus is gon,
Since all men know, he long was drawing on.
Thus rest in peace thou everlasting swain,
And supream waggoner, next *Charles* his wain.

Vpon John Crop, *who dyed by taking a vomit.*

Mans life's a game at tables, and he may
Mend his bad fortune by his wiser play;
Death playes against us, each disease and sore
Are blots, if hit, the danger is the more
To lose the game; but an old stander by
Binds up the blots, and cures the malady,
And so prolongs the game; *John Crop* was he
Death in a rage did challenge for to see
His play, the dice are thrown, when first he drinks,
Casts, makes a blot, death hits him with a sinque:

He casts again, but all in vain, for death
By th'after game did win the prize his breath.
What though his skill was good, his luck was bad,
For never mortall man worse casting had.
But did not death play false to win from such
As he? no doubt, he bare a man too much.

An honest Epitaph.

Here lyes an honest man, reader, if thou seek more,
Thou art not so thy selfe; for honesty is store
Of commendations; and it is more praise,
To dye an honest man, then full of dayes.

On a Cobler.

Here lyes an honest cobler, whom curst fate,
Perceiving nere worn out, would needs translate;
'Twas a good thrifty soul, and time hath bin,
He would well liquor'd wade through thick and thin:
But now he's gone, 'tis all that can be said,
Honest *John* Cobler is here under-laid.

On a proud man.

Good reader know, that comest nigh,
Here lyes he low, that look'd so high.
Both poor and nak'd, that was gay-cloath'd:
Of all forsak'd, who others loath'd,
He once thought all envy'd his worth:
Nor great, nor small, now grudge his turf:
The heavenly cope was his ambition:
Three cubits scope is his fruition.

He was above all; God above him:
He did not love all; nor God love him:
He that him taught first to aspire,
Now hath him caught, and payes his hire.

On an irefull and angry man.

Here lyes a *Fury*, hight Sir *Ire*,
That bred, and earn'd immortall fire.
He 'gan to wrangle from the womb;
And was a wrangler to his tomb.
A peevish, and a foolish elfe,
Foe to his God, his saints, his selfe.
He hated men, men did not love him:
No evill but his own might move him.
He was, and was earths load and care:
He is, and is hells brand, and share.

On John Dawson Butler.

Dawson the butler's dead, although I think
Poets were nere infus'd with single drink,
Ile spend a farthing Muse, a watery verse,
Will serve the turn to cast upon his herse.
If any cannot weep among us here,
Take off his cup, and so squeeze out a teare.
Weep O ye barrels let your drippings fall
In trickling streams, make wast more prodigal,
Then when our beer was good, that *John* may float
To *Stix* in beer, and lift up *Charons* boat,
With wholsome waves: and as the conduits ran
With clarret, at the coronation,

So let your channels flow with single tiff,
For *John* I hope is crown'd : take off your whiff,
Ye men of *Rosemary*, and drink up all,
Remembring 'tis a *butlers* funeral :
Had he been master of good double beer,
My life for his, *John Dawson* had been here.

On Turn-Coat.

Passenger, Stay, Reade, Walk. Here Lyeth, ANDREW TURNCOAT, WHO WAS NEITHER SLAVE, NOR SOULDIER, NOR PHYSITIAN, NOR FENCER, NOR COBLER, NOR FILCHER, NOR LAWYER, NOR USURER, BUT ALL; WHO LIVED NEITHER IN CITY, NOR COUNTREY, NOR AT HOME, NOR ABROAD, NOR AT SEA, NOR AT LAND, NOR HERE, NOR ELSEHERE, BUT EVERY WHERE; WHO DIED NEITHER OF HUNGER, NOR POYSON, NOR HATCHET, NOR HALTER, NOR DOGGE, NOR DISEASE, BUT OF ALL TOGETHER I. I. H. BEING NEITHER HIS DEBTOR, NOR HEIRE, NOR KINSMAN, NOR FRIEND, NOR NEIGHBOUR, BUT ALL, IN HIS MEMORY HAVE ERECTED, THIS NEITHER MONUMENT, NOR TOMB, NOR SEPULCHER, BUT ALL, WISHING NEITHER EVIL, NOR WEL, NEITHER TO THEE, NOR TO ME, NOR HIM, BUT ALL UNTO ALL.

On a Dyer.

Though death the dyer colour-lesse hath made,
Yet he dies pale, and will not leave his trade;

But being dead, the means yet doth not lack,
To dye his friends cloth into mourning black,
Some sure foresaw his death, for they of late
Us'd to exclaim upon his dying fate.
And weak, and faint, he seem'd oft times t'have been,
For to change colours often he was seen;
Yet there no matter was so foul, but he
Would set a colour on it handsomely:
Death him no unexpected stroke could give,
That learnt to dye, since he began to live.
He shall yet prove, what he before had try'd,
And shall once more live after he hath dy'd.

On a disagreeing Couple.

Hic jacet ille, qui centies & mille
  Did scold with his wife:
Cum illo jacet illa, quæ communis in villa
  Did quittance his life:
His name was Nick, the which was sick,
  And that very male,
Her name was Nan, who loved well a man,
  So gentlemen, vale.

On a Foot-boy that dyed with overmuch running.

Base tyrant death, thus to assail one tir'd,
Who scarce his latest breath being left expir'd;
And being too too cruell thus to stay
So swift a course, at length ran quite away.
But pretty boy, be sure it was not death
'That left behind thy body out of breath:

Thy soule and body running in a race,
Thy soule held out, thy body tir'd apace,
Thy soul gained and left that lump of clay
To rest it self untill the latter day.

On a Scrivener.

Here to a period is the scrivener come,
This is the last sheet, his full point this tomb.
Of all aspersions I accuse him not,
'Tis known he liv'd not, without many a blot;
Yet he no ill example shew'd to any,
But rather gave good copies unto many.
He in good letters hath alwaies been bred,
And hath writ more then many men have read.
He rulers had at his command by law,
And though he could not hang yet he could draw
He far more bond-men had and made, then any;
A dash alone of his pen ruin'd many;
That not without good reason, we might call
His letters great or little, capitall.
Yet is the scriveners fate as sure as just,
When he hath all done then he falls to dust.

On Mr. P. Gray.

Reader stay,
And if I had no more to say,
But here doth lye till the last day,
All that is left of *Philip Gray;*
It might thy patience richly pay:
For, if such men as he could dye,
What surety of life have thou and I?

On a Chandler.

How might his dayes end that made weaks? or he
That could make light, here laid in darknesse be?
Yet since his weeks were spent, how could he chuse
But be depriv'd of light, and his trade lose?
Yet dead the chandler is, and sleeps in peace,
No wonder, long since melted was his greace:
It seems that he did evill, for day-light
He hated, and did rather wish the night:
Yet came his works to light, and were like gold
Prov'd in the fire, but could not tryall hold;
His candle had an end, and deaths black night
Is an extinguisher of all his light.

On a Smith.

Farewell stout Iron-side, not all thine art
Could make a shield against deaths envious dart,
Without a fault, no man his life doth passe,
For to his vice the smith addicted was.
He oft (as choler is increast by fire)
Was in a fume, and much inclin'd to ire.
He had so long been us'd to forge, that he
Was with a black-coal markt for forgery:
But he for witnesse needed not to care,
Who but a black-smith was, though ne'r so fair;
And opportunities he needed not,
That knew to strike then when the ir'n was hot;
As the door-nailes he made, hee's now as dead;
He them and death-him, hath knockt on the head.

On a man drown'd in the Snow.

Within a fleece of silent waters drown'd,
Before my death was known, a grave I found;
The which exil'd my life from her sweet home,
For grief straight froze it self into a tombe.
One element my angry fate thought meet
To be my death, grave, tomb, and winding sheet:
Phœbus himself, an epitaph had writ,
But blotting many ere he thought one fit;
He wrote untill my grave, and tomb were gone,
And 'twas an epitaph that I had none;
For every one that passed by that way,
Without a sculpture read that there I lay.
Here now the second time untomb'd I lye,
And thus much have the best of destiny:
Corruption, from which onely one was free,
Devour'd my grave, but did not feed on me:
My first grave took me from the race of men,
My last shall give me back to life agen.

On Doctor Hackets wife.

Drop mournfull eyes your pearly trickling tears,
Flow streams of sadness down the spangled sphears,
Fall like the tumbling cataracts of *Nile*,
Make deaf the world with cryes; let not a smile
Appear, let not an eye be seen to sleep
Nor slumber, onely let them serve to weep
Her dear lamented death, who in her life
Was a religious, loyall, loving wife,

Of children tender, to an husband kind,
Th'undoubted symtomes of a vertuous mind :
Which makes her glorious, 'bove the highest pole,
Where angels sing sweet *requiems* to her soule,
She liv'd a none-such, did a none-such dye,
Ne'r *none-such* here her corps interred lye.

On a beautifull Virgin.

In this marble buri'd lyes
  Beauty may inrich the skyes,
And adde light to *Phœbus* eyes,

Sweeter then *Aurora's* aire,
  When she paints the lillies faire,
And gilds cowslips with her haire.

Chaster then the virgin spring,
  Ere her blossomes she doth bring,
Or cause *Philomel* to sing.

If such goodnesse live 'mongst men,
  Bring me it; I know then
She is come from heaven agen.

But if not, ye standers by
  Cherish me, and say that I
Am the next design'd to dy.

An ancient Epitaph on Mamin Mar-Prelate.

The Welshman is hanged,
Who at our kirk flanged,
And at her state banged,
And breaded are his bukes :
And though he be hanged,
Yet he is not wranged,
The devill has him fanged
In his kruked klukes.

Vpon Hodge Pue's Father.

Oh cruell death that stopt the view
Of *Thoms* parishoner good man *Pue,*
Who lived alwaies in good order,
Untill that death stopt his recorder,
Which was betwixt Easter and Pentecost,
In the year of the great frost :
At *New-Market* then was the king,
When as the bells did merrily ring ;
The minister preached the day before
Unto his highnesse and no more,
Returning home, said prayers and
Buried the man as I understand.

On our prime English Poet Geffery Chaucer, an ancient
Epitaph.

My Master Chaucer, with his fresh comedies
Is dead, alas! chiefe poet of Brittaine,
That whilome made full piteous tragedies :

The fault also of princes did complaine,
As he that was of making soberaigne;
Whom all this land should of right preferre,
Sith of our language he was the load-sterre.

On Mr. Edm: Spencer, the famous Poet.

At *Delphos* shrine, one did a doubt propound,
Which by the Oracle must be released,
Whether of poets were the best renown'd,
Those that survive, or they that are deceased?
  The gods made answer by divine suggestion,
  While *Spencer* is alive, it is no question.

On John Owen.

Well had these words been added to thy herse,
What e'r thou spak'st (like *Ovid*) was a verse.

On Michael Drayton buryed in Westminster.

Do pious marble, let thy readers know,
  What they, and what their children ow
  To *Draytons* sacred name, whose dust
  We recommend unto thy trust.
Protect his memory, preserve his story,
And a lasting monument of his glory,
  And when thy ruines shall disclaime
  To be the treasury of his name:
His name which cannot fade, shall be
An everlasting monument to thee.

On Mr. Beaumont.

He that hath such acutenesse, and such wit,
As well may ask six lives to manage it;
He that hath writ so well, that no man dare
Deny it for the best; let him beware:
Beaumont is dead, by whose sole death appears,
Wit's a disease consumes men in few years.

On William Shakespeare.

Renowned *Spencer* lye a thought more nigh
To learned *Chaucer*, and rare *Beaumont* lye
A little nearer *Spencer*, to make room
For *Shakespeare* in your threefold, fourfold tomb,
To lodge all four in one bed make a shift
Untill Dooms-day, for hardly will a fifth
Betwixt this day and that, by fates be slain,
For whom your curtains may be drawn again.
If your precedency in death do bar
A fourth place in your sacred sepulcher;
Under this sacred marble of thine owne,
Sleep rare tragœdian *Shakespeare!* sleep alone.
Thy unmolested peace in an unshared cave,
Possesse as lord, not tenant of thy grave,
That unto us, and others it may be,
Honour hereafter to be laid by thee.

On Ben: Johnson.

Here lyes *Johnson* with the rest
Of the poets; but the best.

Reader, wo'dst thou more have known?
Ask his story, not this stone;
That will speak what this can't tell
Of his glory.   So farewell.

Another on Ben: J.

The Muses fairest light, in no dark time;
The wonder of a learned age; the line
That none can passe; the most proportion'd wit
To nature : the best judge of what was fit :
The deepest, plainest, highest, clearest pen :
The voyce most eccho'd by consenting men :
The soul which answer'd best to all well said
By others : and which most requitall made :
Tun'd to the highest key of ancient *Rome*,
Returning all her musick with her own.
In whom with nature, study claim'd a part,
And yet who to himselfe ow'd all his art;
Here lyes *Ben: Johnson*, every age will look
With sorrow here, with wonder on his book.

On Mr. Francis Quarles.

To them that understand themselves so well,
As what, not who lyes here, to ask, I'l tell,
What I conceive, envy dare not deny,
Far both from falshood, and from flattery.
  Here drawn to land by death, doth lye
  A vessell fitter for the sky,
  Then *Jasons Argo*, though to *Greece*,
  They say, it brought the golden fleece.

The skilfull pilot steer'd it so,
Hither and thither, to and fro,
Through all the seas of poetry,
Whether they far or near doe lye,
And fraught it so with all the wealth,
Of wit and learning not by stealth,
Or piracy, but purchase got,
That this whole lower world could not
Richer commodities, or more
Afford to adde unto his store.
To heaven then with an intent
Of new discoveries, he went,
And left his vessell here to rest
Till his return shall make it blest.
   The bill of lading he that looks
   To know, may find it in his books.

On Doctor Donnes Death.

He that would write an epitaph for thee,
And do it well, must first begin to be
Such as thou wert ; for none can truly know
Thy worth, thy life, but he that hath liv'd so,
He must have wit to spare, and to hurle down :
Enough to keep the gallants of the town.
He must have learning plenty ; both the laws,
Civill, and common, to judge any cause ;
Divinity great store, above the rest ;
None of the worst edition, but the best ;
He must have language, travail, all the arts ;
Judgement to use ; or else he wants thy parts.

He must have friends the highest, able to do;
Such as *Mæcenas* and *Augustus* too;
  He must have such a sicknesse, such a death,
  Or else his vain descriptions come beneath.
    Who then shall write an epitaph for thee,
    He must be dead first; let alone for me.

On Doctor Whaly.

What? is the young *Apollo* grown of late
Conscious his tender years are nothing fit
To rule the now large *Heliconian* state,
Without a sage competitor in it?
And therefore sent death, who might *Whaly* bring
To be a guardian to this stripling king;
Sure so it is, but if we thought it might
Be worse then this: namely, that th'gods for spight
To earth, had ta'n him hence; wee'd weep amain,
Wee'd weep a *Phlegethon*, an ocean;
Which might without the help of *Charon's* oares,
Ferry his soule to the *Elysian* shoars.

On Doctor Bambrigg.

Were but this marble vocall, there
Such an *elogium* would appear
As might, though truth did dictate, move
Distrust in either faith or love;
As ample knowledge as could rest
Inshrined in a mortals brest,
Which ne'rthelesse did open lye,
Uncoverd by humility.

A heart which piety had chose,
To be her altar, whence arose
Such smoaking sacrifices, that
We here can onely wonder at;
A honey tongue that could dispence,
Torrents of sacred eloquence;
That 'tis no wonder if this stone
Because it cannot speak, doth groan;
For could mortality assent,
These ashes would prove eloquent.

On Sir Walter Rawleigh at his Execution.

Great heart who taught thee so to dye?
Death yielding thee the victory?
Where took'st thou leave of life? if there,
How couldst thou be so freed from feare?
But sure thou dyest and quit'st the state
Of flesh and blood before the fate.
Else what a miracle were wrought,
To triumph both in flesh and thought?
I saw in every stander by,
Pale death, life onely in thine eye:
Th'example that thou left'st was then,
We look for when thou dy'st agen.
　Farewell, truth shall thy story say,
　We dy'd, thou onely liv'dst that day.

On Sir Horatio Palvozeene.

Here lyes Sir *Horatio Palvozeene,*
Who rob'd the pope to pay the queene,

And was a thief.   A thief? thou ly'st;
For why? he rob'd but antichrist.
Him death with his beesome swept from *Babram,*
Into the bosome of old *Abraham:*
But then came *Hercules* with his club,
And struck him down to *Belzebub.*

On Sir Francis Drake drowned.

Where *Drake* first found, there last he lost his fame:
And for tomb left nothing but his name.
His body's bury'd under some great wave,
The sea that was his glory, is his grave:
Of him no no man true epitaph can make,
For who can say, *Here lyes Sir Francis Drake.*

Sir Ph. Sidney on himself.

It is not I that dye, I doe but leave an inn,
Where harbour'd was with me, all filthy sin;
It is not I that dye, I doe but now begin
Into eternall joy by faith to enter in.
  Why mourn you then my parents, friends, and kin?
Lament you when I lose, not when I win.

On Sir Walter Rawleigh.

If spight be pleas'd, when as her object's dead,
Or malice pleas'd, when it hath bruis'd the head,
Or envy pleas'd, when it hath what it would,
Then all are pleas'd, for *Rawleighs* blood is cold,
Which were it warm and active, would o'rcome,
And strike the two first blind, the other dumbe.

On Sir Philip Sidney.

Reader within this ground Sir *Philip Sidney* lyes,
Nor is it fit that more
  I should acquaint;
Lest superstition rise,
  And men adore
A lover, scholler, souldier, and a saint.

On a learned Nobleman.

He that can read a sigh, and spell a tear,
Pronounce amazement, or accent wilde fear,
Or get all grief by heart, he, onely he,
Is fit to write, or read thy elegie.
Unvalued lord! that wert so hard a text,
Read in one age, and understood i'th'next.

On the Tombs in Westminster.

Mortality, behold and feare,
What a change of flesh is here!
Think how many royall bones,
Sleep within these heaps of stones;
Here they lye, had realmes, and lands;
Who now want strength to stir their hands.
Where from their pulpits seal'd with dust,
They preach, in greatnesse is no trust.
Here's an acre sown indeed,
With the richest, royal'st seed,
That the earth did e'r suck in,
Since the first man dy'd for sin:

Here the bones of birth have cry'd,
Though gods they were, as men they dy'd:
Here are sands, ignoble things,
Dropt from the ruin'd sides of kings,
   Here's a world of pomp and state
   Buried in dust, once dead by fate.

On Queen Elizabeth.

Kings, queens, mens, virgins eyes
See where the mirrour lyes.
In whom her friends have seen,
A kings state in a queen:
In whom her foes survai'd,
A mans heart in a maid.
Whom lest men for her piety,
Should grow to think some deity;
Heaven hence by death did summon
Her, to shew that she was woman.

On Queen Anne, who dyed in March, was kept all Aprill, and buried in May.

March with his winds hath struck a cedar tall,
And weeping *Aprill* mourns the cedars fall:
And *May* intends her month no flowers shall bring,
Since she must lose the flow'r of all the spring,
Thy *March* his winds, have caused *Aprill* show'rs,
And yet sad *May* must lose his flow'r of flow'rs.

On Prince Henry.

Reader; wonder think is none,
Though I speak, and am a stone,
Here is shrin'd cœlestial dust,
And I keep it but in trust :
Should I not my treasure tell,
Wonder then you might as well,
How this stone could chuse but break,
If it had not learn'd to speak :
Hence amaz'd and ask not me
Whose these sacred ashes be,
Purposely it is conceal'd,
For alasse ! were that reveal'd,
   All that read would by and by
   Melt themselves to tears and dy.

On King James his death.

We justly, when a meaner subject dyes,
Begin his epitaph with, Here he lyes,
But when a king, whose memory remains
Triumphant over death ; with, here he reignes :
Now he is dead, to whom the world imputes
Deservedly, eternall attributes.
For shall we think his glory can decease,
That's honour'd with the stile, The King of Peace :
Whose happy union of Great Britany,
Calls him the blessed King of Unity.
And in whose royall title it ensu'th,
Defender of the Faith, and King of Truth,

These girt thy brows with an immortal crown,
(Great *James*) and turn thy tomb into a throne.

On the King of Sweden.

The world expects *Swedes* monumental stone
Should equall the philosophers; each groane
Should breath a golden vein, and every verse
Should draw *elixar* from his fatall herse.
No fitter subject where strong lines should meet,
Than such a noble center: could the feet
Of able verse but trace his victories,
Where all's transcendent, who out parallel'd
Plutarchs selected *heroes*, and is held
The tenth of worthies: who hath over-acted
Great *Cæsars German*-Comment, and contracted
His expeditions by preventing aw,
He often overcame before he saw:
And (what of his great son, *Jove* us'd to say)
He alwayes either found or made his way.
Such was his personall and single fight,
As if that death it self had ta'n her flight
Into brave *Swedens* scabbard, when he drew,
Death with that steel inevitably flew.
His camp a church, wherein the gen'ralls life
Was the best sermon, and the onely strife
Amongst his, was to repeat it; bended knee
Was his prime posture, and his enemy
Found this most prevalent; his discipline
Impartiall and exact, it did out-shine

Those antique martiall Grecian, Roman lamps,
From which most of the worlds succeeding camps
Have had their borrow'd light; this, this was he,
All this and more; yet even all this can dye.
Death surely ventur'd on the *Swede* to try,
If heav'n were subject to mortality;
And shot his soul to heav'n, as if that she
Could (if not kill) unthrone a deity.
Both Death's deceiv'd, 'tis in another sense
That heaven is said to suffer violence.
No ir'n chain-shot, but 'tis the golden chaine
Of vertue, and the graces are the maine,
That do unhinge the everlasting gates,
All which like yoked undivided mates,
Were link'd in *Sweden;* where then were enchain'd
Like orthodoxall, volumes nothing feign'd:
Though fairly bound, his story is not dipt
In oyle, but in his own true manuscript.
It is enough to name him, surely we
Have got that *Romans* doting lethargy:
And may our names forget, if so we can
Forget the name of *Sweden,* renown'd man,
Thou hadst no sooner made the worthies ten,
But heaven did claim the tenth; jealous that men
Would idolize thee, but their instrument.
Thus thy meridian prov'd thy occident:
Had longer dayes been granted by the Fates,
Rome had heard this *Hanniball* at her gates.

Farewell thou *Austrian* scourge,
  Thou modern wonder,
Strange rain hath followed
  Thy last clap of thunder,
A shower of tears:
  And yet for ought we know,
The horn that's left,
  May blow down *Jericho.*

To Death.

Death, art thou mad? or having lost thine eyes,
Now throw'st thy dart at wild uncertainties?
Which hits those men, who hadst thou eyes or sense
Would challenge from thee mild obedience.
Their prudent looks gilt with divinity,
Thy trembling hand would cast thy dart away,
And grant the wearied bells a holy day;
And thou griev'd for thy former cruelty.
Wouldst to the world proclaim a jubilee.
But thou art blind and deaf: yet one or two
At most, methinks, had been enow
To satisfie thy bloody tyranny.
But thou wouldst fain rob poor mortality
Of all true worth, that men might be as base
As thou art, and the devils of thy race.
Art thou coward grown? why didst not dart
Thy spight at lusty youth? whose valiant heart
Would scorn thy fond alarum, and would slight
Thy mighty malice, and thy puny might.

This had been fair enough ; but thou goest further
That had been but man-slaughter, this is murther ;
To kill those rich-soul'd men, who sweetly do
Whisper unto their willing souls to goe.
But knowledge of thy weaknesse makes thee wise,
Thou seek'st not triumphs now, but sacrifice.
Thy malice fools thee too, thou hop'st they'd grieve
Because they should be forc'd behind to leave
Their honour'd worth ; but (fond fool) they be
Now crown'd and cloath'd with immortality.
Nor shalt thou kill their fames ; here we will raise
A monument to them, shall out-last dayes ;
Nor shall decay, untill the trumpets call
The world to see thy long-wish'd funerall :
Till then sleep blest souls, freed from hopes and fears,
Whilst we do write your *epitaphs* in tears.

Fancies and Fantasticks.

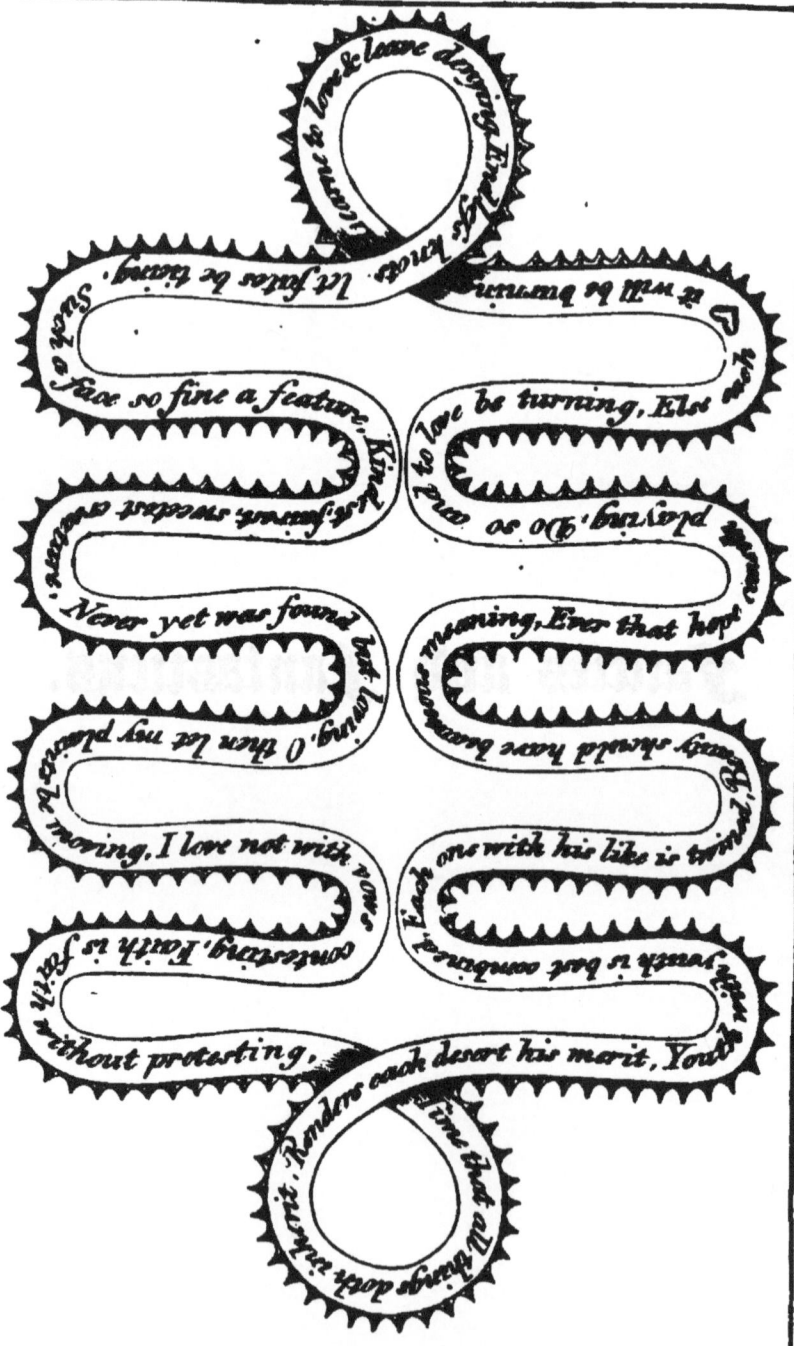

Come to love & leave denying, End
Such faiths hated. Let fates be trying. it will be burning,
Face so fine a feature, Kind to love be turning, Else such
Kind & favour, sweetest creature. playing, Do so
Never yet was found but meaning, Ever that hopt
Loving, O then let my plaints be Beauty should have become
moving, I love not with vows one with his like is twind,
confessing, Faith is Faith Youth is best combind,
without protesting, Renders each desert his merit, Youth
...ance doth inherit. ...time that all things doth inherit.

Annagrams.

Thomas Egerton.

1. ANAGR.

Honors met age.

Honors met age; and seeking where to rest,
Agreed to lodge, and harbour in thy brest.

*On Captaine John
Came-age.*

2. ANAGR.

Age came.

When perils I by land and sea had past,
Age came to summon me to death at last.

Christopher Lindall.

3. ANAGR.

I offer, lend Christ all.

That with this epigram thy deeds agree,
They well know, that did ever well know thee.

John Rysden.

4. ANAGR.

In honors dy.

Thy actions, friend, declare thy noble mind,
And to the world thy reall worth proclaime,
That fame her self cannot thy equall find,
To paralell thy glory, and thy name,
    On, onward still from no good action fly,
    Who lives like thee, cann't but in honors dy.

On the same.

I ne're will credit any powerfull fate
Can turn thy glory to a waning state;
Thou still wilt be thy self; therefore say I,
In honors thou shalt live, but never dy.

Phineas Fletcher.

5. ANAGR.

Hath Spencer life?
Or *Spencer hath life.*

That *Spencer* liveth, none can ignorant be,
That reads his works (*Fletcher*) or knoweth thee.

Mrs. Elizabeth Noell.

6. ANAGR.

Holinesse be still my star.

The safest conduct to the port of blisse,
Lyes not in brittle honor, for by this

We often loose our way, to shun this bar
To heaven, holines be still my star.

My lot is blisse eternall.

The world's a lottery, full of various chances,
Whereof each draws a share as fortune fancies,
Among the rest they ayme at things supernall,
I've drawn, and find my lot is blisse eternall.

I shall smite no ill brest.

The common way to wound mens hearts I shun,
Nor with meere outside am I to be won,
Vertue may move me, for it crowns the best,
But I shall smite no ill or lustfull brest.

My blisse on earth's little.

Honors are faire but fading flowers, which give
Delight to those that gather them, but live
Not ever flowrishing; this truth I find
Too truely in my selfe, by fate assign'd
For having all, I see that all's but brittle,
And even at best my blisse on earth's but little.

See my heart is still noble:

Though fortune frowns and fate suppres my will,
Yet see the lucke, my heart is noble still.

Domina Margarita Sandis.

ANAGRAMMA.

Anne domi das Margaritas?
Why do wee seek and saile abroad to find
Those pearls, which do adorn the female-kind?
Within our seas there comes unto our hands
A matchlesse Margaryte among the Sands.

The Church Papist.

I hold as faith	What England's church allows
What Rome's church saith	My conscience disavowes
Where th' king is head	The church can have no seame
The flocks misled	Where the pope's supreame
Where th' alter's drest	There's service scarce divine
The peoples blest	Where's table bread and wine
Hee's but an asse	Who the communion flies
Who shuns the masse	Is catholique and wise
Who charity preach	Their church with error's fraught
They heav'n soon reach	Where only faith is taught
On faith t'rely	No matter for good works
Is heresie	Make's Christians worse thenTurks.

The declining of a Gallant.

Singulariter.
{
Nominativo *hic* gallant asse.
Genitivo *hujus* brave.
Dativo *huic* if he get a licke.
Accusativo *hunc* of a taffaty punck.
Vocativo *O* he's gone if he cry so.
Ablativo *ab hoc* he hath got the pock.
}

Pluraliter.

> *Nominativo hi gallanti,* if the pike can defie.
> *Genitivo horum,* yet he is a begger in *corum.*
> *Dativo his,* his gilt rapier he doth misse.
> *Accusativo hos,* without a cloack he goes.
> *Vocativo O,* woe to the hole he must goe.
> *Ablativo ab his,* thus a gallant declined is.

Cupid unto thy altar and thy lawes
like those twin doves thy mothers chariot drawe
wee have beene bound, yet can our service finde
no recompence *Cupid* wilt nere be kind;
shall we still kneele, still pray, yet be
as farre to seeke, as we'd nere praid to thee.
why didst thou kindle fires
in our once cold desires,
or being kindled, why
doe they not sympothie
what credit can accrew still
erring God to you by our
contrary sufferings make her then,
love with that heat as maidens should
love men : and by thy mothers name *Cupid*
I vow, each day ile to thine honour'd alter
bow, and pay a 'daily offring; then recover
for pities sake this cold platonicke lover.

To a deserving friend.

Though others know themselves, might I advise,
You should not know your selfe in any wise :
For few or none with such rare gift indude,
If they once know themselves, can but be prou'd.

You have the substance and I live,
But by the shadow which you give,
Substance and shadow, both are due,
And given of mee to none but you,
Then whence is life but from that part
Which is possessor of the heart.

A Lovers departure.

Though envious fortune which could nere have wile,
As yet to grace mee with your pleasing smile :
But ever frown'd, now to augment my griefe,
Barre mee your sight, your refuge and reliefe.
Yet thou'ast my heart, my deere instead of mee :
And as it lives so shall it dye with thee,
Although I part, and parting be a paine,
Keepe thou my heart till I returne againe ;
So that in part, I but depart from thee,
Thou hast my heart, the rest remaines with mee.
Which rest small rest shall find, till having run,
It's wonted course, and where it first begun,
What more remains best thoughts shall you attend,
My love in you began, in you shall end.

A pretty petty parly about a Fart.

Why what's a fart? wind, or aire, or sound, or so,
But presently his back-parts they cry no.
By my fay, saies one, for all your winking,
The answers good, were it not for stinking.
Nay quoth another, in it's no evill,
But that to mee it seeme's so uncivill.
Yet sayes the sagest, young men are too bold,
The priviledge belongs to us that'r old.
Nay quoth an heire this may well be done,
Farts be entaild from the father to the son.
Why sayes another, upon my conscience
It may be reform'd by some frankinsence.
Quoth an astronomer, if you'll not laffe,
I'le measure this fart with my Jacob's staffe:
Fie, sayes Sir *John*, I like not this passage,
Farts interpos'd in midd'st of a message;
Yet gentlemen, this before our departing,
In rhetoricke is no figure of farting.
Nay more than all this, sayes little *Jack Straw*,
A fart's not in compasse of th' civill law,
'Tis true sayes Sir *John*, I dare assure'm,
'Tis *contra modestiam*, not *contra naturam*.
Your words sayes another are all but wind,
For I do not like those motions behind:
I'le lay my cap, quoth *Will* with the red hose,
That the *major* part will goe with the nose.
Well sayes th'other, I'me asham'd to tell it,
For all that are here, may easily smell it,

Then I that stood by said, surely this fart,
Is voyce of the belly and not of the heart.
In compasse of ten mile about,
(Saies one) such a fart there never came out.
A pursevant then humbly on his knees
Would faine have the fart, but it payes no fees:
But sayes the delinquent, pray let mee speake,
Now I assure thee, my shoes did but creake.
O strange quoth one, 'tis most wondrously,
The gentleman speaketh as well as I.
So (gentle reader) our dispute did bend,
To one onely center; and ther's an end.

A Carous-Conto.

The Welshman love's cous pobby,
The French a curtaine sermon,
But I must slash in balderdash,
For I'm a true bred German.

         –

Capape, let us welter, and bouze helter skelter,
Tom-Tinker his tankard, the Fleming his flagon.
   The Irike cough his vasquebough,
   The Dutch-fro his slapdragon.

Ænigma.

As often as I please it changeth forme,
It is no coward, though it do no harme;
'Tis never hurt, nor ever doth it feed;
'Tis nothing worth, yet nothing doth it need.
Swiftly it runs, yet never maketh sound,
And once being lost; again 'tis never found.
'Tis a fit servant for a gentleman,
And a true pattern for a serving-man.
'Tis born a gyant, lives a dwarfe, and nigh
Unto its death, a gyant doth it dye.

Another on the six Cases.

No. *Nanta* was nominated for a **W.**
Gen. For she that had been *Genitive* before :
Da. Notice hereof was *to the Justice* given,
Acc. *Who her accus'd,* that she had loosely liven.
Voc. But she *cry'd mercy,* and her fault up ript,
Abl. And so was *ta'n away* and soundly whipt.
    Her case was ill : yet will the question be,
    Being thus declin'd, in what a case was she.

If V 2 I, as I 2 V am true,

V̇ must lye, and **V̇**

Thoughts—⎱
Searching ⎰c

    Valued⎱
Love———⎰may   **B**

 Truth never ties
Too A foole yy

If  have part

And  V bb

Y'have 1. 2. many then I. C.
And R not worth

   Write ⎱   QQ
I'le——— ⎰ not yours V·V

A Riddle.

A beggar once exceeding poore,
A penny pray'd me give him,
And deeply vow'd ne'r to ask more
And I ne'r more to give him,
Next day he begg'd again, I gave,
Yet both of us our oaths did save.

Another.

There was a man bespake a thing,
Which when the owner home did bring,
He that made it, did refuse it,
He that bought it, would not use it;
He that hath it doth not know
Whether he hath it, yea or no.

Another.

One evening, as cold, as cold might be,
With frost and snow, and pinching weather,
Companions about three times three,
Lay close all in a bed together;
   Yet one after other they took heat,
   And dy'd that night all in a sweat.

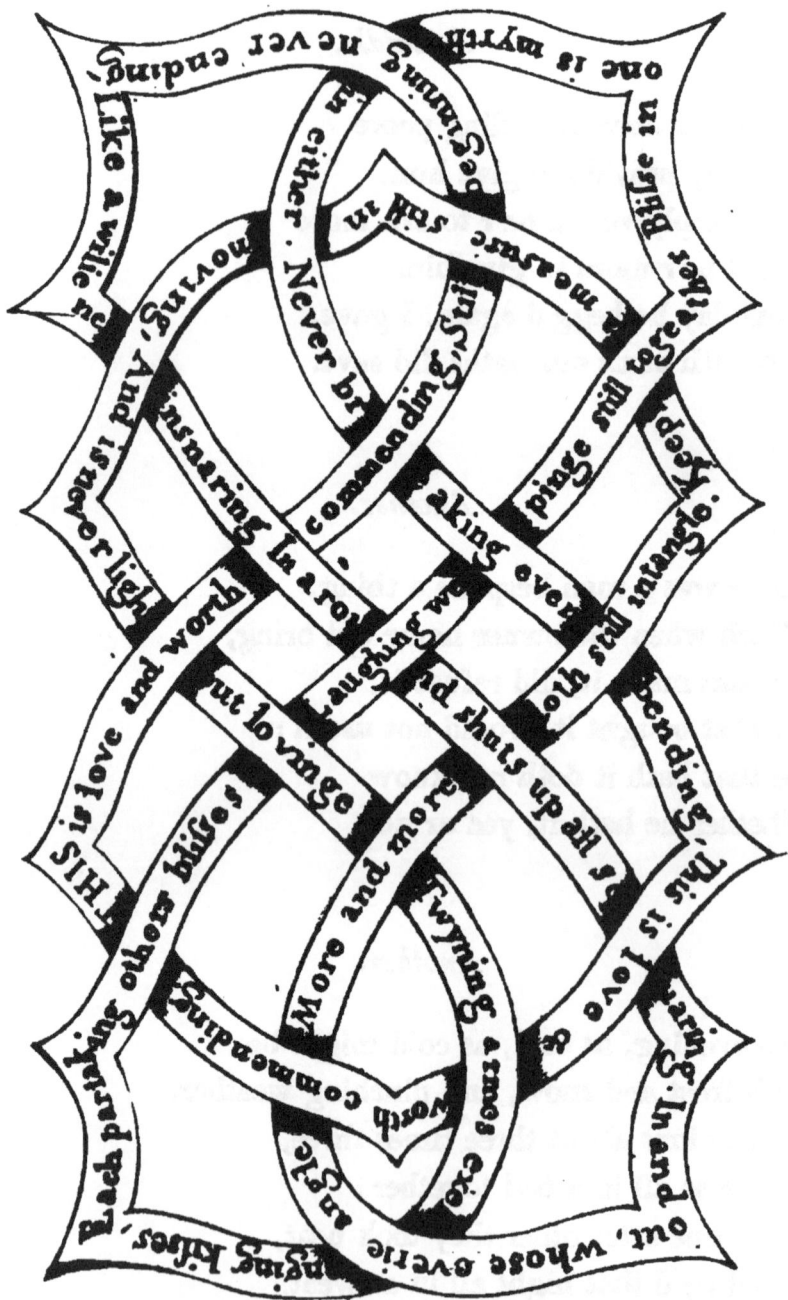

Beginning never ending. Like a wilie ne

one is myrth Blisse in

either. Never br moving, And is never ligh

commanding Suf measure still in piage still together Keep intangle.

Insnaring In a ro aking ever bending, This

Laughing nd shuts up all is love

THIS is love and worth ut lovinge more and more Twyning a

Each partaking others blisse worth commending

nging kisses out, whose overie angle

A doubtfull meaning.

The *Fæminine* kind is counted ill :
And is I swear : The contrary ;
No man can find : That hurt they will ;
But every where : Doe show pity ;
To no kind heart : They will be curst ;
To all true friends : They will be trusty ;
In no part : They work the worst ;
With tongue and mind : But honesty ;
They do detest : Inconstancy ;
They do embrace : Honest intent ;
They like least : Lewd fantasie ;
In every case : Are penitent ;
At no season : Doing amisse ;
To it truly : Contrary ;
To all reason : Subject and meek ;
To no body : Malicious ;
To friend or foe : Or gentle sort ;
They be never : Doing amisse ;
In weale and woe : Of like report ;
They be ever : Be sure of this ;
The *Fæminine* kind : Shall have my heart ;
Nothing at all : False they wil be ;
In word and mind : To suffer smart ;
And ever shall : Believe you me.

2 A

.goe

That doth .

That's
rul'd by 1.

whose sayes no :

I'le try ere trust
ward · lest

my

Find slight regard.

The  a

whilst

1  2 Lovers

That
  gazed me.

There was nor

nor loathsome

That might disturb or break delight,

Nor  nor

  in that same road,
And yet to me they seem'd affright.
  favour
Then   them I told,
True love cannot be
              bold

These may be read two or three wayes.

Your face	Your tongue	your wit
so faire	so smooth	so sharp
first drew	then mov'd	then knit
mine eye	mine eare	my heart
Mine eye	Mine eare	My heart
thus drawn	thus mov'd	thus knit
affects	hangs on	yeelds to
Your face	Your tongue	your wit

These may be read backward or forward.

Joy, mirth, triumphs, I do defie,
Destroy me death; fain would I dye:
Forlorn am I, love is exil'd,
Scorn smiles thereat; hope is beguil'd:
  Men banish'd blisse, in woe must dwell,
  Then joy, mirth, triumphs, all farewell.

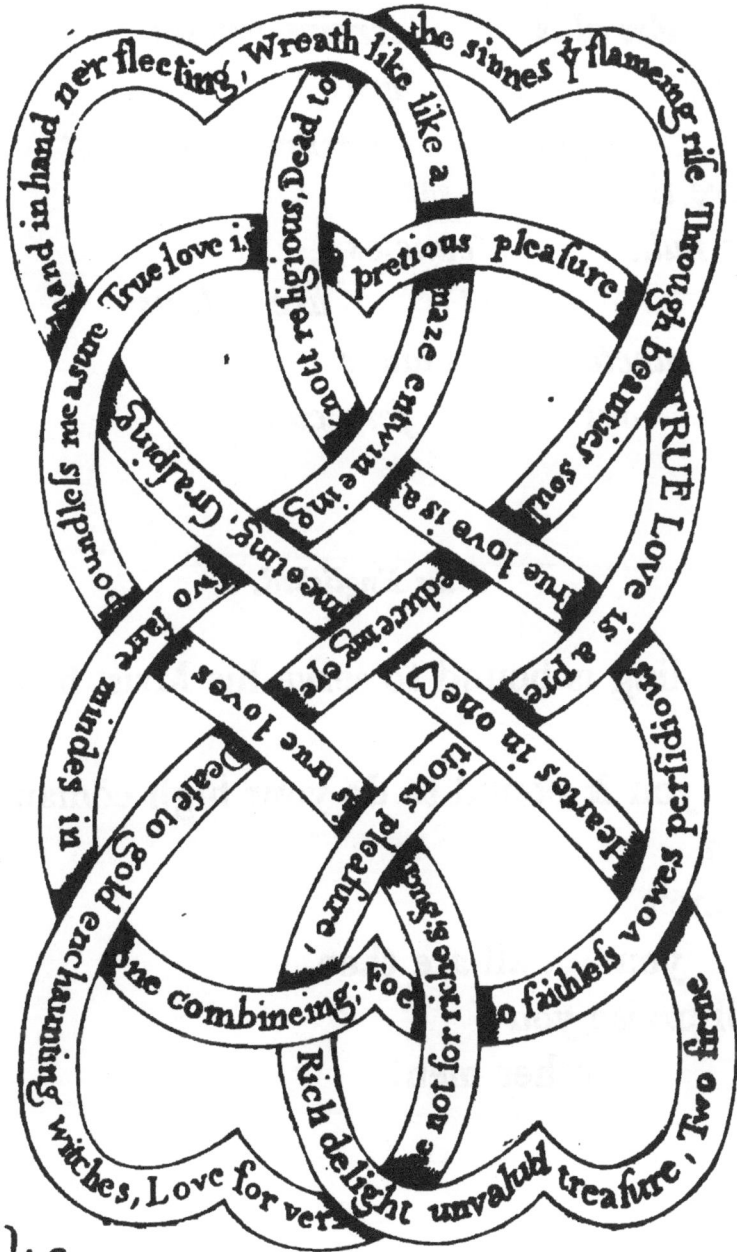

ner fleeting, Wreath like a the sinnes & flameing rise

Dead to Through beauties sou...

True love is pretious pleasure TRUE Love is a pre

maze entwineing

hand in hand vast measure True love is

Graspinge boundles in

two fair mindes in breeting, true love is a

...ducing eye Hearts in one

Deafe to Gold true loves ...ious pleasure faithles vowes periured

one combineing; Foe nor for riches

enchaunting witches, Love for ver Rich delight unvalud treasure, Two firme

    Est aliis   *servire tenetur*
Jure   *qui*
     sum   *servire necesse est*
Jure tibi   *me*
Te nulli   *cunctos*
    aut   *are videris*
Qui cunctos *hos laude*
    aut   ' *fero cunctis.*

Thus Englished.

    -ling is bound to serve his Mris. hands
An-
    you & bound to do your high cōmands
I'm
None's   you
    you   all are then
I'll praise you
    other men.

A New years Gift.

That our loves may never alter,
Tye it fast with this strong halter.

The Answer.

The rope is old, the jest is new,
I'll take the jest, the rope take you.

A Gentleman to his Love.

Tell her I love; and if she ask how well;
Tell her my tongue told thee no tongue can tell.

Her Answer.

Say not you love, unlesse you do,
For lying will not honour you.

His Reply.

Madam, I love, and love to do,
And will not lye, unless with you.

To his Mistresse.

A constant heart within a womans breast,
Is Ophir gold within an ivory chest.

Her Answer.

Of such a treasure then thou art possest,
For thou hast such a heart in such a chest.

On Chloris walking in the Snow.

I saw fair *Chloris* walk alone,
When feather'd rain came softly down,
Then *Jove* descended from his tower,
To court her in a silver shower:
The wanton snow flew to her brest,
Like little birds into their nest;
But overcome with whiteness there
For grief it thaw'd into a teare;
Then falling down her garment hem,
To deck her, froze into a gem.

Vpon Clarinda, begging a lock of her Lovers hair.

Fairest *Clarinda*, she whom truth calls faire,
Begg'd my heart of me, and a lock of haire;
Should I give both, said I, how should I live?
The lock I would, the heart I would not give:
For that, lest theeving love should steal away;
Discretion had lock'd up, and kept the key;
As for the lock of hair which lovers use,
My head laid on her knee, I pray'd her chuse,
Taking her sizars by a cunning art,
First pick'd the lock, and then she stole my heart.

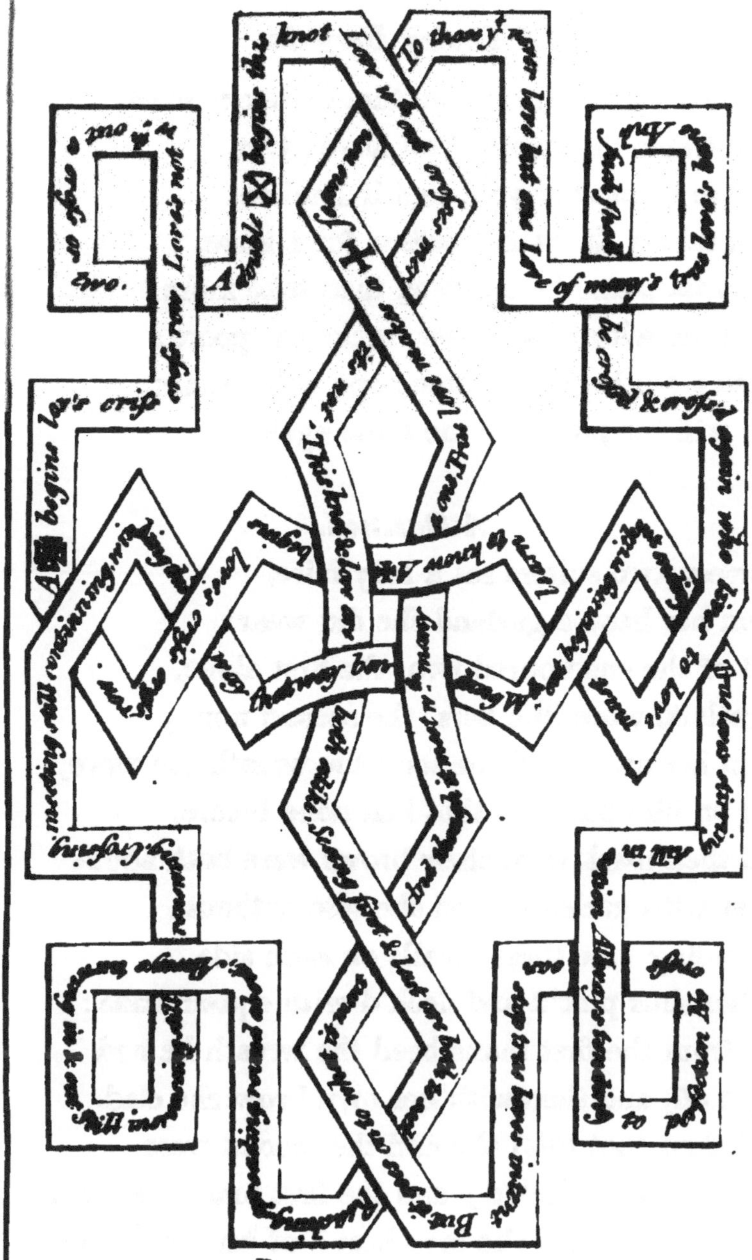

A double ⊠ begins this knot
This knot & love are
Learn to know
crossed & crossed again
True love stirring still in

A Loving Bargain.

Give me a kisse, I'll make that odde one even,
Then treble that which you have given;
Be sure I'l answer you, and if I misse,
Then take a thousand forfeits for a kisse,
And a thousand be too few, then take more:
Kisse me with your kisses, make me poore:
When I am begger'd some hope will remain,
You will for pity give me some again.

A Question.

Between two suiters sat a lady faire,
Upon her head a garland she did wear:
And of the enamoured two, the first alone,
A garland wore like hers, the second none;
From her own head she took the wreath she wore,
And on him plac'd it that had none before.
And then mark this, their brows were both about
Beset with garlands, and she sate without:
Beholding now these rivalls on each side
Of her thus plac'd and deck'd with equall pride:
She from the first mans head the wreath he had
Took off, and therewith her own brow she clad.
And then (not this) she and the second were
With garlands deck'd; and the first man sate bare.
  Now which did she love best? of him to whom
  She gave the wreath? or him she took it from?

The Answer.

In my conceit, she would him soonest have,
From whom she took, not him to whom she gave.
For to bestow, many respects may move :
But to receive, none can perswade but love.
She grac'd him much on whom the wreath she plac'd ;
But him whose wreath she wore, she much more grac'd
For where she gives, she there a servant makes,
But makes her self a servant where she takes.
Then where she takes, she honours most : and where
She doth most honour, she most love doth bear.

An incomparable kisse.

Give me a kisse from those sweet lips of thine,
And make it double by enjoyning mine,
Another yet, nay yet another,
And let the first kisse be the seconds brother.
Give me a thousand kisses, and yet more ;
And then repeat those that have gone before ;
Let us begin while day-light springs in heav'n
And kisse till night descends into the ev'n,
And when that modest secretary, night,
Discolours all but thy heav'n-beaming bright,
We will begin revels of hidden love ;
In that sweet orbe where silent pleasures move.
In high, new strains, unspeakable delight,
We'll vent the dull hours of the silent night.
Were the bright day no more to visit us,
O then for ever would I hold thee thus ;

Naked, inchain'd, empty of idle feare,
As the first lovers in the garden were.
I'll dye betwixt thy breasts that are so white,
For, to dye there, would do a man delight.
Embrace me still, for time runs on before,
And being dead we shall embrace no more.
Let us kisse faster then the hours do flye,
Long live each kisse, and never know to dye.
Yet if that fade, and fly away too fast,
Impresse another, and renew the last;
Let us vie kisses, till our eye-lids cover,
And if I sleep, count me an idle lover,
Admit I sleep, I'll still pursue the theam,
And eagerly I'l kisse thee in a dream.
O give me way; grant love to me thy friend,
Did hundred thousand suiters all contend
For thy virginity, there's none shall woe
With heart so firm as mine; none better do
Then I with your sweet sweetnesse; if you doubt,
Pierce with your eyes my heart, or pluck it out.

To his Mistresse.

Dearest, thy twin'd haires are not threds of gold,
Nor thine eyes diamonds; nor do I hold
Thy lips for rubies, nor thy cheeks to be
Fresh roses; nor thy dugs of ivory;
The skin that doth thy dainty body sheath,
Not alablaster is; nor dost thou breath
Arabian odours; these the earth brings forth,
Compar'd with thine, they would impair thy worth;

Such then are other mistresses; but mine
Hath nothing earth, but all divine.

The Answer.

If earth doth never change, nor move,
There's nought of earth sure in thy love;
Sith heavenly bodies with each one,
Concur in generation;
And wanting gravity are light,
Or in a borrowed lustre bright;
If meteors and each falling starre,
Of heavenly matter framed are,
Earth hath my mistresse, but sure thine
All heavenly is, though not divine.

To his Mistresse.

I love, because it comes to me by kind;
And much, because it much delights my mind:
And thee because thou art within my heart:
And thee alone, because of thy desert.
    I love, and much, and thee, and thee alone,
    By kind, mind, heart, and every one.

Her Answer.

Thou lov'st not, because thou art unkind,
Nor much, cause it delighteth not thy mind:
Nor me, because I am not in thy heart:
Nor me alone, because I want desert:
    Thou lov'st nor much, nor me, nor me alone,
    By kind, mind, heart, desert, nor any one.

Clownish Courtship.

Excellent mistresse, brighter than the moon,
Then scoured pewter, or the silver-spoon,
Fairer then *Phœbus*, or the morning starre;
Dainty faire mistresse, by my troth you are,
As far excelling *Dian* and her nymphs,
As lobsters crawfish, and as crawfish shrimps:
Thine eyes like diamonds, do shine most clearly,
As I'm an honest man, I love thee dearly.

A Comparison.

Like to the self-inhabiting snaile,
Or like a squirrell pent-hous'd under his taile,
  Even such is my mistresse face in a vaile:
Or like to a carp that's lost in mudding,
Nay, more like to a black-pudding:
  For as the pudding, the skin lies within,
  So doth my mistresse beauty in a taffity gin.

A Question.

Tell me (sweet-heart) how spell'st thou *Jone,*
Tell me but that, 'tis all I crave;
I shall not need to be alone,
If such a lovely mate I have;
That thou art one, who can deny?
And all will grant that I am I,
If I be I, and thou art one,
Tell me (sweet-heart) how spell'st thou *Jone.*

The Answer.

I tell you sir, and tell you true,
That I am _J_, and I am _one_,
So can I spell _Jone_ without you,
And spelling so, can lye alone:
My eye to one is consonant,
But as for yours it is not so.;
If that your eye agreement want,
I to your eye must answer no;
   Therefore leave off your loving plea,
   And let your I be I _per se._

Loves prime.

Dear love, do not your fair beauty wrong
With thinking still you are too young,
The rose and lilly in your cheek
Do flourish, and no ripening seek:
Those flaming beams shot from your eye,
Do show loves midsomer is nigh.
Your cherry-lip, red, soft and sweet,
Proclaim such fruit for tast is meet:
   Then lose no time, for love hath wings,
   And flies away from aged things.

Another to his Mistresse.

When first I saw thee, thou didst sweetly play
The gentle thief, and stol'st my heart away;
Render me mine again, or leave thy owne,
Two are too much for thee, since I have none:

But if thou wilt not, I will swear thou art
A sweet-fac'd creature with a double heart.

Another.

Sweetest fair be not too cruell,
Blot not beauty with disdain,
Let not those bright eyes adde fewell
To a burning heart in vain ;
Lest men justly when I dye,
Deem you the candle, me the flye.

Another.

I cannot pray you in a studyed stile,
Nor speak words distant from my heart a mile ; .
I cannot visit Hide-Park every day,
And with a hackney court my time away ;
I cannot spaniolize it week by week,
Or wait a month to kisse your hand or cheek ;
If when you'r lov'd, you cannot love again,
Why, do but say so, I am out of pain.

Excuse for absence.

You'll ask perhaps wherefore I stay,
(Loving so much,) so long away ?
I do not think 'twas I did part,
It was my body, not my heart :
For like a compasse in your love,
One foot was fixt, and cannot move ;
Th'other may follow the blind guide
Of giddy fortune, but cannot slide

Beyond your service; nor will venter
To wander far from you the center.

To a fair, but unkind Mistresse.

I prethee turn that face away,
Whose splendor but benights my day;
Sad eyes like mine, and wounded hearts,
Shun the bright rayes that beauty darts;
Unwelcome is the sun that pries
Into those shades where sorrow lyes.
Go shine on happy things, to me
The blessing is a misery;
For your bright sun, not warms, but burns;
Like that the Indian sooty turns.
I'l serve the night, and there confin'd,
Wish thee lesse fair, or else more kind.

To himselfe.

Retreat sad heart, breed not thy further pain;
Admire, but fonder thoughts seek to refrain.

To some Ladies.

Ladies, you that seem so nice,
And in show as cold as ice,
And perhaps have held out thrice,
Do not think, but in a trice,
One or other may entice;
And at last by some device,
Set your honour at a price.

You whose smooth and dainty skin,
Rosie lips, or cheeks, or chin,
All that gaze upon you win,
Yet insult not, sparks within
Slowly burn e'r flames begin, .
And presumption still hath bin
Held a most notorious sin.

A heart lost.

Good folk, for love or hire,
But help me to a cryer,
For my poor heart is gone astray
After two eyes that went that way.
O yes! if there be any man
In town or country, can
Bring me my heart again,
I'll pay him for his pain.
And by these marks I will you show,
That onely I this heart do owe:
It is a wounded heart,
Wherein yet sticks the dart,
Every part sore hurt throughout:
Faith and troth writ round about.
It is a tame heart and a deare,
That never us'd to roame,
But having got a haunt, I feare
Will never stay at home,
For love-sake walking by this way,
If you this heart do see;
Either impound it for a stray,
Or send it home to me.

The sad Lover.

Why should I wrong my judgement so,
As for to love where I do know
   There is no hold for to be taken?

For what her wish thirsts after most,
If once of it her heart can boast,
   Straight by her folly 'tis forsaken.

Thus whilst I still pursue in vaine,
Me thinks I turn a child again,
   And of my shadow am a chasing.

For all her favours are to me
Like apparitions which I see,
   But never can come neer th'embracing.

Oft had I wish'd that there had been
Some almanack whereby to have seen,
   When love with her had been in season.

But I perceive there is no art
Can find the epact of the heart,
   That loves by chance, and not by reason.

Yet will I not for this despaire,
For time her humor may prepare
   To grace him who is now neglected.

And what unto my constancie
She now denies: one day may be
   From her inconstancy expected.

A Watch sent to a Gentlewoman.

Goe and count her happy hours,
They more happy are than ours :
That day that gets her any blisse,
Make it twice as long as 'tis :
The houre she smiles in, let it be
By thine art increas'd to three :
But if she frown on thee or me,
Know night is made, by her, not thee :
Be swift in such an houre, and soon
Make it night, though it be noon :
Obey her time, who is the free,
Faire sun that governs thee and me.

On a Fairing.

Let them whose heart distrusts a mistresse faith,
Bribe it with gifts : mine no suspition hath :
It were a sin of as much staine in me,
To think you false, as so my selfe to be.
If to reward that thou hast exprest,
Thou dost expect a present : 'tis confest
'Twere justice from another, but I am
So poore ; I have not left my selfe a name
In substance ; not made thine by gift before :
He that bestowes his heart, can give no more.
If thou wouldst have a fairing from me, then
Give me my selfe back, I'll give it thee agen.

Posies for Rings.

We are agreed
In time to speed.

I trust in time
Thou wilt be mine.

In thy breast
My heart doth rest.

This and the giver
Are thine for ever.

'Tis love alone
Makes two but one.

Loves knot once tyde
Who can divide?

Where hearts agree
No strife can be.

God above
Increase our love.

Though time do slide,
Yet in true love abide.

Nought so sweet,
As when we greet.

Thy affection,
My perfection.

With a ◯ *to Julia.*

Julia, I bring
To thee this ring,
Made for thy finger fit;
To shew by this,
That our love is
(Or sho'd be) like to it.

Close though it be,
Thy joynt is free:
So when lov's yoke is on,
It must not gall,
Or fret at all
With hard oppression.

But it must play
Still either way;
And be too, such a yoke,
As not too wide,
To over-slide;
Or be so straite to choake,

So we, who beare
This beame, must reare
Our selves to such a height:
As that the stay
Of either may
Create the burden light.

And as this round
Is no where found
To flaw or else to sever:
So let our love
As endlesse prove;
And pure as gold for ever.

True Beauty.

May I finde a woman faire,
And her mind as clear as aire;
If her beauty goe alone,
'Tis to me, as if 'twere none.

May I find a woman rich,
And not of too high a pitch;

If that pride should cause disdain,
Tell me, lover, where's thy gain ?

May I finde a woman wise,
And her falshood not disguise ;
Hath she wit, as she hath will ?
Double arm'd she is to ill.

May I finde a woman kind,
And not wavering like the wind :
How should I call that love mine,
When 'tis his, and his, and thine ?

May I find a woman true,
There is beauties fairest hue ;
There is beauty, love and wit,
Happy he can compasse it.

Choice of a Mistresse.

Not that I wish my mistris
More or lesse than what she is,
Write I these lines, for 'tis too late
Rules to prescribe unto my fate.

But yet as tender stomachs call
For some choice meat, that bears not all :
A queazie lover may impart,
What mistresse 'tis that please his heart.

First I would have her richly spred,
With natures blossomes white and red;
For flaming hearts will quickly dye,
That have not fewell from the eye.

Yet this alone will never win,
Except some treasure lies within;
For where the spoile's not worth the stay,
Men raise their siege and go away.

I'd have her wise enough to know
When, and to whom a grace to show:
For she that doth at randome chuse,
She will, as soon her choice refuse.

And yet me thinks I'd have her mind
To flowing courtesie inclin'd:
And tender hearted as a maid,
Yet pity onely when I pray'd.

And I would wish her true to be,
(Mistake me not) I mean to me;
She that loves me, and loves one more,
Will love the kingdome o'r and o'r.

And I could wish her full of wit,
Knew she how to huswife it:
But she whose wisdome makes her dare
To try her wit, will sell more ware.

Some other things, delight will bring,
As if she dances, play, and sing.
So they be safe, what though her parts
Catch ten thousand forreign hearts.

But let me see, should she be proud;
A little pride should be allow'd.
Each amorous boy will sport and prate
Too freely, where he finds not state.

I care not much though she let down
Sometime a chiding, or a frown.
But if she wholly quench desire,
'Tis hard to kindle a new fire.

To smile, to toy, is not amisse,
Sometimes to interpose a kisse;
But not to cloy; sweet things are good,
Pleasant for sawce, but not for food.

Wishes to his supposed Mistresse.

Who e'r she be,
That is the onely she,
That shall command my heart and me.

Might you hear my wishes
Bespeak her to my blisses,
And be call'd my absent kisses.

I wish her beauty,
That owes not all his duty
To gawdy tire, or some such folly.

A face that's best
By its own beauty drest;
And can alone command the rest.

Smiles, that can warme
The blood, yet teach a charme
That chastity shall take no harme.

Joyes that confesse
Vertue her mistresse,
And have no other head to dresse.

Dayes, that in spight
Of darknesse, by the light
Of a cleare minde, are day all night.

Life that dares send
A challenge to his end,
And when it's come, say, Welcome friend.

Soft silken howers,
Open sunnes; shady bowers,
Bove all; nothing within that lowers.

I wish her store
Of wealth may leave her poore
Of wishes; and I wish no more.

Now if time knows,
That her whose radiant browes,
Weave them a garlant of my vows.

Her that dare be,
What these lines wish to see,
I seek no further, it is she.

Such worth as this is,
Shall fix my flying wishes
And determine them to kisses.

Let her full glory,
(My fancies) fly before ye,
Be ye my fiction, but her my story.

To a Lady.

Madam,
Should I not smother this ambitious fire,
Which actuates my verse: it would aspire
To blear your vertues, in a glimm'ring line;
And your perfections in its measures twine.
But I have check'd my fancie Muse, nor dares
Dull poetry attempt to scan the spheares;
Or in a cloudy rime invaile the light,
Or court the trembling watchmen of the night;
Some vulgar vertue, or a single blaze,
Might stand in verse; and would endure a gaze:
But when both art, and nature, shall agree
To summe them all in one epitome:

When the perfections of both sexes, are
Lock'd in one female store-house; who shall dare
In an audacious rapture, to untwine
Into loose numbers, what heaven doth enshrine,
In one rich breast? Dazled invention say,
Canst thou embowell either *India*,
In one poor rime? Or can thy torch-light fire,
Shew us the sunne; or any star that's higher?
If thou wilt needs spend thy officious flame,
Do it in admiration: but disclaime
Thy power to praise: thy senders wishes, beare,
And be the herauld of the new-born yeare:
Wish that each rising sunne, may see her more
Happy, then when he rose the morne before;
And may, when e'r he gilds the envious west,
Leave her more blest, then when he grac'd the feast;
Wish higher yet, that her felicity
May equalize her vertues: Poetry
Thou art too low; canst thou not swell a straine
May reach my thoughts: good madam since 'tis vain,
(And yet my verse to kisse your hand presum'd)
Let it to be your sacrifice be doom'd:
And what it wants in true poetique fire,
Let the flame adde, till so my Muse expire.

An Eccho.

Come Eccho I thee summon,
Tell me truly what is woman?
  If worne, she is a feather,
  If woo'd she's frosty weather;

If wonne, the winde not slighter:
If weigh'd the moon's not lighter:
If lain withall, she's apish:
If not laine with, she's snappish.

Come Eccho I thee summon,
Tell me once more what is woman?
  If faire, she's coy in courting,
  If witty, loose in sporting,
  If ready, she's but cloathing,
  If naked, she's just nothing,
  If not belov'd, she horns thee;
  If lov'd too well, she scorns thee.
The Eccho still replyed,
But still me thought she lyed.

Then for my mistresse sake,
I againe reply did make.
  If worn, she is a jewell,
  If woo'd, she is not cruell,
  If wonne, no rock is surer,
  If weigh'd, no gold is purer,
  If laine withall, delicious;
  If not, yet no way vitious.
False Eccho go, you lye.
See your errours I discry.

And for the second summon I
This for woman do reply.
  If faire she's heavenly treasure,
  If witty, she's all pleasure,

If ready, she's quaintiest.
If not ready, she's dantiest,
If lov'd, her heart she spares not,
If not belov'd, she cares not.
False Eccho, go you lye.
See your errours I discry.

To Fortune.

Since Fortune thou art become so kinde,
To give me leave to take my mind,
　　　　Of all thy store.
First it is needfull that I finde
Good meat and drink of every kinde
　　　　I ask no more.
And then that I may well digest
Each severall morsel of the feast :
　　　　See thou my store.
To ease the care within my breast,
With a thousand pound at least :
　　　　I ask no more.
A well born and a pleasing dame,
Full of beauty, void of shame ;
　　　　Let her have store
Of wealth, discretion, and good fame ;
And able to appease my flame.
　　　　I ask no more.
Yet one thing more do not forget,
Afore that I do do this feat,
　　　　Forgot before ; 　.

That she a virgin be, and neat,   .
Of whom two sonnes I may beget;
           I aske no more.
Let them be barons, and impart
To each a million for his part;
           I thee implore.
That when I long life have led,
I may have heaven when I am dead:
           I ask no more.

A Dialogue between Icarus, and surprized Phillida.

Phil. Prette sweet-one look on me,
     Faine I would thy captive be,
    Bound by thee is *liberty*.

Icar. Be not so unkindly wise,
     For your looks will bribe my eyes,
    To divulge where my heart lyes.

Phil. If they doe, thou need'st not feare,
     By my innocence I sweare,
    I'll but place another there.

Icar. That's my feare, I dare not prove,
     Nor my resolution move.
    'Cause I know you are in love.

Phil. Lov'd *Icarus*, and if I be,
     I know it cannot injure thee:
    Love and beauty will agree.

Icar. Oh you do my hearing wrong,
    I have turn'd my eyes thus long
  To be captiv'd by your tongue.

Phil. Then my hours are happy spent,
    If my tongue give such content,
  It shall be thy *instrument.*

Icar. But be sure you use it then,
    Thus unto no other men,
  Lest that I grow deaf agen.

    Fidelius and his silent Mris. Flora.

Fid. My dearest *Flora* can you love me ?
        Flo. Prethee prove me.
Fid. Shall I have your hand to kisse ?
        Flo. Yes, yes.
Fid. On this whitenesse let me sweare,
        Flo. No, pray forbeare.
Fid. I love you dearer than mine eyes.
        Flo. Be wise.
Fid. I prize no happinesse like you.
        Flo. Will you be true ?
Fid. As is the turtle to her mate.
        Flo. I hate.
Fid. Who my divinest *Flora*, me ?
        Flo. No flattery.
Fid. He that flatters, may he dye,
        Flo. Perpetually.

Fid. And his black urne be the cell,
        Flo. Where furies dwell.
Fid. May his name be blasphemous,
        Flo. To us.
Fid. His memory for ever rot;
        Flo. And be forgot.
Fid. Lest it keep our age and youth,
        Flo. From love and truth.
Fid. Thus upon your virgin hand,
        Flo. Your vows shall stand.
Fid. This kisse confirmes my act and deed:
        Flo. You may exceed.
Fid. Your hand, your lip, I'll vow on both;
        Flo. A dangerous oath.
. *Fid.* My resolution ne'r shall start;
        Flo. You have my heart.

Fears and Resolves of two Lovers.

A. What wouldst thou wish? tell me dear lover.
I. How I might but thy thoughts discover.
A. If my firme love I were denying,
Tell me, with sighes wouldst thou be dying?
I. Those words in jest to heare thee speaking,
For very grief, this heart is breaking.
A. Yet wouldst thou change? I prethee tell me.
In seeing one that doth excell me?
I. O no, for how can I aspire,
To more than to my own desire?

This my mishap doth chiefly grieve me;
Though I do swear't, you'l not believe me.

A. Imagine that thou dost not love me;
But some beauty that's above me.

I. To such a thing sweet do not will me;
The naming of the same will kill me.

A. Forgive me faire one, Love hath feares:
I. I do forgive, witnesse these tears.

A Sonnet.

Who can define, this all things, nothing love,
Which hath so much of every thing in it?
Which watry, with the planets oft doth move,
And with the zoane it hath a fiery fit;
Oft seizes men, like massy stupid earth,
And with the aire, it filleth every place;
Which had no midwife, nor I think no birth,
No shrine, no arrowes, but a womans face.
A god he is not, for he is unjust;
A boy he is not, for he hath more power;
A fiction 'tis not, all will yeeld I trust;
What is it then, that is so sweetly sower?
No law so wise, that can his absence prove?
But (ah) I know there is a thing call'd love.

A love-sick sonnet.

Love is a sicknesse full of woes,
    All remedies refusing:
A plant that with most cutting growes,
    Most barren with best using.

Why so ?
More we enjoy it, more it dyes,
If not enjoy'd, it sighing cryes
Hey ho !

Love is a torment of the mind,
  A tempest everlasting ;
And *Jove* hath made it of a kinde,
  Not well, nor full nor fasting.
            Why so ?
More we enjoy it, more it dyes,
If not enjoy'd, it sighing cryes
            Hey ho !

A Question.

Fain would I learn of men the reason why
They swear they dye for love, yet lowly ly ?
Or why they fondly dote on, and admire
A painted face, or a fantastick tyre ?
  For while such idols they fall down before,
  They prove more fools than those they thus adore.

Answer.

The reason why men loving lowly ly ;
Is hope to gain their purposes thereby.
And that they fondly dote on paint and tires ;
'Tis just in love, to shew mens fond desires.
  And for the rest, this have I heard from schools,
  That love, makes foolish wise, and wise men fools.

Sighs.

All night I muse, all day I cry,
      ay me.
Yet still I wish, though still deny.
      ay me.
I sigh, I mourn, and say that still,
I onely live my joyes to kill.
      ay me.
I feed the pain that on me feeds;
      ay me.
My wound I stop not, though it bleeds;
      ay me.
Heart be content, it must be so,
For springs were made to overflow.
      ay me.
Then sigh and weep, and mourn thy fill,
      ay me.
Seek no redresse, but languish still.
      ay me.
Their griefs more willing they endure,
That know when they are past recure.
      ay me.

To Celia weeping.

Fairest, when thine eyes did poure
      A chrystall shower;
I was perswaded, that some stone
      Had liquid grown;

And thus amazed; sure thought I
When stones are moist, some raine is nigh.

Why weep'st thou? cause thou cannot be
    More hard to me?
So lionesses pitty, so
    Do tygers too:
So doth that bird, which when she's fed
On all the man, pines o're the head.

Yet I'le make better omens till
    Event beguile;
Those pearly drops, in time shall be
    A precious sea;
And thou shalt like thy corall prove,
Soft under water, hard above.

An Hymne to Love.

  I will confesse
  With cheerfulnesse,
Love is a thing so likes me,
  That let her lay
  On me all day,
I'le kisse the hand that strikes me.

  I will not, I,
  Now blubb'ring cry,
It (ah!) too late repents me,

That I did fall
To love at all,
Since love so much contents me.

No, no, I'le be
In fetters free ;
While others they sit wringing
  Their hands for paine ;
  I'le entertaine
The wounds of love with singing.

With flowers and wine
And cakes divine,   ,
To strike me I will tempt thee :
  Which done ; no more
  I'le come before
Thee and thine altars empty.

Loves Discoveryes.

With much of paine, and all the art I knew,
  Have I endeavor'd hitherto
To hide my love ; and yet all will not do.

The world perceives it, and it may be, she ;
  Though so discreet, and good she be,
By hiding it, to teach that skill to me.

Men without love have oft so cunning growne,
   That something like it they have showne,
But none that had it ever seem'd t'have none.

Love's of a strangely open, simple kind,
   Can no arts or disguises find,
But thinks none sees it cause it self is blind.

The very eye betrayes our inward smart;
   Love of himself left there a part,
When through it he past into the heart.

Or if by chance the face betray not it,
   But keep the secret wisely, yet,
Like drunkennesse into the tongue 'twill get.

Heart-breaking.

It gave a piteous groan, and so it broke;
   In vaine it something would have spoke:
   The love within too strong for't was
Like poyson put into a Venice glasse.

I thought that this some remedy might prove,
   But, oh, the mighty serpent love,
   Cut by this chance in pieces small,
In all still liv'd, and still it stung in all.

And now (alas) each little broken part
  Feels the whole pain of all my heart:
  And every smallest corner still
Lives with that torment which the whole did kill.

Even so rude armies when the field they quit,
  And into severall quarters get;
  Each troop does spoyle and ruine more
Then all joyn'd in one body did before.

How many loves reigne in my bosome now?
  How many loves, yet all of you?
  Thus have I chang'd with evill fate
My monarch love into a tyrant state.

A Tear sent his Mistresse.

Glide gentle streams, and bear
Along with you my tear
  To that coy girle;
  Who smiles, yet slayes
  Me with delayes;
And strings my tears as pearle.

See! see she's yonder set,
Making a carkanet
  Of mayden-flowers!
  There, there present
  This orient,
And pendant pearl of ours.

Then say, I've sent one more
Jem, to enrich her store;
　　And that is all
　　Which I can send,
　　Or vainly spend,
For tears no more will fall.

Nor will I seek supply
Of them, the springs once dry;
　　But I'le devise,
　　(Among the rest)
　　A way that's best
How I may save mine eyes,

Yet say, sho'd she condemn
Me to surrender them;
　　Then say; my part
　　Must be to weep
　　Out them; to keep
A poor, yet loving heart.

Say too, she wo'd have this;
She shall: Then my hope is,
　　That when I'm poore,
　　And nothing have
　　To send, or save;
I'm sure she'l ask no more.

A Song.

To thy lover,
Dear discover
That sweet blush of thine that shameth
   (When those roses
   It discloses)
All the flowers that nature nameth.

In free ayre,
Flow thy haire;
That no more summers best dresses,
   Be beholden
   For their golden
Locks to *Phœbus* flaming tresses.·

O deliver
Love his quiver,
From thy eyes he shoots his arrowes,
   Where *Apollo*
   Cannot follow:
Feathered with his mothers sparrows.

O envy not
(That we dye not)
Those deer lips whose door encloses
   All the graces
   In their places,
Brother pearles, and sister roses.

From these treasures
Of ripe pleasures
One bright smile to clear the weather.
Earth and heaven
Thus made even,
Both will be good friends together.

The aire does wooe thee,
Winds cling to thee,
Might a word once fly from out thee;
Storm and thunder
Would sit under,
And keep silence round about thee.

But if natures
Common creatures,
So dear glories dare not borrow;
Yet thy beauty
Owes a duty,
To my loving lingring sorrow.

When my dying
Life is flying;
Those sweet aires that often slew me;
Shall revive me,
Or reprive me,
And to many deaths renew me.

The Cruell Maid.

And cruell maid, because I see
You scornfull of my love, and me:
Ile trouble you no more; but go
My way, where you shall never know
What is become of me: there I
Will find me out a path to dye;
Or learn some way to forget
You and your name, for ever: yet
Ere I go hence, know this from me,
What will, in time, your fortune be :
This to your coynesse I will tell;
And having spoke it once, Farewell.
The lilly will not long endure;
Nor the snow continue pure :
The rose, the violet, one day
See, both these lady-flowers decay :
And you must fade, as well as they.
And it may chance that love may turn,
And (like to mine) make your heart burn.
And weep to see't; yet this thing do,
That my last vow commends to you :
When you shall see that I am dead,
For pitty let a tear be shed;
And (with your mantle o're me cast)
Give my cold lips a kisse at last :
If twice you kisse, you need not feare,
That I shall stir, or live more here.

Next hollow out a tomb to cover
Me; me, the most despised lover;
And write thereon, *This, reader, know,*
Love kill'd this man. No more but so.

Silence.

No; to what purpose should I speak ?
No, wretched heart, swell till you break !
She cannot love me if she would ;
And to say truth, 'twere pity that she should.
No, to the grave thy sorrows beare,
  As silent as they will be there ;
Since that lov'd hand this mortal wound doth give,
  So handsomely the thing contrive.
  That she may guiltlesse of it live.
  So perish, that her killing thee
May a chance medley, and no murther be.

  'Tis nobler much for me that I
  By her beauty, not her anger dye ;
  This will look justly, and become
An execution, that a martyrdome.
  The censuring world will ne're refraine
  From judging men by thunder slaine.
She must be angry sure, if I should be
  So bold to ask her to make me
  By being hers, happier than she ;
  I will not ; 'tis a milder fate
To fall by her not loving, than her hate.

And yet this death of mine, I fear,
Will ominous to her appear:
When, sound in every other part, .
Her sacrifice is found without an heart;
For the last tempest of my death
Shall sigh out that too, with my breath.

His Misery.

Water, water I espy
Come, and cool ye, all who fry
In your loves; but none as I.

Though a thousand showers be
Still a falling, yet I see
Not one drop to light on me.

Happy you, who can have seas
For to quench ye, or some ease
From your kinder mistresses.

I have one, and she alone
Of a thousand thousand known,
Dead to all compassion.

Such an one, as will repeat
Both the cause, and make the heat
More by provocation great.

Gentle friends, though I despaire
Of my cure, do you beware
Of those girles, which cruell are.

The Call.

Marina stay,
And run not thus like a young roe away,
        No enemy
Pursues thee (foolish girle) 'tis onely I,
        Ile keep off harmes,
If thou'll be pleas'd to garrison mine arms;
        What dost thou feare
Ile turn a traytour? may these roses here
        To palenesse shred,
And lillies stand disguised in new red,
        If that I lay
A snare, wherein thou wouldst not gladly stay;
        See, see the sun
Doth slowly to his azure lodging run;
        Come sit but here,
And presently hee'l quit our hemisphere;
        So still among
Lovers, time is too short, or else too long;
        Here will we spin
Legends for them, that have love martyrs been;
        Here on this plaine
Wee'l take *Narcissus* to a flower again;

Come here and chose
On which of these proud. plats thou wouldst repose,
Here mayest thou shame
The rusty violets, with the crimson flame,
Of either cheek ;
And primroses white as thy fingers seek ;
Nay, thou mayst prove
That mans most noble passion, is to love.

A Check to her delay.

Come come away,
Or let me goe ;
Must I here stay,
Because y'are slow ;
And will continue so ?
Troth lady, no.

I scorne to be
A slave to state :
And since I'm free
I will not wait
Henceforth at such a rate,
For needy fate.

If you desire
My spark sho'd glow,
The peeping fire
You must blow ;
Or I shall quickly grow
To frost or snow.

The Lure.

Farewell, nay prethee turn again,
Rather then loose thee, Ile arraign
My self before thee; thou (most faire) shall be
     Thy self the judge;
     Ile never grudge
A law, ordain'd by thee.

Pray do but see, how every rose
A sanguine visage doth disclose,
O see, what aromatick gusts they breath;
     Come here wee'l sit,
     And learn to knit,
Them up into a wreath.

With that wreath, crowned shalt thou be;
Not grac't by it, but it thee;
Then shall the fawning zephirs wait to hear
     What thou shalt say,
     And softly play,
While newes to me they bear.

Come prethee come, wee'l now assay
To piece the scantnesse of the day;
Wee'l pluck the wheels from th'charry of the sun,
     That he may give
     Us time to live;
Till that our scene be done.

Wee'l suffer viperous thoughts, and cares,
To follow after silver haires;
Let's not anticipate them long before;
        When they begin,
        To enter in,
Each minute they'l grow more.

No, no, *Marina*, see this brook
How't would its posting course revoke,
Ere it shall in the ocean mingled lye,
        And what I pray,
        May cause this stay;
But to attest our joy?

Far be't from lust; such wild fire, ne're
Shall dare to lurk or kindle here;
Diviner flames shall in our fancies roule,
        Which not depresse
        To earthlinesse,
But elevate the soule.

Then shall a grandiz'd love, confesse,
That souls can mingle substances;
That hearts can easily counter-changed be,
        Or at the least,
        Can alter breasts,
When breasts themselves agree.

To Julia.

'Tis ev'ning my sweet,
And dark ; let us meet ;
Long time w'have here been a toying :
And never as yet,
That season co'd get,
Wherein t'have had an enjoying.

For pitty or shame,
Then let not loves flame,
Be ever and ever a spending ;
Since now to the port
The path is but short ;
And yet our way has no ending.

Time flyes away fast ;
Our howres do wast ;
The while we never remember,
How soon our life, here,
Grows old with the yeere,
That dyes with the next *December.*

Of Beauty.

What do I hate, what's beauty ? lasse
How doth it passe ?
As flowers, assoon as smelled at
Evaporate,
Even so this shadow, ere our eyes
Can view it, flies.

What's colour ? 'las the sullen night
    Can it affright ;
A rose can more vermilion speak,
    Then any cheek ;
A richer white on lillies stands,
    Then any hands.

Than what's the worth, when any flower
    Is worth far more ?
How constant's that which needs must dye
    When day doth flye ?
Glow-worms, can lend some petty light,
    To gloomy night.

And what's proportion ? we discry
    That in a fly ;
And what's a lip ? 'tis in the test
    Red clay at best.
And what's an eye ? an eglets are
    More strong by farre.

Who can that specious nothing heed,
    Which flies exceed ?
Who would his frequent kisses lay
    On painted clay ?
Wh'would not if eyes affection move
    Young eglets love ?

Is beauty thus ? then who would lye
    Love-sick and dye ?

And's wretched self annihilate
    For knows not what?
And with such sweat and care invade
    A very shade?

Even he that knows not to possesse
    True happinesse,
But has some strong desires to try
    What's misery,
And longs for tears, oh he will prove
    One fit for love.

Farewell to Love.

Well-shadow'd landskip, fare-ye-well:
How I have lov'd you, none can tell,
    At least so well
  As he, that now hates more
  Then e're he lov'd before.

But my dear nothings, take your leave,
No longer must you me deceive,
    Since I perceive,
  All the deceit, and know
  Whence the mistake did grow.

As he whose quicker eye doth trace
A false star shot to a market-place,
    Do's run apace,
  And thinking it to catch,
  A gelly up do's snatch.

So our dull souls tasting delight
Far off, by sence, and appetite,
 Think that is right
 And reall good; when yet
 'Tis but the counterfeit.

Oh! how I glory now; that I
Have made this new discovery?
 Each wanton eye
 Enflam'd before: no more
 Will I increase that score.

If I gaze, now, 'tis but to see
What manner of deaths-head 'twill be,
 When it is free
 From that fresh upper-skin,
 The gazers joy and sin.

A quick coarse me-thinks I spy
In ev'ry woman: and mine eye,
 At passing by,
 Check, and is troubled, just
 As if it rose from dust.

They mortifie, not heighten me:
These of my sins the glasses be:
 And here I see,
 How I have lov'd before,
 And so I love no more.

To a proud Lady.

Is it birth puffs up thy mind ?
Women best born are best inclin'd.
Is it thy breeding ? No, I ly'de ;
Women well bred are foes to pride.
Is it thy beauty, foolish thing ?
Lay by thy cloaths, there's no such thing ?
Is it thy vertue ? that's deny'd,
Vertue's an opposite to pride.
Nay, then walk on, I'le say no more,
Who made thee proud, can make thee poore.
   The devill onely hath the skill
   To draw fair fools to this foule ill.

On Women.

Find me an end out in a ring,
Turn a stream backwards to its spring,
Recover minutes past and gone,
Undoe what is already done,
Make heaven stand still, make mountains fly,
And teach a woman constancy.

An Apologetique Song.

Men, if you love us, play no more
The fools, or tyrants, with your friends,
To make still sing o're and ore,
Our own false praises, for your ends.

We have both wits and fancies too,
And if we must, let's sing of you.

Nor do we doubt, but that we can,
If we would search with care and pain,
Find some one good, in some one man;
So going through all your strain,
  We shall at last of parcells make
  One good enough for a song sake.

And as a cunning painter takes
In any curious piece you see,
More pleasure while the thing he makes,
Then when 'tis made; why, so will we.
  And having pleas'd our art, wee'l try
  To make a new, and hang that by.

Canto.

Like to a ring without a finger,
Or a bell without a ringer;
Like a horse was never ridden,
Or a feast and no guest bidden,
Like a well without a bucket,
Or a rose if no man pluck it:
  Just such as these may she be said,
  That lives, not loves, but dyes a maid.

The ring if worn, the finger decks,
The bell pull'd by the ringer speaks,

The horse doth ease, if he be ridden,
The feast doth please, if guest be bidden,
The bucket draws the water forth,
The rose when pluck'd, is still most worth :
    Such is the virgin in my eyes,
    That lives, loves, marries, ere she dyes.

Like a stock not graffed on,
Or like a lute not playd upon,
Like a jack without a weight,
Or a bark without a fraight,
Like a lock without a key,
Or a candle in the day :
    Just such as these may she be said,
    That lives, not loves, but dyes a. maid.

The graffed stock doth bear best fruite,
There's musick in the finger'd lute ;
The weight doth make the jack go ready,
The fraight doth make the bark go steady ;
The key the lock doth open right,
A candle's useful in the night :
    Such is the virgin in my eyes,
    That lives, loves, marries, ere she dyes.

Like a call without a non-sir,
Or a question without an answer,
Like a ship was never rigg'd,
Or a mine was never digg'd ;

Like a cage without a bird,
Or a thing not long preferr'd.
  Just such as these may she be said,
  That lives, not loves, but dyes a maid.

The non-sir doth obey the call,
The question answer'd pleaseth all,
Who rigs a ship sailes with the wind,
Who digs a mine doth treasure find,
The wound by wholsome tent hath ease,
The box perfum'd the senses please:
  Such is the virgin in my eyes,
  That lives, loves, marries, ere she dies.

Like marrow-bone was never broken,
Or commendation and no token,
Like a fort and none to win it,
Or like the moon, and no man in it;
Like a school without a teacher,
Or like a pulpit and no preacher.
  Just such as these may she be said,
  That lives, ne'r loves, but dyes a maid.

The broken marrow-bone is sweet,
The token doth adorn the greet,
There's triumph in the fort being won,
The man rides glorious in the moon;
The school is by the teacher still'd,
The pulpit by the preacher fill'd.

Such is the virgin in mine eyes,   .
That lives, loves, marries, ere she dyes.

Like a cage without a bird,
Or a thing too long defer'd :
Like the gold was never try'd,
Or the ground unoccupi'd ;
Like a house that's not possessed,
Or the book was never pressed.
    Just such as these may she be said,
    That lives, ne'r loves, but dyes a maid.

The bird in cage doth sweetly sing,
Due season prefers every thing,
The gold that's try'd from drosse is pur'd,
There's profit in the ground manur'd,
The house is by possession graced ;
The book when prest, is then embraced.
    Such is the virgin in mine eyes,
    That lives, loves, marries, ere she dyes.

A Disswasive from Women.

Come away, do not pursue
A shadow that will follow you.
Women lighter than a feather,
Got and lost and altogether :
Such a creature may be thought,
Void of reason, a thing of nought. · · ·

2.

Come away, let not thine eyes
Gaze upon their fopperies,
Nor thy better genius dwell
Upon a subject known so well:
For whose folly at the first
Man and beast became accurst.

3.

Come away, thou canst not find,
One of all that's faire and kind,
Brighter be she then the day,
Sweeter then a morne in *May*;
Yet her heart and tongue agrees
As we and the *Antipodes*.

4.

Come away, or if thou must
Stay a while: yet do not trust,
Nor her sighs, nor what she swears,
Say she weep, suspect her tears.
Though she seem to melt with passion,
'Tis old deceipt, but in new fashion.

5.

Come away, admit there be
A naturall necessity;
Do not make thy selfe a slave
For that which she desires to have.
What she will, or do, or say,
Is meant the clean contrary way.

6.

Come away, or if to part
Soon from her, affects thy heart,
Follow on thy sports a while,
Laugh and kisse, and play a while :
Yet as thou lov'st me, trust her not,
Lest thou becom'st a—I know not what.

An Answer to it.

Stay, O stay, and still pursue,
Bid not such happinesse adue,
Know'st thou what a woman is ?
An image of cœlestial bliss.
Such a one is thought to be
The nearest to divinity.

2.

Stay, O stay, how can thine eye
Feed on more felicity ?
Or thy better genius dwell
On subjects that do this excell ?
Had it not been for her at first,
Man and beast had liv'd accurst.

3.

Stay, O stay, has not there been
Of beauty, and of love a queen ?
Does not sweetnesse terme a shee
Worthy its onely shrine to thee ?

And where will vertue chuse to dye,
If not in such a treasury?

4.

Stay, O stay, wouldst thou live free?
Then seek a nuptiall destinie:
'Tis not natures blisse alone,
(She gives) but heavens and that in one;
What she shall, or do, or say,
Never from truth shall go astray.

5.

Stay, O stay, let not thine heart
Afflicted be, unlesse to part
Soone from her. Sport, kiss and play
Whilst no howers enrich the day:
And if thou dost a cuckold prove,
Impute it to thy want of love.

The Postscript.

Good women are like starres in darkest night,
Their vertuous actions shining as a light
To guide their ignorant sex, which oft times fall,
And falling oft, turns diabolicall.
Good women sure are angels on the earth,
Of these good angels we have had a dearth:
And therefore all you men that have good wives,
Respect their vertues equall with your lives.

THE DESCRIPTION OF WOMEN.

Whose head befringed with be-scattered tresses,
Shews like *Apolloes*, when the morn he dresses :
Or like *Aurora* when with pearle she sets,
Her long discheveld rose-crown'd trammelets :
Her forehead smooth, full, polish'd, bright and high,
Bears in it self a gracefull majesty ;
Under the which, two crawling eye-brows twine
Like to the tendrills of a flatt'ring vine :

Under whose shade, two starry sparkling eyes
Are beautifi'd with faire fring'd canopies.
Her comely nose with uniformall grace,
Like purest white, stands in the middle place,
Parting the paire, as we may well suppose,
Each cheek resembling still a damask rose :
Which like a garden manifestly shown,
How roses, lillies, and carnations grown ;
Which sweetly mixed both with white and red,
Like rose-leaves, white and red, seem mingled.
Then nature for a sweet allurement sets
Two smelling, swelling, bashfull cherry-lets ;
The which with ruby-rednesse being tip'd,
Do speak a virgin merry, cherry-lip'd.
Over the which a neat sweet skin is drawne,
Which makes them shew like roses under lawne.
These be the ruby-portals and divine,
Which ope themselves, to shew an holy shrine,
Whose breath is rich perfume, that to the sense
Smells like the burn'd *Sabean* frankincense ;
In which the tongue, though but a member small,
Stands guarded with a rosie-hilly-wall.
And her white teeth, which in the gums are set,
Like pearl and gold, make one rich cabinet.
Next doth her chin, with dimpled beauty strive
For his white, plumpe, and smooth prerogative.
At whose faire top, to please the sight there grows
The fairest image of a blushing rose ;
Mov'd by the chin, whose motion causeth this,
That both her lips do part, do meet, do kiss.

Her ears, which like two labyrinths are plac'd
On either side, with which rare jewels grac'd :
Moving a question whether that by them
The jem is grac'd, or they grac'd by the jem.
But the foundation of the architect,
Is the swan-staining, faire, rare, stately neck,
Which with ambitious humblenesse stands under,
Bearing aloft this rich-round world of wonder.
Her breast a place for beauties throne most fit,
Bears up two globes, where love and pleasure sit ;
Which headed with two rich round rubies, show
Like wanton rose-buds growing out of snow,
And in the milky valley that's between,
Sits *Cupid* kissing of his mother queen.
Then comes the belly, seated next below,
Like a faire mountain in *Riphean* snow ;
Where nature in a whitenesse without spot,
Hath in the middle tide a Gordian knot.
Now love invites me to survey her thighes,
Swelling in likenesse like two chrystall skyes ;
Which to the knees by nature fastned on,
Derive their ever well 'greed motion.
Her legs with two clear calves, like silver try'd,
Kindly swell up with little pretty pride ;
Leaving a distance for the comely small
To beautifie the leg and foot withall.
Then lowly, yet most lovely stand the feet,
Round, short and cleer, like pounded spices sweet ;
And whatsoever thing they tread upon,
They make it scent like bruised cinnamon.

The lovely shoulders now allure the eye,
To see two tablets of pure ivorie:
From which two arms like branches seem to spread
With tender vein'd, and silver coloured,
With little hands, and fingers long and small,
To grace a lute, a violl, virginall.
In length each finger doth his next excell,
Each richly headed with a pearly shell.
Thus every part in contrariety
Meet in the whole, and make an harmony:
As divers strings do singly disagree,
But form'd by number make sweet melodie.

Her supposed Servant, described.

I would have him if I could,
Noble; or of greater blood:
Titles, I confesse, do take me;
And a woman God did make me,
French too boote, at least in fashion,
And his manners of that nation.

Young I'd have him to, and faire,
Yet a man; with crisped haire
Cast in a thousand snares, and rings
For loves fingers, and his wings:
Chestnut colour, or more slack
Gold, upon a ground of black.
Venus, and *Minerva's* eyes
For he must look wanton-wise.

Eye-brows bent like *Cupids* bow,
Front, an ample field of snow;
Even nose, and cheeke (withall)
Smooth as is the biliard ball:
Chin, as wholly as the peach;
And his lip should kissing teach,
Till he cherish'd too much beard,
And make love or me afeard.

He should have a hand as soft
As the downe, and shew it oft;
Skin as smooth as any rush,
And so thin to see a' blush
Rising through it e're it came,
All his blood should be a flame
Quickly fir'd as in beginners
In loves schoole, and yet no sinners.

'Twere too long to speak of all
What we harmonie do call
In a body should be there.
Well he should his cloaths to weare;
Yet no taylor help to make him
Drest, you still for man should take him;
And not think h'had eate a stake,
Or were set up in a brake.

Valiant he should be as fire,
Shewing danger more than ire.
Bounteous as the clouds to earth;
And as honest as his birth.

All his actions to be such
As to do nothing too much.
Nor o're praise, nor yet condemn :
Nor out-value, nor contemne ;
Nor do wrongs, nor wrongs receive ;
Nor tie knots, nor knots unweave ;
And from basenesse to be free,
As he durst love truth and me.

Such a man with every part,
I could give my very heart ;
But of one, if short he came,
I can rest me where I am.

Another Ladyes exception.

For his minde, I do not care,
That's a toy, that I could spare ;
Let his title be but great,
His clothes rich, and band sit neat,
Himselfe young, and face be good,
All I wish tis understood.
What you please, you parts may call,
'Tis one good part I'd lye withall.

Abroad with the Maids.

Come sit we under yonder tree,
Where merry as the maids we'l be,
And as on primroses we sit,
We'l venter (if we can) at wit :
If not, at draw-gloves we will play ;
So spend some minutes of the day ;

Or else spin out the threed of sands,
Playing at questions and commands :
Or tell what strange tricks love can do,
By quickly making one of two.
Thus we will sit and talke; but tell
No cruell truths of *Philomell*,
Or *Phillis*, whom hard fate forc't on,
To kill her selfe for *Demophon.*
But fables we'l relate; how *Jove*
Put on all shapes to get a love;
As now a satyr, then a swan ;
A bull but then ; and now a man.
Next we will act how young men wooe;
And sigh, and kisse, as lovers do,
And talk of brides ; and who shall make
That wedding smock, this bridal-cake;
That dress, this sprig, that leafe, this vine;
That smooth and silken columbine.
This done, we'l draw lots, who shall buy
And guild the bayes, and rosemary :
What posies, for our wedding rings ;
What gloves we'l give and ribonings :
And smiling at our selves, decree,
Who then the joyning priest shall be.
What short sweet prayers shall be said ;
And how the posset shall be made
With cream of lillies (not of kine)
And maidens-blush, for spiced wine,
Thus having talkt, we'l next commend
A kiss to each; and so we'l end.

THE SHEPHEARDS HOLY DAY.

Mopso and Marina.

Mop. Come *Marina* let's away,
    For both bride, and bridegroom stay:
    Fie for shame, are swains so long
    Pinning of their head-geare on?
        Prethee see,
        None but we
    'Mongst the swaines are left unready:

Fie, make hast,
Bride is past,
Follow me, and I will lead thee.

Mar. On, my loving *Mopsus*, on,
I am ready, all is done
From my head unto my foot,
I am fitted each way too't ;
Buskins gay,
Gowne of gray,
Best that all our flocks do render ;
Hat of straw,
Platted through,
Cherry lip, and middle slender.

Mop. And I think you will not find
Mopsus any whit behind,
For he loves as well to goe,
As most part of shepheards do.
Cap of browne,
Bottle-crowne,
With the legge I won at dancing,
And a pumpe,
Fit to jumpe,
When we shepheards fall a prancing.

And I know there is a sort,
Will be well provided for't,
For I heare, there will be there,
Liveliest swaines within the shire ;

Jetting *Gill,*
Jumping *Will ;*
O'r the floore will have their measure :
Kit and *Kate*
There will waite,
Tib and *Tom* will take their pleasure.

Mar. But I fear ;
Mop. What dost thou fear ?
Mar. *Crowd* the fidler is not there :
And my mind delighted is
With no stroke so much as his.
    Mop. If not he,
    There will be
Drone the piper that will trounce it.
    Mar. But if *Crowd*
    Struck alowd,
Lord me thinks how I could bounce it.

Mop. Bounce it *Mall* I hope thou will,
For I know that thou hast skill ;
And I am sure, thou there shalt find
Measures store to please thy mind.
    Roundelayes,
    Irish hayes,
Cogs and Rongs, and Peggie Ramsy,
    Spaniletto,
    The Venetto,
John come kisse me, Wilsons fancy.

Mar. But of all there's none so sprightly
　　To my eare, as *Touch me lightly;*
　　For it's this we shepheards love,
　　Being that which most doth move;
　　　　There, there, there,
　　　　To a haire;
　　O *Tim Crowd,* methinks I hear thee,
　　　　Young nor old,
　　　　Ne're could hold,
　　But must leak if they come near thee.

Mop. Blush *Marina,* fie for shame,
　　Blemish not a shepheards name;
Mar. Mopsus, why, is't such a matter,
　　Maids to shew their yeelding nature?
　　　　O what then,
　　　　Be ye men,
　　That will hear your selves so forward,
　　　　When you find
　　　　Us inclin'd
　　To your bed and board so toward?

Mop. True indeed, the fault is ours,
　　Though we term it oft times yours.
Mar. What would shepheards have us doe,
　　But to yeeld when they do woo?
　　　　And we yeeld
　　　　Them the field,
　　And endow them with their riches.

Mop. Yet we know
      Oft times too,
You'll not stick to weare the breeches.

Mar. Fools they'l deem them, that do hear them
      Say their wives are wont to weare them;
      For I know, there's none has wit,
      Can endure or suffer it;
            But if they
            Have no stay,
      Nor discretion (as 'tis common)
            Then they may
            Give the sway,
      As is fitting, to the woman.

Mop. All too long (deare love) I ween,
      Have we stood upon this theatre:
      Let each lasse, as once it was,
      Love her swain, and swain his lasse:
            So shall we
            Honour'd be,
      In our mating, in our meeting,
            While we stand
            Hand in hand,
      Honest swainling, with his sweeting.

Alvar and Anthea.

Come *Anthea* let us two
Go to feast as others do.
Tarts and custards, cream and cakes,
Are the junkets still at wakes :
Unto which the tribes resort,
Where the businesse is the sport :
Morris-dancers thou shalt see,
Marian too in pagentrie :
And a mimick to devise
Many grinning properties.
Players there will be, and those
Base in action as in clothes :
Yet with strutting they will please
The incurious villages.
Neer the dying of the day
There will be a cudgel-play,
Where a coxcomb will be broke,
Ere a good word can be spoke :
But the anger ends all here,
Drencht in ale, or drown'd in beere.
Happy rusticks, best content
With the cheapest merriment :
And possesse no other feare,
Then to want the wake next yeare.

The Wake.

I, and whither shall we go?
. To the wake I trow:
'Tis the village Lord Majors show,
Oh! to meet I will not faile;
  For my pallate is in hast,
  Till I sip again and tast
Of the nut-brown lass and ale.

  Feele how my temples ake
  For the lady of the wake;
Her lips are as soft as a medlar,
  With her posies and her points,
  And the ribbons on her joynts,
The device of the fields and the pedler.

Enter Maurice-Dancer.

With a noyse and a din,
Comes the maurice-dancer in :
With a fine linnen shirt, but a buckram skin.
　　Oh! he treads out such a peale
　　From his paire of legs of veale,
The quarters are idols to him.

　　Nor do those knaves inviron
　　Their toes with so much iron,
'Twill ruine a smith to shooe him.
　　I, and then he flings about,
　　His sweat and his clout,
The wiser think it two ells :　.
　　While the yeomen find it meet,
　　That he jingle at his feet,
The fore-horses right eare jewels.

Enter Fidler.

But before all be done,
With a Christopher strong,
Comes musick none, though fidler one,
While the owle and his grandchild,
With a face like a manchild,
Amaz'd in their nest,
Awake from the rest,
And seek out an oake to laugh in.
Such a dismall chance,
Makes the church-yard dance,
When the screech owles guts string a coffin,
When a fidlers coarse,
Catches cold and grows hoarse,
Oh ye never heard a sadder,
When a rattle-headed cutter,
Makes his will before supper,
To the tune of the Nooze and the Ladder.

Enter the Taberer.

I, but all will not·do, ·
   Without a passe or two,
From him that pipes and tabers the tattoo.
      He's a man that can tell 'em,
      Such a jigge from his vellam ;
      With his whistle and his club,
      And his brac't half tub,
That I think there ne're came before ye,
      Though the mothes lodged in't,
      Or in manuscript or print.
Such a pitifull parchment storie.
      He that hammers like a tinker
      Kettle musick is a stinker,
Our taberer bids him heark it ;
      Though he thrash till he sweats,
      And out the bottome beats
Of his two dosser drummes to the market.

Enter Bag-piper.

Bag-piper good luck on you,
 Th'art a man for my money;
Him the bears love better than honey.
 How he tickles up his skill,
 With his bladder and his quill;
 How he swells till he blister,
 While he gives his mouth a glister,
Nor yet does his physick grieve him;
 His chops they would not tarry,
 For a try'd apothecary,
But the harper comes in to relieve him.
 Whose musick took its fountain,
 From the bogge or the mountain,
For better was never afforded.
 Strings hoppe and rebound,
 Oh the very same sound
May be struck from a truckle-bed coarded.

Cock-throwing.

Cock a-doodle do, 'tis the bravest game,
Take a cock from his dame,
And bind him to a stake,
How he strutts, how he throwes,
How he swaggers, how he crowes,
As if the day newly brake.
How his mistriss cackles,
Thus to find him in shackles,
And ty'd to a pack-threed garter;
Oh the bears and the bulls,
Are but corpulent gulls
To the valiant Shrove-tide martyr.

Canto.

Let no poet critick in his ale,
Now tax me for a heedlesse tale,
For ere I have done, my honest *Ned*,
I'll bring my matter to a head.

The brazen head speaks through the nose,
More logick then the colledge knowes:
Quick-silver heads run over all,
But dunces heads keep *Leaden-hall.*

A quiristers head is made of aire,
A head of wax becomes a player,

So pliant 'tis to any shape,
A king, a clowne, but still an ape.

A melancholy head it was,
That thought it selfe a Venice glasse;
But when I see a drunken sot,
Methinks his head's a chamberpot.

A poets head is made of match,
Burnt sack is apt to make it catch;
Well may he grind his houshold bread,
That hath a wind-mill in his head.

There is the tongue of ignorance,
That hates the time it cannot dance;
Shew him deare wit in verse or prose,
In reeks like brimstone in his nose;
But when his granhams will is read,
O dear (quoth he) and shakes his head.
   French heads taught ours the gracefull shake,
   They learn'd it in the last earth-quake.

The head gentle makes mouths in state,
At the mechanick beaver pate.
The empty head of meer esquire,
Scornes wit; as born a title higher.
In *capite* he holds his lands,
His wisdome in fee-simple stands.
   Which he may call for, and be sped,
   Out of the footmans running head.

The Saracens, not Gorgons head,
Can look old ten in th'hundred dead,
But deaths head on his fingers ends,
Afflicts him more then twenty fiends;
An *Oxford* cook that is well read,
Knows how to dresse a criticks head.
    Take out the brains, and stew the noats,
    O rare calves-head for pupills throats.

Prometheus would be puzled,
To make a new projectors head :
He hath such subtile turnes and nookes,
Such turn-pegs, mazes, tenter-hooks :
A trap-doore here, and there a vault,
Should you go in, you'ld sure be caught;
    This head, if e'r the heads-man stick,
    Hee'll spoile the subtile politick.

Six heads there are will ne'r be seen,
The first a maids past twice sixteen :
The next is of an unicorne,
Which when I see, I'll trust his horne;
A beggar's in a beaver; and
A gyant in a pigmies hand;
    A coward in a ladies lap,
    A good man in a fryers cap.

The plurall head of multitude,
Will make good hodg-podge when 'tis stude;
    Now I have done my honest *Ned*,
    And brought my matter to a head.

Interrogativa Cantilena.

If all the world were paper,
And all the sea were inke ;
If all the trees were bread and cheese,
How should we do for drinke ?

If all the world were sand'o,
Oh then what should we lack'o ;
If as they say there were no clay,
How should we take tobacco ?

If all our vessels ran'a,
If none but had a crack'a ;
If Spanish apes eat all the grapes,
How should we do for sack'a ?

If fryers had no bald pates,
Nor nuns had no dark cloysters,
If all the seas were beans and pease,
How should we do for oysters ?

If there had been no projects,
Nor none that did great wrongs ;
If fidlers shall turne players all,
How should we doe for songs ?

If all things were eternall,
And nothing their end bringing ;
If this should be, then how should we,
Here make an end of singing ?

The seven Planets.

♄ . ♃ . ♂ . ☉ . ♀ . ☿ . ☾ .

SATURNE diseas'd with age, and left for dead;
Chang'd all his gold, to be involv'd in lead.

JOVE, *Juno* leaves, and loves to take his range;
From whom, man learnes to love, and loves to change.

JUNO checks *Jove*, that he to earth should come,
Having her selfe to sport withall at home.

MARS is disarmed, and is to *Venus* gon,
Where *Vulcans* anvill must be struck upon.

SOL sees, yet 'cause he may not be allow'd,
To say he sees, he hides him in a cloud.

VENUS tels *Vulcan, Mars* shall shooe her steed,
For he it is that hits the naile o'th head.

The aery-nuntius sly MERCURIUS,
Is stoln from heaven to *Galobelgicus.*

LUNA is deemed chast, yet she's a sinner,
Witnesse the man that she receives within her:
But that she's horn'd it cannot well be sed,
Since I ne'r heard that she was married.

The 12. *Signes of the Zodiack.*

♈

Venus to *Mars*, and *Mars* to *Venus* came,
Venus contriv'd, and *Mars* confirm'd the same :
Ida, the place, the game what best did please,
Whiles *Vulcan* found the sunne in ARIES.

♉

TAURUS, as it hath bean alledg'd by some,
Is fled from *Neck* and *Throat* to roare at *Rome :*
But now the *Bull* is growne to such a rate,
The price has brought the *Bull* quite out of date.

♋

CANCER the backward *Crab* is figured here,
O'r stomach, breast and ribs to domineer.
Eve on a rib was made, whence we may know,
Women from *Eve,* were crab'd and backward too.

♍

VIRGO the phœnix signe (as all can tell ye)
Has regiment o'r bowels, and o'r belly.
But now since *Virgo* could not her belly tame,
Belly has forc'd *Virgo* to lose her name.

♏

SCORPIO serpent-like, most slily tenders,
What much seduceth men, his privie members :

Which mov'd our grandam *Eve* give ear unto
That secret-member-patron *Scorpio.*

♑

The goatish CAPRICORNE that us'd to presse
'Mongst naked mermaidens, now's faln on's knees,
Where crest-faln too (poor snake) he lies as low,
As those on whom he did his horns bestow.

II

With arme in arme our GEMINI enwreath,
Their individuate parts in life and death :
The arms and shoulders sway, O may I have
But two such friends to have me to my grave.

♌

LEO a port-like prelate now become,
Emperiously retires to th'sea of *Rome :*
A sea, and yet no Levant-sea, for than
He were no *Leo,* but *Leviathan.*

♎

LIBRA the reines, which we may justly call
A signe which tradesmen hate the worst of all :
For she implies even weights, but do not look
To find this signe in every grocers-book.

♐

If thou wouldst please the lasse that thou dost marry,
The sign must ever be in SAGITTARY :

Which rules the thighs, an influence more common,
'Mongst marmosites and monkies then some women.

≡

AQUARIUS (as I informed am)
Kept *Puddle Wharfe*, and was a waterman,
But being one too honest for that kind,
He *row'd* to heaven, and left those knaves behind.

♓

PISCIS the fish is said to rule the feet,
And socks with all that keep the feet from sweat;
One that purveyes provision enough,
Of *Ling, Poore-John,* and other lenten stuffe.

A Hymne to Bacchus.

I sing thy praise *Bacchus,*
Who with thy *Thyrse* dost thwack us:
And yet thou só dost back us.

With boldnesse that we feare
No *Brutus* entring here;
Nor *Cato* the severe.

What though the *Lictors* threat us,
We know they dare not beat us;
So long as thou dost heat us.

When we thy *orgies* sing,
Each cobler is a king;
Nor dreads he any thing.

And though he doth not rave,
Yet he'l the courage have
To call my lord major knave;
Besides too, in a brave.

Although he has no riches,
But walks with dangling breeches,
And skirts that want their stitches;
And shews his naked flitches;

Yet he'l be thought or seen;
So good as *George-a-green;*
And calls his blouze, his queene,
And speaks in a language keene.

O *Bacchus!* let us be
From cares and troubles free;
And thou shalt hear how we
Will chant new hymnes to thee.

THE WELSH MANS PRAISE OF WALES.

I's not come here to tauke of *Prut*,,
From whence the *Welse* does take hur root;
Nor tell long pedegree of Prince *Camber*,
Whose linage would fill full a chamber,
Nor sing the deeds of old Saint *Davie*,
The ursip of which would fill a navie.
But hark you me now, for a liddel tales
Sall make a gread deal to the creddit of *Wales*.

B B 2

For hur will tudge your eares,
With the praise of hur thirteen seers;
And make you as clad and merry,
As fourteen pot of perry.

'Tis true, was weare him sherkin frieze,
But what is that? we have store of seize;
And Got is plenty of coats milk
That sell him well, will buy him silk
Inough, to make him fine to quarrell
At *Herford* sizes in new apparell;
And get him as much green melmet perhap,
Sall give it a face to his Momouth cap.
    But then the ore of *Lemster*,
    Py Cot is uver a sempster;
    That when he is spun, or did
    Yet match him with hir thrid.

Aull this the backs now, let us tell ye,
Of some provisions for the belly:
As cid and goat, and great goats mother,
And runt, and cow, and good cows uther.
And once but 'tast on the Welse mutton;
Your *Englis* seeps not worth a button.
And then for your fiss, sall shoose it your diss,
Look but about, and there is a trout.
    A salmon, cor, or chevin,
    Will feed you six or seven;
    As taull man as ever swagger
    With *Welse* club, and long dagger.

But all this while, was never think
A word in praise of our *Welse* drink :
Yet for aull that, is a cup of *Bragat*,
Aull *England* seer may cast his cap at.
And what you say to ale of *Webley*,
Toudge him as well, you'll praise him trebly,
As well as *Metheglin*, or *Syder*, or *Meath*,
S'all sake it your dagger quite out o'the seath.

   And oate-cake of *Guarthenion*,
   With a goodly leek or onion,
   To give as sweet a rellis
   As e'r did harper *Ellis.*

And yet is nothing now all this,
If of our musicks we do miss ;
Both harpes, and pipes too, and the crowd,
Must aull come in, and tauk alowd,
As lowd as *Bangu, Davies* bell,
Of which is no doubt you have here tell :
As well as our lowder *Wrexam* organ,
And rumbling rocks in the seer of *Glamorgan*,
   Where look but in the ground there,
   And you sall see a sound there ;
   That put her all to gedder,
   Is sweet as measure pedder.

Hur in Love.

A modest shentle when hur see
The great laugh hur made on me,
And fine wink that hur send
To hur come to see hur friend :
Hur coud not strose py Got apove,
Put was entangle in hur love.
A hundred a time hur was about
To speak to hur, and have hur out,
Put hur being a *Welshman* porne,
And therefore was think, hur woud hur scorne ;
Was fear hur think, nothing petter,
Then cram hur love into a letter ;
Hoping he will no ceptions take
Unto hur love, for country sake :
For say hur be *Welshman*, whad ten ?
Py Got they all be shentlemen,
Was decend from *Shoves* nown line,
Par humane, and par divine ;
And from *Venus*, that fair goddess,
And twenty other shentle poddys :
Hector stout, and comely *Parris*,
Arthur, *Prute*, and king of *Fayris*,
Was hur nown cosins all a kin
We have the *Powels* issue in :
And for ought that hur con see,
As goot men, as other men pee :

But whot of that ? Love is a knave,
Was make hur do whot he woud have;
Was compell hur write the rime,
That ne'r was writ before the time.
And if he will nod pity hur paine,
As Got shudge hur soul, sall ne'r write again :
For love is like an ague-fit,
Was brin poore *Welseman* out on hur wit :
Till by hur onswer hur do know
Whother hur do love hur, ai or no.
Hur has not bin in *England* lung,
And conna speak the Englis tongue :
Put hur is hur friend, and so hur will prove,
Pray a send hur word, if hur con love.

OF MELANCHOLY.

When I go musing all alone,
Thinking of divers things fore-known,
When I build castles in the aire,
Void of sorrow and voide of feare,
Pleasing my self with phantasmes sweet,
Me thinks the time runs very fleet.

All my joyes to this are folly,
Naught so sweet as melancholy.

:

When I lie waking all alone,
Recounting what I have ill done,
My thoughts on me then tyrannise,
Fear and sorrow me surprise,
Whether I tarry still or go,
Me thinks the time moves very slow.
 All my griefs to this are jolly,
 Naught so sad as melancholy.

When to my self I act and smile,
With pleasing thoughts the time beguile,
By a brook side or wood so green,
Unheard, unsought for, or unseen,
A thousand pleasures do me blesse,
And crown my soul with happinesse.
 All my joyes besides are folly,
 None so sweet as melancholy.

When I lye, sit, or walk alone,
I sigh, I grieve, making great moane,
In a dark grove, or irkesome denne,
With discontents and furies then,
A thousand miseries at once,
Mine heavy heart and soul ensconce.
 All my griefs to this are jolly,
 None so soure as melancholy.

Me thinks I hear, me thinks I see,
Sweet musick, wondrous melodie,
Townes, places and cities fine;
Here now, then there, the world is mine,
Rare beauties, gallant ladies shine,
What e're is lovely or divine.
    All other joyes to this are folly,
    None so sweet as melancholy.

Me thinks I hear, methinks I see
Ghosts, goblins, feinds, my phantasie
Presents a thousand ugly shapes,
Headlesse beares, black-men and apes,
Dolefull outcries, and fearefull sights,
My sad and dismall soule affrights.
    All my griefs to this are jolly,
    None so damn'd as melancholy.

Me thinks I court, me thinks I kisse,
Me thinks I now embrace my mistriss.
O blessed dayes, O sweet content,
In Paradise my time is spent.
Such thoughts may still my fancy move,
So may I ever be in love.
    All my joyes to this are folly,
    Naught so sweet as melancholy.

When I recount loves many frights,
My sighs and tears, my waking nights,

My jealous fits; O mine hard fate,
I now repent, but 'tis too late.
No torment is so bad as love,
So bitter to my soul can prove.
   All my griefs to this are jolly,
    Naught so harsh as melancholy.

Friends and companions get you gone,
'Tis my desire to be alone,
Ne're well but when my thoughts and I,
Do domineer in privacie.
No gemme, no treasure like to this,
'Tis my delight, my crown, my blisse,
   All my joyes to this are folly,
    Naught so sweet as melancholy.

'Tis my sole plague to be alone,
I am a beast, a monster growne,
I will no light nor company,
I find it now my misery,
The scene is turn'd, my joyes are gone,
Feare, discontent, and sorrows come.
   All my griefs to this are jolly,
    Naught so fierce as melancholy.

I'le not change life with any king,
I ravisht am : can the world bring
More joy, then still to laugh and smile,
In pleasant toyes time to beguile ?

Do not, O do not trouble me,
So sweet content I feel and see.
  All my joyes to this are folly,
   None so divine as melancholy.

Il'e change my state with any wretch,
Thou canst from goal or dunghill fetch:
My paines past cure, another hell,
I may not in this torment dwell,
Now desperate I hate my life,
Lend me an halter or a knife.
  All my griefes to this are jolly,
   Naught so dam'd as melancholy.

ON THE LETTER O.

Runne round my lines, whilst I as roundly show
The birth, the worth, the extent of my round O . . .
That O which in the indigested mass
Did frame it selfe, when nothing framed was.
But when the worlds great masse it selfe did show,
In largenesse, fairenesse, roundnesse, a great O .
The heavens, the element, a box of O's,
Where still the greater doth the lesse inclose.

The imaginary center in ○'s made,
That speck which in the world doth stand or fade.
The zodiack, colours, and equator line,
In tropique and meridian ○ did shine,
The lines of bredth, and lines of longitude,
Climate from climate, doth by ○ seclude.
And in the starry spangled sky the ○
Makes us the day from night distinctly know.
And by his motion, round as in a ring,
Light to himselfe, light to each ○ doth bring :
In each dayes journey, in his circle round,
The framing of an ○ by sense is found.
The moon hath to the ○'s frame, most affection ;
But the sunne's envy grudgeth such perfection.
Yet *Dian* hath each moneth, and every yeare,
Learned an ○'s frame in her front to beare.
And to requite *Sol's* envie with the like,
With oft eclipses at his ○ doth strike.
In our inferiour bodies there doth grow
Matter enough to shew the worth of ○ .
Our brains and heart, either in ○ doth lye,
So that the nest of ○'s the sparkling eye.
The ribs in meeting, fashion an ○'s frame,
The mouth and eare, the nostrills beare the same.
The Latins honouring the chiefest parts,
Gloryed to make our ○ the heart of hearts ;
Fronting it with three words of deepest sense,
Order, opinion, and obedience.
Oft have I seen a reverend dimmed eye,
By the help of ○ to read most legibly.

Each drop of rain that fals, each flower that grows :
Each coyne that's currant doth resemble O's.
Into the water, if a stone we throw,
Marke how each circle joyns to make an O.
Cut but an orange, you shall easily find,
Yellow and white, and watery O's combind,
O doth preserve a trembling conjurer,
Who from his circle O doth never stirre.
O from a full throat cryer, if it come,
Strikes the tumultuous roaring people dumbe,
The thundering cannon from this dreadfull O,
Ruine to walls, and death to men doth throw.
O utters woes, O doth expresse our joyes,
O wonders shews, O riches, or O toyes.
And O ye women which do fashions fall,
O ruffe, O gorget, and O farthingall,
And O ye spangles, O ye golden O's
That art upon the rich embroydered throws.
Think not we mock, though our displeasing pen
Sometime doth write, you bring an O to men.
'Tis no disparagement to you ye know,
Since *Ops* the gods great grandame bears an O ;
Your sexes glory (Fortune) though she reel,
Is ever constant to her O, her wheele,
And you carroches through the street that glide,
By art of foure great O's do help you ride.
When tables full, and cups do overflow,
Is not each cup, each salt, each dish an O ?
What is't that dreadfull makes a princes frown,
But that his head bears golden O the crowne ?

Unhappy then th'arithmetician, and
He that makes ⚪ a barren cipher stand.
Let him know this, that we know in his place,
An ⚪ addes number, with a figures grace;
And that ⚪ which for a cipher he doth take,
One dash may easily a thousand make.
  But ⚪ enough, I have done my reader wrong,
  Mine ⚪ was round, and I have made it long.

Pure Nonsence.

When *Neptune's* blasts, and *Boreas* blazing storms,
When *Tritons* pitchfork cut off *Vulcans* horns,
When *Eolus* boyst'rous sun-beams grew so dark,
That *Mars* in moon-shine could not hit the mark:
Then did I see the gloomy day of *Troy*,
When poor *Æneas* leglesse ran away:
Who took the torrid ocean in his hand,
And sailed to them all the way by land:
An horrid sight to see *Achilles* fall,.
He brake his neck, yet had no hurt at all.
But being dead, and almost in a trance,
He threatned forty thousand with his lance.
Indeed 'twas like such strange sights then were seen
An ugly, rough, black monster all in green.
That all about the white, blew, round, square sky,
The fixed starrs hung by geometry.
Juno amazed, and *Jove* surpriz'd with wonder,
  Caus'd heaven to shake, and made the mountains
    thunder.

Which caus'd *Æneas* once again retire,
Drown'd *Ætna's* hill, and burnt the sea with fire.
Nilus for feare to see the ocean burn,
Went still on forward in a quick return.
Then was that broyl of *Agamemnon's* done,
When trembling *Ajax* to the battell come,
He struck stark dead (they now are living still)
Five hundred mushrooms with his martial bill.
Nor had himselfe escaped, as some men say,
If he being dead, he had not run away.
O monstrous, hideous troops of dromidaries,
How bears and buls from monks and goblins varies!
Nay would not *Charon* yeeld to *Cerberus*,
But catch'd the dog, and cut his head off thus:
Pluto rag'd, and *Juno* pleas'd with ire,
Sought all about, but could not find the fire:
But being found, well pleas'd, and in a spight
They slept at *Acharon*, and wakt all night:
Where I let passe to tell their mad bravadoes,
Their meat was tosted cheese and carbonadoes.
Thousands of monsters more besides there be
Which I fast hoodwink'd, at that time did see;
  And in a word to shut up this discourse,
  A rugd-gowns ribs are good to spur a horse.

A messe of Non-sense.

Like to the tone of unspoke speeches,
Or like a lobster clad in logick breeches,
Or like the gray freeze of a crimson cat,
Or like a moon-calfe in a slipshooe-hat,
Or like a shadow when the sunne is gon,
Or like a thought that ne'r was thought upon :
  Even such is man, who never was begotten,
  Untill his children were both dead and rotten.

Like to the fiery touchstone of a cabbage,
Or like a crablouse with his bag and baggage,
Or like th'abortive issue of a fizle,
Or the bag-pudding of a plow-mans whistle,
Or like the foursquare circle of a ring,
Or like the singing of hey down a ding ;
  Even such is man, who breathles, without doubt,
  Spake to small purpose when his toague was out.

Like to the green fresh fading rose,
Or like to rime or verse that runs in prose,
Or like the humbles of a tinder-box,
Or like a man that's sound, yet hath the pox,
Or like a hob-naile coyn'd in single pence,
Or like the present preterperfect tense :
  Even such is man who dy'd, and then did laugh
  To see such strong lines writ on's epitaph.

An Encomium.

I sing the praises of a fart;
That I may do't by rules of art,
I will invoke no deity
But butter'd pease and furmity,
And think their help sufficient
To fit and furnish my intent.
For sure I must not use high straines
For fear it bluster out in graines :
When *Virgils* gnat, and *Ovids* flea,
And *Homers* frogs strive for the day ;
There is no reason in my mind,
That a brave fart should come behind ;
Since that you may it parallel
With any thing that doth excell :
Musick is but a fart that's sent
From the guts of an instrument :
The scholler but farts, when he gains
Learning with cracking of his brains.
And when he has spent much pain and toile,
Thomas and *Dun* to reconcile ;
And to learn the abstracting art,
What does he get by't ? not a fart.
The souldier makes his foes to run
With but the farting of a gun ;
That's if he make the bullet whistle,
Else 'tis no better then a fizle :

And if withall the wind do stir up
Rain, 'tis but a fart in syrrup.
They are but farts, the words we say,
Words are but wind, and so are they.
Applause is but a fart, the crude
Blast of the fickle multitude.
Five boats that lye the *Thames* about,
Be but farts severall docks let out.
Some of our projects were, I think,
But politick farts, foh how they stink!
As soon as born, they by and by,
Fart-like but only breath, and dy.
Farts are as good as land, for both
We hold in taile, and let them both:
Onely the difference here is, that
Farts are let at a lower rate.
I'll say no more, for this is right,
That for my guts I cannot write,
Though I should study all my dayes,
Rimes that are worth the thing I praise,
What I have said, take in good part,
If not, I do not care a fart.

THE DRUNKEN. HUMORS.

One here is bent to quarrell, and he will
(If not prevented) this his fellow kill:
He fumes, and frets, and rages; in whose face
Nothing but death and horror taketh place.
    But being parted, 'tother odd jugg, or two,
    Makes them all friends again with small adoe.

Another he makes deaf your ears to heare
The vain tautologies he doth declare;
That, had you as many ears as *Argus* eyes;
He'd make them weary all with tales, and lyes:
  And at the period of each idle fable,
  He gives the on-set to out-laugh the table.

One he sits drinking healths to such a friend,
Then to his mistriss he a health doth send:
This publick captains health he next doth mean,
And then in private to some nasty quean;
  Nothing but healths of love is his pretence,
  Till he himself hath lost both health and sense.

To make the number up amongst the crew,
Another being o're-fill'd, begins to spue
Worse then the brutish beast; (O fy upon it!)
It is a qualme forsooth doth cause him vomit.
  So that his stomack being over-prest,
  He must disgorge it, e're he can have rest.

Here sits one straining of his drunken throat
Beyond all reason, yet far short of note:
Singing is his delight, then hoops and hallows,
Making a garboyle worse then *Vulcans* bellows.
Now for a counter-tenor he takes place,
But straining that too high, falls to a base.
Then screws his mouth an inch beyond his forme,
To treble it, just like a gelders-horne:

He's all for singing, and he hates to chide,
Till blithfull *Bacchus* cause his tongue be tide.

One like an ape shews many tricks and toys,
To leap, and dance, and sing with ruefull noise;
O're the foorme skips, then crosse-legd sits
Upon the table, in his apish fits.
From house to house he rambles in such sort,
That no baboon could make you better sport:
He pincheth one, another with his wand
He thrusts, or striketh, or else with his hand:
    Pisses the room, and as he sleeping lyes,
    Waters his couch (not with repenting eyes.)

A seaventh, he sits mute, as if his tongue
Had never learn'd no other word but mum;
And with his mouth he maketh mops and mews,
Just like an ape his face in form he screws:
Then nods with hum, and hah; but not one word
His tongue-tide foolish silence can afford.
To note his gesture, and his snorting after,
'Twould make a horse break all his girts with laughter.
    But questionlesse he'd speak more were he able,
    Which you shall hear, having well slept at table.

Sir reverence, your stomacks do prepare
Against some word, or deed, ill-scent doth beare.
So this most sorded beast being drunk, doth misse
The chamber-pot, and in his hose doth pisse.

Nay, smell but near him, you perhaps may find,
Not onely piss'd before, but — behind ;
Each company loaths him, holding of their nose,
Scorning, and pointing at his filthy hose :
  As no condition of a drunkard's good,
  So this smels worst of all the loathsome brood.

THE POST OF THE SIGNE.

Though it may seem rude
For me to intrude,
    With these my bears by chance a;
'Twere sport for a king,
If they could sing
    As well as they can dance-a.

Then to put you out
Of fear or doubt,
   He came from St. *Katherine*-a.
These dancing three,
By the help of me,
   Who am the post of the signe-a.

We sell good ware,
And we need not care,
   Though court and countrey knew it;
Our ale's o'th best:
And each good guest
   Prayes for their souls that brew it.

For any alehouse,
We care not a louse,
   Nor tavern in all the town-a:
Nor the Vintry Cranes,
Nor St. *Clement Danes*,
   Nor the *Devill* can put us down-a.

Who has once there been,
Comes hither agen,
   The liquor is so mighty.
Beer strong and stale,
And so is our ale;
   And it burns like aqua-vitæ.

To a stranger there,
If any appeare,
  Where never before he has bin;
We shew th'iron gate,
The wheele of St. *Kate*,
  And the place where they first fell in.

The wives of *Wapping*,
They trudge to our tapping,
  And still our ale desire;
And there sit and drink,
Till they spue and stink,
  And often pisse out the fire.

From morning to night,
And about to day-light,
  They sit and never grudge it;
Till the fish-wives joyne
Their single coyne,
  And the tinker pawns his budget.

If their brains be not well,
Or bladders do swell,
  To ease them of their burden;
My lady will come
With a bowl and a broom,
  And their handmaid with a jourden.

From court we invite,
Lord, lady, and knight,
  Squire, gentleman, yeoman, and groom,
And all our stiffe drinkers,
Smiths, porters, and tinkers,
  And the beggers shall give ye room.

If you give not credit,
Then take you the verdict,
  Of a guest that came from St. *Hallows;*
And you then will sweare,
The man has been there,
  By his story now that follows.

A BALLADE.

A Discourse between two Countrey-men.

I tell thee *Dick* where I have been,
Where I the rarest things have seen ;
   Oh things beyond compare !
Such sights again cannot be found
In any place on English ground,
   Be it at wake or faire.

At *Charing-Crosse*, hard by the way
Where we (thou know'st) do sell our hay,
      There is a house with stairs;
And there did I see coming down
Such volk as are not in our town,
      Vortie at least in pairs.

Amongst the rest, on pest'lent fine,
(His beard no bigger though then thine)
      Walkt on before the rest:
Our landlord looks like nothing to him:
The king (God blesse him) 'twould undo him
      Should he go still so drest.

At Course-a-Park, without all doubt,
He should have first been taken out
      By all the maids i'th town:
Though lusty *Roger* there had been,
Or little *George* upon the green,
      Or *Vincent* of the Crown.

But wot you what? the youth was going
To make an end of all his wooing;
      The parson for him staid:
Yet by his leave (for all his hast)
He did not so much wish all past
      (Perchance) as did the maid.

The maid (and thereby hangs a tale)
For such a maid no Widson-ale
    Could ever yet produce :
No grape that's kindly ripe, could be
So round, so plump, so soft as she,
    Nor half so full of juice.

Her finger was so small, the ring
Would not stay on which he did bring,
    It was too wide a peck :
And to say truth (for out it must)
It lookt like the great collar (just)
    About our young colts neck.

Her feet beneath her peticoat,
.Like little mice stole in and out,
    As if they fear'd the light :
But *Dick* she dances such a way !
No sun upon an Easter day
    Is half so fine a sight.

He would have kist her once or twice,
But she would not, she was so nice
    She would not do't in sight,
And then she lookt as who would say
I will do what I list to day ;
    And you shall do't at night.

Her cheeks so rare a white was on,
No dazy make comparison
    (Who sees them is undone)
For streaks of red were mingled there,
Such as are on a Katherine peare,
    The side that's next the sun.)

Her lips were red, and one was thin
Compar'd to that was next her chin ;
    (Some bee had stung it newly)
But (*Dick*) her eyes so guard her face,
I durst no more upon them gaze,
    Then on the sun in *July*.

Her mouth so small when she does speak,
Thou'dst swear her teeth her words did break,
    That they might passage get,
But she so handled still the matter,
They came as good as ours, or better,
    And are not spent a whit.

If wishing should be any sin
The parson himself had guilty bin,
    (She lookt that day so purely)
And did the youth so oft the feat
At night, as some did in conceit,
    It would have spoil'd him surely. . .

Passion oh me! how I run on!
There's that that would be thought upon,
   (I trow) besides the bride.
The businesse of the kitchin's great,
For it is fit that men should eat;
   Nor was it there deny'd.

Just in the nick the cook knockt thrice,
And all the waiters in a trice
   His summons did obey,
Each serving-man with dish in hand,
Marcht boldly up like our train'd band,
   Presented and away.

When all the meat was on the table,
What man of knife, or teeth, was able
   To stay to be intreated?
And this the very reason was
Before the parson could say grace,
   The company was seated.

Now hats fly off, and youths carrouse;
Healths first go round, and then the house,
   The brides came thick and thick;
And when 'twas nam'd another health,
Perhaps he made it hers by stealth;
   (And who could help it Dick)

O'th sudain up they rise and dance;
Then sit again, and sigh, and glance:
   Then dance again and kisse:
Thus sev'rall wayes the time did passe,
Whil'st every woman wisht her place,
   And every man wisht his.

By this time all were stoln aside,
To councell and undresse the bride;
   But that he must not know:
But 'twas thought he guest her mind,
And did not mean to stay behind
   Above an houre or so.

When in he came (*Dick*) there she lay
Like new-faln snow melting away,
   ('Twas time I trow to part)
Kisses were now the onely stay,
Which soon she gave, as who would say,
   God b'w'y'! with all my heart.

But just as heavens would have to crosse it,
In came the bride-maids with the posset:
   The bridegroom eat in spight;
For had he left the women to't
It would have cost two houres to do't,
   Which were too much that night.

At length the candle's out, and now,
All that they had not done, they do :
    What that is, who can tell ?
But I beleeve it was no more
Then thou and I have done before
    With *Bridget*, and with *Nell*.

The Good Fellow.

When shall we meet again to have a tast
Of that transcendent ale we drank of last ?
What wild ingredient did the woman chose
To make her drink withall ? it made me lose
My wit, before. I quencht my thirst ; there came
Such whimsies in my brain, and such a flame
Of fiery drunkennesse had sing'd my nose,
My beard shrunk in for fear ; there were of those
That took me for a comet, some afar
Distant remote, thought me a blazing star ;
The earth me thought, just as it was, it went
Round in a wheeling course of merriment.
My head was ever drooping, and my nose
Offering to be a suiter to my toes. . . .
My pock-hole face, they say, appear'd to some,
Just like a dry and burning honey-comb :
My tongue did swim in ale, and joy'd to boast
Itself a greater sea-man than the toast.
My mouth was grown awry, as if it were
Lab'ring to reach the whisper in mine eare,

My guts were mines of sulphur, and my set ·
Of parched teeth, struck fire as they met.
Nay, when I pist, my urine was so hot,
It burnt a hole quite through the chamber-pot:
Each brewer that I met, I kiss'd, and made
Suit to be bound apprentice to the trade:
One did approve the motion, when he saw,
That my own legs could my indentures draw.
Well sir, I grew stark mad, as you may see
By this adventure upon poetry.
You easily may guesse, I am not quite
Grown sober yet, by these weak lines I write:
Onely I do't for this, to let you see,
Whos'ere paid for the ale, I'm sur't paid me.

CANTO,

In the praise of Sack.

Listen all I pray,
To the words I have to say,
In memory sure insertum:
Rich wines do us raise
To the honour of bayes,
Quem non fecere disertum?

Of all the juice,
Which the gods produce,
Sack shall be preferr'd before them;

'Tis sack that shall
Create us all,
Mars, Bacchus, Apollo, virorum.

We abandon all ale,
And beer that is stale,
Rosa-solis, and damnable hum :
But we will rack
In the praise of sack,
'Gainst *Omne quod exit in um.*

This is the wine,
Which in former time,
Each wise one of the Magi
Was wont to carouse
In a frolick blouse.
Recubans sub tegmine fagi.

Let the hope be their bane,
And a rope be their shame,
Let the gout and collick pine um,
That offer to shrink,
In taking their drink,
Seu Græcum, sive Latinum.

Let the glasse go round,
Let the quart-pot sound ;
Let each one do as he's done to :

Avaunt ye that hugge
The abominable jugge,
'Mongst us *Heteroclita sunto.*

There's no such disease,   ·.
As he that doth please
His palate with.beer for to shame us :
　'Tis sack makes us sing,
　Hey down a down ding,
Musa paulo majora canamus.

He is either mute,
Or doth poorly dispute,
That drinks ought else but wine O,   ·
　The more wine a man drinks,
　Like a subtile sphinx
Tantum valet ille loquendo.

'Tis true, our souls,
By the lowsie bowles
Of beer that doth naught but swill us,
　Do go into swine,
　(*Pythagoras* 'tis thine)
Nam vos mutastis & illas.

When I've sack in my brain,
I'm in a merry vain,
And this to me a blisse is :

Him that is wise,
I can justly despise :
Mecum confertur Vlysses ?

How it chears the brains,
How it warms the veins,
How against all crosses it arms us !
How it makes him that's poor,
Couragiously roar,.
Et mutatus dicere formas.

Give me the boy, ·
My delight and my joy,
To my *tantum* that drinks his *tale :*
By sack he that waxes
In our syntaxes.
Est verbum personale.

Art thou weak or lame,
Or thy wits to blame ?
Call for sack, and thou shalt have it.
'Twill make thee rise,
And be very wise,
Cui vim natura negavit.

We have frolick rounds,
We have merry go downs,
Yet nothing is done at randome,

For when we are to pay,
We club and away,
Id est commune notandum.

The blades that want cash,
Have credit for crash,
They'll have sack what ever it cost um,
They do not pay;
Till another day,
Manet alta mente repostum.

Who ne'r failes to drink,
All clear from the brink,
With a smooth and even swallow,
I'll offer at his shrine,
And call it divine,
Et erit mihi magnus Apollo.

He that drinks still,
And never hath his fill,
Hath a passage like a conduit,
The sack doth inspire,
In rapture and fire,
Sic æther æthera fundit.

When you merrily quaffe,
If any do off,
And then from you needs will passe thee,

Give their nose a twitch,
And kick them in the britch,
Non componuntur ab asse.

I have told you plain,
And tell you again,
Be he furious as *Orlando,*
  He is an asse,
  That from hence doth passe,
Nisi bibit ad ostia stando.

The vertue of Sack.

Fetch me *Ben Johnsons* skull, and fill't with sack,
Rich as the same he drank, when the whole pack
Of jolly sisters pledg'd, and did agree,
It was no sin to be as drunk as he:
If there be any weaknesse in the wine,
There's vertue in the cup to mak't divine;
This muddy drench of ale does tast too much
Of earth, the malt retains a scurvy touch
Of the dull hand that sows it; and I fear
There's heresie in hops; give block-heads beer,
And silly *Ignoramus,* such as think
There's powder treason in all *Spanish* drink,
Call sack an idoll; we will kisse the cup,
For fear the conventicle be blown up
With superstition; away with the brew-house alms,
Whose best mirth is six shillings beer and qualms.

Let me rejoyce in sprightly sack, that can
Create a brain even in an empty pan.
Canary! it's thou that dost inspire,
And actuate the soul with heavenly fire.
Thou that sublim'st the genius-making wit,
Scorn earth, and such as love, or. live by it.
Thou mak'st us lords of regions large and faire,
Whilst our conceits build castles in the aire:
Since fire, earth, aire, thus thy inferiours be,
Henceforth I'll know no element but thee :.
Thou precious *elixar* of all grapes,
Welcome by thee our muse begins her scapes,
Such is the worth of sack; I am (me thinks)
In the *Exchequer* now, hark how it chinks,
And do esteem my venerable selfe
As brave a fellow, as if all the pelfe
Were sure mine own; and I have thought a way
Already how to spend it; I would pay.
No debts, but fairly empty every trunk ;
And change the gold for sack to keep me drunk ;
And so by consequence till rich *Spaines* wine
Being in my crown, the *Indies* too were mine
And when my brains are once afoot (heaven bless us !)
I think my self a better man than *Cræsus.*
And now I do conceit my selfe a judge,
And coughing laugh to see my clients trudge
After my lordships coach unto the hall
For justice, and am full of law withall,
And do become the bench as well as he
That fled long since for want of honesty :

But I'll be judge no longer, though in jest,
For fear I should be talkt with like the rest,
When I am sober; who can chuse but think
Me wise, that am so wary in my drink?
Oh admirable sack! here's dainty sport,
I am come back from *Westminster* to court;
And am grown young again; my ptisick now
Hath left me, and my judges graven brow
Is smooth'd; and I turn'd amorous as *May,*
When she invites young lovers forth to play
Upon her flowry bosome: I could win
A vestall now, or tempt a queen to sin.
Oh for a score of queens! you'd laugh to see,
How they would strive which first should ravish me:
Three goddesses were nothing: sack has tipt
My tongue with charms like those which *Paris* sipt
From *Venus,* when she taught him how to kisse
Faire *Helen,* and invite a fairer blisse:
Mine is *Canary rhetorick,* that alone
Would turn *Diana* to a burning stone.
Stone with amazement, burning with loves fire;
Hard to the touch, but short in her desire.
Inestimable sack! thou mak'st us rich,
Wise, amorous, any thing; I have an itch
To t'other cup, and that perchance will make
Me valiant too, and quarrell for thy sake.
If I be once inflam'd against thy foes
That would preach down thy worth in small-beer prose.
I shall do miracles as bad, or worse,
As he that gave the king an hundred horse:

T'other odd cup, and I shall be prepar'd
To snatch at stars, and pluck down a reward
With mine own hands from *Jove* upon their backs
That are, or *Charls* his enemies, or sacks;
Let it be full, if I do chance to spill
Over my standish by the way, I will
Dipping in this diviner ink, my pen,
Write my self sober, and fall to't agen.

The Answer of Ale to the Challenge of Sack.

Come, all you brave wights,
That are dubbed ale-knights
    Now set out your selves in fight:
And let them that crack
In the praises of sack,
    Know *malt* is of mickle might.
Though sack they define
To holy divine,
    Yet it is but natural liquor:
Ale hath for its part
An addition of art,
    To make it drink thinner or thicker
Sacks fiery fume
Doth wast and consume
    Mens *humidum radicale;*
It scaldeth their livers,
It breeds burning feavers,
    Proves *vinum venenum reale.*

But history gathers,
From aged fore-fathers,
    That ale's the true liquor of life:
Men liv'd long in health,
And preserv'd their wealth,
    Whilst barley-broth onely was rife.
Sack quickly ascends,
And suddenly ends.
    What company came for at first:
And that which yet worse is,
It empties mens purses
    Before it half quencheth their thirst.
Ale is not so costly,
Although that the most lye
    Too long by the oyle of barley,
Yet may they part late
At a reasonable rate,
    Though they came in the morning early.
Sack makes men from words
Fall to drawing of swords,
    And quarrelling endeth their quaffing;
Whilst dagger-ale barrels
Bear off many quarrels,
    And often turn chiding to laughing.
Sack's drink for our masters:
All may be ale-tasters.
    Good things the more common the better.
Sack's but single broth:
Ale's meat, drink, and cloth,
    Say they that know never a letter.

But not to entangle
Old friends till they wrangle,
   And quarrel for other mens pleasure;
Let ale keep his place,
And let sack have his grace,
   So that neither exceed the due measure.

The Tryumph of Tobacco over Sack and Ale.

Nay, soft, by your leaves,
Tobacco bereaves
   You both of the garland: forbear it:
You are two to one,
Yet tobacco alone
   It is like both to win it, and wear it.
Though many men crack,
Some of ale, some of sack,
   And think they have reason to do it;
Tobacco hath more,
That will never give o're
   The honour they do unto it.
Tobacco engages
Both sexes, all ages,
   The poor as well as the wealthy,
From the court to the cottage,
From childhood to dotage,
   Both those that are sick and the healthy.
It plainly appears
That in a few years
   Tobacco more custom hath gained,

Then sack, or then ale,
Though they double the tale
    Of the times, wherein they have reigned.
And worthily too,
For what they undoe
    Tobacco doth help to regaine,
On fairer conditions,
Than many physitians,
    Puts an end to much grief and paine.
It helpeth digestion,
Of that there's no question,
    The gout, and the toothach, it easeth :
Be it early, or late,
'Tis never out of date,
    He may safely take it that pleaseth.
Tobacco prevents
Infection by scents,
    That hurt the brain, and are heady,
An antidote is,
Before you're amisse,
    As well as an after remedy.
The cold it doth heat,
Cools them that do sweat,
    And them that are fat maketh lean :
The hungry doth feed,
And, if there be need,
    Spent spirits restoreth again.
Tobacco infused
May safely be used
    For purging, and killing of lice :

Not so much as the ashes
But heals cuts and slashes,
    And that out of hand, in a trice.
The poets of old,
Many fables have told,
    Of the gods and their *Symposia :*
But tobacco alone,
Had they known it, had gone
    For their *nectar* and *ambrosia*.
It is not the smack
Of ale, or of sack,
    That can with tobacco compare :
For taste, and for smell,
It bears away the bell
    From them both where ever they are :
For all their bravado,
It is Trinidado
    That both their noses will wipe
Of the praises they desire,
Unlesse they conspire
    To sing to the tune of his pipe.

Turpe est difficiles habere nugas.

A Farewell to Sack.

Farewell thou thing, time past so true and dear
To me, as blood to life, and spirit, and near,
Nay thou more near then kindred, friend, or wife,
Male to the female, soul to the body, life

To quick action, or the warm soft side
Of the yet chast, and undefiled bride.
These and a thousand more could never be
More near, more dear, then thou wert once to me.
'Tis thou above, that with thy mystick faln
Work'st more then wisdome, art, or nature can;
To raise the holy madnesse, and awake
The frost-bound blood and spirits, and to make
Them frantick with thy raptures, stretching through
The souls like lightning, and as active too.
But why, why do I longer gaze upon
Thee, with the eye of admiration,
When I must leave thee, and inforc'd must say,
To all thy witching beauties, go away?
And if thy whimpering looks do ask me, why?
Know then, 'tis Nature bids thee hence, not I;
'Tis her erroneous self hath form'd my brain,
Uncapable of such a soveraigne,
As is thy powerfull selfe; I prethee draw in
Thy gazing fires, lest at their sight the sin
Of fierce idolatry shoot into me, and
I turn apostate to the strict command
Of Nature; bid me now farewell, or smile
More ugly, lest thy tempting looks beguile   (thee,
My vows pronounc't in zeal, which thus much shows
That I have sworn, but by thy looks to know thee.
Let others drink thee boldly, and desire
'Thee, and their lips espous'd, while I admire
And love, but yet not tast thee: let my Muse
Faile of thy former helps, and onely use

Her inadulterate strength, whats done by me,
Shall smell hereafter of the lamp, not thee.

A fit of Rime against Rime.

Rime the rack of finest wits,
That expresseth but by fits
　　　True conceit.
Spoyling senses of their treasure,
Cousening judgement with a measure,
　　　But false weight.
Wresting words from their true calling,
Propping verse for fear of falling
　　　To the ground.
Joyning syllables, drowning letters,
Fastning vowells, as with fetters
　　　They were bound.
Soon as lazie thou wer't known.
All good poetry hence was flown,
　　　And art banish'd.
For a thousand years together,
All *Parnassus* green did wither.
　　　And wit vanish'd.
Pegasus did fly away,
At the wells no Muse did stay,
　　　But bewayl'd
So to see the fountaine dry,
And *Apollo's* musick dye ;
　　　All light fail'd !

Starveling rimes did fill the stage,
Not a poet in an age
    Worth crowning.
Not a work deserving bayes,
Nor a line deserving praise;
    Pallas frowning.
Greek was free from rimes infection,
Happy Greek by this protection
    Was not spoyled.
Whilst the Latine, queen of tongues,
Is not free from rimes wrongs;
    But rests soiled.
Scarce the hill again doth flourish,
Scarce the world a wit doth nourish,
    To restore
Phœbus to his crown again,
And the Muses to their brain,
    As before.
Vulgar languages that want
Words, and sweetnesse, and be scant
    Of true measure,
Tyran rime hath so abused,
That they long since have refused
    Other ceasure.
He that first invented thee,
May his joynts tormented be,
    Cramp'd for ever.
Still may syllables joyn with thee,
Still may reason war with rime,
    Resting never.

May his sense when it would meet,
The cold tumor in his feet,
   Grow unsounder.
And his title be long foole,
That in rearing such a schoole,
   Was the founder.

A Letany.

From a proud woodcock, and a peevish wife,
A pointlesse needle, and a broken knife,
From lying in a ladies lap,
Like a great fool that longs for pap,
   And from the fruit of the three corner'd tree,
   Vertue and goodnesse still deliver me.

From a conspiracy of wicked knaves,
A knot of villains, and a crew of slaves,
From laying plots for to abuse a friend,
From working humors to a wicked end,
   And from the wood where wolves and foxes be,
   Vertue and goodnesse still deliver me.

From rusty bacon, and ill rosted eeles,
And from a madding wit that runs on wheels,
A vap'ring humour, and a beetle head,
A smoaky chimney, and a lowsie bed,
   A blow upon the elbow and the knee,
   From each of these, goodnesse deliver me.

From setting vertue at too low a price;
From losing too much coyn at cards and dice.
From surety-ship, and from an empty purse,
Or any thing that may be termed worse;
   From all suoh ill, wherein no good can be,
   Vertue and goodnesse still deliver me.

From a fool, and serious toyes,
From a lawyer three parts noise;
From impertinence like a drum
   Beat at dinner in his room,
From a tongue without a file,
   Heaps of *phrases* and no stile,
From a fiddler out of tune,
   As the *cuckoo* is in *June*.
From a lady that doth breath
   Worse above, than underneath.
From the bristles of a hog,
   Or the ring-worm in a dog:
From the courtship of a bryer,
   Or St. *Anthonies* old fire.
From the mercy of some jaylors,
From the long bills of all taylors,
From parasites that will stroak us,
From morsells that will choak us,
From all such as purses cut,
From a filthy durty slut,
From canters and great eaters,
From patentees and cheaters,

From men with reason tainted,
From women which are painted,
From all far-fetch'd new fangles,
From him that ever wrangles,
From rotten cheese, and addle eggs,
From broken shins, and gowty legs,
From a pudding hath no end,
From bad men that never mend,
From the Counter or the Fleet,
From doing penance in a sheet,
From jesuites, monks, and fryers,
From hypocrites, knaves, and lyers,
From *Romes* pardons, bulls, and masses,
From bug-bears, and broken glasses,
From *Spanish* pensions and their spies,
From weeping cheese with *Argus* eyes,
From forain foes invasions,
From papistical perswasions,
From private gain, by publick loase,
From coming home by weeping crosse,
From all these I say agen,
Heaven deliver me.   Amen.

THE GYPSIES.

The Captain sings.

From the famous *Peak of Darby,*
And the *Devils-Arse* there hard-by,
Where we yearly keep our musters,
Thus the *Ægyptians* throng in clusters.
Be not frighted with our fashion,
Though we seem a tattered nation;
We account our rags, our riches,
So our tricks exceed our stitches.

Give us bacon, rinds of wallnuts,
Shells of cockels, and of small nuts ;
Ribands, bells, and saffrand linnen,
All the world is ours to win in.
Knacks we have that will delight you,
Slight of hand that will jnvite you
To endure our tawny faces
Quit your places, and not cause you cut your laces.

All your fortunes we can tell ye,
Be they for the back or belly ;
In the moods too and the tences,
That may fit your fine five senses.

Draw but then your gloves we pray you,
And sit still, we will not fray you ;
For though we be here at *Burley*,
Wee'd be loath to make a hurley.

Another sings.

Stay my sweet singer,
The touch of thy finger,
A little and linger ;
For me that am bringer
Of bound to the border,
The rule and recorder,
And mouth of the order,
As prist of the game,
And prelate of the same.

There's a *Gentry Cove* here;
Is the top of the shire,
Of the Bever *Ken*,
A man among men ;
You need not to feare,
I have an eye, and an eare
That turns here and there,
To look to our geare.
   Some say that there be,
   One or two, if not three,
   That are greater than he.
And for the *Rome-Morts*,
I know by their ports
And their jolly resorts
They are of the sorts
That love the true sports
Of King *Ptolomeus*,
Or great *Coriphæus*,
And Queen *Cleopatra*,
The *Gypsies* grand *Matra*.
   Then if we shall shark it,
   Here faire is, and market.
Leave pig py and goose,
And play fast and loose,
A short cut and long,
Some inch of a song,
Pythagoras lot,
Drawn out of a pot ;
With what says *Alkindus*
And *Pharaotes Indus*,

John de Indagine
With all their *Pagiue*,
Of faces and palmestrie,
    And this is *Allmysterie*.
Lay by your wimbles,
Your boring for thimbles,
Or using your nimbles,
In diving the pockets,
And sounding the sockets
Of Simper the *Cockets*;
Or angling the purses,
Of such as will curse us;
But in the strict duell
Be merry, and cruell,
Strike fair at some jewell
That mine may accrew well
For that is the fuell,
To make the town brew well,
And the pot wring well,
And the braine sing well,
Which we may bring well
About by a string well,
And do the thing well.
    It is but a strain
    Of true legerdemain,
    Once twice and againe.
Or what will you say now?
If with our fine play now,
Our knack and our dances,
We work on the fancies

Of some of your Nancies.
These trinckets and tripsies,
And make 'em turn gypsies.
Here's no justice *Lippus*
Will seek for to nip us,
In *Cramp-ring* or *Cippus*,
And then for to strip us,
And after to whip us.
His justice to vary,
While here we do tarry
But be wise, and wary
And we may both carry
The *Kate* and the *Mary*,
And all the bright ae'ry,
Away to the quarry.
Or durst I go further
In method and order,
There's a purse and a seale,
I have a great mind to steal.
That when our tricks are done,
We might seal our own pardon ;
All this we may do,
And a great deal more too,
If our brave *Ptolomee*,
Will but say follow me.

To those that would be Gypsies too.

Friends not to refell ye,
Or any way quell ye,
To buy or to sell ye,
I onely, must tell ye,
Ye aim at a mystery
Worthy a history;
There's much to be done,
Ere you can be a sonne,
Or brother of the moone.
'Tis not so soon
Acquir'd as desir'd.
You must be *Ben-bousie*,
And sleepy and drowsie,
And lasie, and lowsie,
Before ye can rouse ye,
In shape that arowse ye.
And then you may stalk
The *Gypsies* walk;
To the *coops* and the *pens*.
And bring in the hens,
Though the cock be sullen
For losse of the *pullen :*
Take turkie, or capon,
And gammons of bacon,
Let nought be forsaken;
We'l let you go loose
Like a fox to a goose,

And shew you the stye
Where the little pigs lye;
Whence if you can take
One or two, and not wake
The sow in her dreams,
But by the moon beams;
So warily hie,
As neither do cry.
You shall the next day
Have license to play
At the hedge a flirt
For a sheet or a shirt;
If your hand be light,
I'le shew you the slight
Of our *Ptolomies* knot,
It is, and 'tis not.
To change your complexion
With the noble confection.
Of wallnuts and hogs-grease,
Better than dogs-grease:
And to milk the kine,
Ere the milkmaid fine
Hath opened her eine.
Or if you desire
To spit, or fart fire,
Ile teach you the knacks,
Of eating of flax;
And out of their noses,
Draw ribbands and posies.

And if you incline
To a cup of good wine,
When you sup or dine;
If you chance it to lack,
Be it claret or sack;
Ile make this snout,
To deal it about,
Or this to run out,
As it were from a spout.

On a patch'd up Madam.

Pigmaleons fate revers'd is mine,
His marble love took flesh and blood,
What late I worship'd, I decline;
Your beauty now is understood
To have no more in it of life,
Then that whereof he framed his wife.

As women yet who apprehend
Some suddain cause of causeless fear,
Although that seeming cause take end;
And they behold no danger neer,
A shaking through their limbs they find
Like leaves saluted by the wind.

So though your beauties do appear
No beauties which amaz'd me so,

Yet from my breast I cannot teare
The passion which from thence did grow,
Nor yet out of my fancy race
The print of that supposed face.

A real beauty though too neer
The fond *Narcissus* did admire,
I dote on that which is no where
The sign of beauty feeds my fire :
No mortall flame was ere so cruell
As mine which thus survives the fuell.

The Reply on the Contrary.

Not caring to observe the wind,
Or the unfaithful sea explore,
I now no painted colours find,
But settled stand upon the shoar;
And may not here new dangers lye
To conquer and deceive the eye?
No, for she looks so pure, so cleer
That her rich bottom doth appear
Pav'd all with precious things, not torn
From shiprack'd vessels, but there born;
Here sweetness, truth, and every grace
Which time and youth are wont to teach
The eye may in a moment reach
And read distinctly in her face;
Some other nymph with colours faint
And with slow pensils we may paint;

And a weak heart in time destroy,
But she alone can print the boy,
Can with a single look inflame
The coldest breast, the rudest tame.
Then painter say, where couldst thou find
Shades to counterfeit that face?
For colours of this glorious kind,
Come not from any mortal race.
In heaven it self she sure was drest,
With that angel-like guise,
Thus not deluded, we are blest
And see with clearest eyes.

The Melancholy Lover.

It is not I that love you lesse
Then when before your feet I lay,
But to prevent the sad increase
Of hopelesse love, I keep away;
In vain (alas) for every thing
Which I have known, belongs to you;
Your form doth to my fancy bring,
And makes my old wounds bleed anew.
He in the spring who from the sun
Already hath a feaver got,
Too late begins those heats to shun,
Which *Phœbus* through his veins hath shot;
Too late he would the pain asswage,
And to his chamber doth retire;

About with him he bears the rage,
And in his tainted blood the fire;
But vowd I have, and never must
Your banish'd servant trouble you.
For if I break, you may mistrust
The vow I made to love you too.
But tell me lady, dearest foe,
Where your lovely strength doth lye;
Is the power that charms me so
In your soul, or in your eye,
In your snowy neck alone?
Or is that grace in motion seen,
No such wonders can be done,
But in your voyce that's musicks queen;
Whilest I do listen to that voyce
I do feel my life decay
For that sweet and powerful noise
Calls my flitting soule away;
Oh suppresse that magick sound
That destroyes without a wound,
Peace lady, peace, or singing dye
That together you and I
May arm in arm to heaven go,
For all the story we do know,
That the blessed do above
Is that they sing, and that they love.

The Variable Lover ; or a Reply to the Melancholy
Lover.

Thrice happy paire, of whom we cannot know
Which first began to love, and which to woe,
Faire course of passion where two loves impart,
And run together, heart still yoakt in heart ;
Successefull love, whom love hath taught the way
To be victorious in the first assay :
Sure love's an art, best practised at first,
And where the sad and pining prosper worst :
Some with a different fate pursue in vain
Their ladyes loves, whiles others just disdain
Of their neglect, above their passion born,
Do pride to pride oppose, and scorn to scorn ;
Then they relent, but all too late to move
A heart diverted to a nobler love,
The scales are turn'd, her beauties weigh no more
Then th'others vowes, and services before ;
So in some well wrought hangings we may see
How *Hector* leads, and how the *Græcians* flee ;
Here the fierce *Mars* his courage so inspires,
That with bold hands the *Argive* fleet he fires ;
But there from heaven the blew-ey'd virgin falls,
And frighted *Troy* retires within her walls ;
They who are foremost in that bloody place,
Retire anon, and give the conquerours chase ;
So like the chances are of love and war,
That they in this alone distinguished are ;
In love the victors from the vanqushi'd flye,
They fly that wound, and they pursue that dye.

The Ladyes Slave to his Mistresse.

Fairest piece of well form'd earth,
Urge not thus your haughty birth;
The power which you have o're us lyes
Not in your face, but in your eyes;
None but a lord! Alas that voice
Confines you to a narrow choice;
Should you no honey vow to tast,
But what the master bees have plac'd
In compasse of their cells, how small
A portion to your share would fall?
Nor all appear amongst those few
Worthy the stock from whence they grew;
The sap which at the root is bred
In trees, through all the boughes is spread;
But vertues which in beauties shine,
Make not like progresse through the line;
'Tis not from whom, but where we live,
The place doth oft the graces give;
Had *Cæsar* on the mountain bred
A flock perhaps, or herd had led,
He who the world subdu'd, had been
But the best wrestler on the green:
'Tis art and knowledge which draw forth
The hidden seeds of humane worth;
They blow the sparks, and make them rise
Into such flames, as touch the skyes:

To the old *heroes* hence was given
A pedigree that touch'd the heaven;
Of mortal seed they were not held,
Which other mortals so excell'd;
And beauty too in such excesse
As yours (fair lady) claimes no lesse.
Smile but on me, and you shall scorn
Henceforth to be of princes born;
Your slave I am, can paint the grove
Where your lov'd mother slept with *Jove*,
And yet excuse the faultlesse dame,
Caught with her spouses shape, and name;
Your matchless form will credit bring
To all the wonders I shall sing.

The Reply.

At last here for your sake I part
With all that grew so neer my heart;
The passion which you had for me,
The faith, the love, the constancy;
And that all may successeful prove,
I'le turn my self to what you love.
Too much I do confesse I priz'd
That which you thought all grace compriz'd;
Too much I with my arrowes strove
To reach, or hurt a yeelding dove;
It was your constancy that still
Declin'd my force, and mock'd my skill;

No more I'le wander through the aire,
Nor mount, nor shop at every faire;
And with a fancy unconfin'd,
And lawlesse as the sea, or wind,
Pursue you wheresoe're you fly,
And with your various thoughts comply;
The formall starres do travail so,
As we their names, and courses know,
And he who on their aspects looks,
Would think them governed by our books;
But never were the clouds reduc'd
To any art their motion us'd;
For those free vapours are so light
And frequent, that the conquer'd fight
Despaire to find the rules that guide
Those guilded shadows, as they slide;
And therefore of the spacious aire,
Joves royal consort had the care;
And by that power did once escape
The amorous bold *Ixions* rape;
And she with her resemblance grac'd
A shining cloud which he imbrac'd;
Such was the image, so it smil'd
With seeming kindness, which beguild
Your hugging thoughts, when as you thought
That you had me your mistress caught;
So shap'd it was, but for the faire,
You fill'd your arms with yeelding aire;
For which you sure may grieve the lesse
Because the gods had like successe;

For in their story, one we see
Pursues a nymph, and takes a tree ;
A second, with a lovers hast,
Soon overtakes whom he had chac'd ;
But she that did a virgin seem,
Did prove to be a gliding stream ;
For his supposed love a third
Layes greedy hold upon a bird,
And stands amaz'd to find his deare
A wild inhabitant of th'ayre ;
To these bold tales such youths as you
Give credit, and still make them new.
But *Sir*, if you do apprehend
These words of your repenting friend,
Again, deceive me, and again,
For I do swear, Il'e not complain ;
For still to be deluded so,
Is all the pleasure lovers know ;
Who like good faulkners take delight
Not in the quarry, but the flight.

The cunning Curtezan.

Sir tell me, why should we delay
Pleasures shorter than the day ?
Could we, which we never can,
Stretch our lives beyond their span ;
Beauty, like a shadow flyes,
And our youth before us dyes ;

Or would youth and beauty stay,
Love hath wings, and will away;
Love hath swifter wings than time,
Change in love, to heaven doth clime;
Gods who never change their state,
Varied oft their love and hate.
Sir, unto this truth we owe
All the love betwixt us two;
Let not you and I enquire
What hath been our past desire,
On what maidens you have smil'd,
Or what youths I have beguil'd;
Leave it to the planets too,
What we shall hereafter do;
And for the joyes we now shall prove
Take advice of present love.

The Reply.

See how the willing earth gives way
To take th'impression where she lay;
See how the ground as loath to leave
So sweet a burden, still doth cleave
Close to her stained garments; here
The coming spring would first appeare,
And all this place with roses strow
If busie feet would let them grow;
Thus the first lovers on the clay
Of which they were composed lay,
And in their prime, with equall grace
Met the first patterns of our raee;

Then blush not lady, nor yet frown
Nor wonder how you both came down;
The young man could not choose but bend,
When all his heav'n upon him lean'd;
If ought by him amisse were done,
'Twas, that he let you rise so soon.

On the French English Ape.

Mark him once more, and tell me if you can
Look, and not laugh, on yonder gentleman.
Could I but work a transformation strange
On him whose pride doth swell and rankle so,
I would his carrion to a thistle change,
Which asses feed on, and which rusticks mow.

Another on the same.

What dost thou mean to revell, roare, and spend,
And drink, and drab, and swear so? wilt thou rend
Thy way to hell? the devil will spy day,
And at a small hole snatch thee quite away.

On a Brede of divers colours, woven by four Maids of Honour, and presented to the Queen on New-yeers Day last.

Twice twenty slender virgin fingers twine
This curious web, where all their fancies shine;
As nature them, so they this brede have wrought,
Soft as their hands, and various as their thoughts;

Not *Juno's* bird when he his train doth spread,
And woes the female to his painted bed ;
No, nor the bow which so adorns the skyes,
So glorious is, or boasts so many dies.
    But now 'tis done, O let me know
    Where those immortal colours grow,
    That could this deathless peice compose
    In lillyes, or the fading rose ?
    No for this art they have climb'd higher,
    Then did *Prometheus* for his fire.

On deaf Small, the Ale-Wife.

She prates to others, yet can nothing hear,
Just like a sounding jugge that wants an eare.

Another.

Small my host doth to me such reckoning make,
That I of *Small* my host small reckoning take,
Henceforth, good *Small*, let reckonings lesser be,
And greater reckoning I shall make of thee.

On a Tell-tale.

Such glowing tongues to hot contention bent,
Are not unlike red herrings broyl'd in Lent.

Cherry-pit.

Nicholas and *Nell* did lately sit
Playing for sport at Cherry-pit ;
They both did throw, and having thrown,
He got the pit, and she the stone.

A vow to Cupid.

Cupid I do love a girle
Ruby lip'd, and tooth'd like pearl;
If so be that I may prove
Lucky in this maid I love,
I do promise there shall be
Myrtles offer'd up to thee.

On the Rose.

Go lovely rose,
Tell her that wasts her time and me,
  That now she knows
When I resemble her to thee
How sweet, and fair she seems to be.
  Tell her that's young
And shuns to have her graces spy'd,
  That hadst thou sprung
In desarts where no men abide,
Thou must have uncommended dy'd.
  Small is the worth
Of beauty from the light retir'd,
  Bid her come forth
Suffer her self to be desir'd,
And blush not to be so admir'd.
  Then dye that she,
The common fate of all things rare
  May read in thee
How small a part of time they share
That are so wondrous sweet, and faire.

Another.

Lately on yonder fragrant bush,
Big with many a coming rose,
This early bud began to blush,
And did but half it self disclose ;
   I pluck'd it, though no better grown,
   Yet now you see how full 'tis blown.
Still as I did the leaves inspire,
With such a purple light they shone
As if they had been made of fire,
And spreading so, would flame anon ;
   All that was meant by aire, or sun,
   To the young flower my breath hath done.
And if loose breath so much can do,
It may as well inform of love,
Of purest love, and musick too,
When once your beauties it shall move,
   That breath may have the happy power
   To work on you, as on a flower.

Another.

Go happy rose, and interwove
With other flowers bind my love ;
Tell her too, she must not be
Longer peevish, longer free,
That so long hath fetter'd me.

Say, if she frets, that I have bands
Of pearl, and gold to bind her hands ;

Tell her if she struggles still,
I have myrtle rods at will
That can tame, although not kill.

Take thou my blessing now, and go
And tell her this, but do not so,
Least a handsome anger fly
Like a lightning from her eye,
And burn thee up, as well as I.

On the two Dwarfs that were marryed at Court, not long before Shrovetide.

The sign or chance makes others wive,
But nature did this match contrive;
Eve might as well have *Adam* fled,
As she denyed her little bed
To him, for whom heaven seem'd to frame
And measure out this little dame.

Thrice happy is this humble paire,
Beneath the level of all care;
For o're their heads all arrowes fly
Of sad distrust, and jealousie,
Secured in as high extream,
As if the world held none but them.

To him the fairest nymphs do show
Like moving mountains topt with snow;

And every man a *Polypheme,*
Doth to his *Galatœa* seem :
None may presume her faith to prove,
He proffers death, who proffers love.

On the approaching Spring.

Chl. *Hilas,* oh *Hilas* why sit we mute
    Now that each bird saluteth the spring ?
    Wind up the slackned strings of thy lute ;
    Never canst thou want matter to sing ?
    For love thy breast doth fill with such a fire,
    That whatsoe're is fair, moves thy desire.

Hil. Sweetest you know the sweetest of things
    Of various flowers which the bees do compose,
    Yet no particular tast it brings
    Of violet, wood-bine, pink or rose ;
    So love's the resultance of all the graces
    Which flow from a thousand several faces.

Chl. *Hilas* the birds which chant in this grove
    Could we but know the language they use,
    They would instruct us better in love,
    And reprehend thy inconstant muse ;
    For love their breasts doth fill with such a fire,
    That what they do chuse, bounds their desire.

Hil. *Chloris* this change the birds do approve,
    Which the warm season hither does bring,

Time from your self does further remove
You, then the winter from the gay spring ;
She that like lightning shin'd whiles her face lasted,
Looks like an oak being old, which lightning hath
(blasted.

To be ingraven under the Queens Picture.

Such *Helen* was, and who can blame the boy
That in so bright a flame consum'd his *Troy* ?
But had like vertue shin'd in that fair Greek,
The amorous shepheard had not dar'd to seek
Or hope for pity, but with silent moan
And better fate, had perished alone.

How the Violets came blew.

The violets, as poets tell,
With *Venus* wrangling went
Whither the violets did excell
Or she in sweetest scent ;
But *Venus* having lost the day
Poor girle, she fell on you,
And beat you so, as some do say
Her blowes did make you blew.

Violets in a Ladyes Bosome.

Twice happy violets, that first had birth
In the warm spring, when no frosts nip the earth ;
Thrice happy now, since you transplanted are
Unto the sweeter bosome of my faire ;

And yet poor flowers, I pity your hard fate;
You have but chang'd, not better'd your estate:
What boots it you t'have scap'd cold winters breath
To find like me, by flames a suddain death?

An old Man, to a young Maid.

Scorn me not fair, because you see
My hairs are white; what if they be?
Think not, 'cause in your cheeks appear
Fresh springs of roses, all the year;
And mine, like winter, wan and old,
My love like winter, should be cold;
See in the garland which you weare,
How the sweet blushing roses there
With palest lillyes do combine,
Be taught by them, and so lets joyn.

To the Wife, being married to that old Man.

Since thou wilt needs, bewitch'd with some ill charms
Be buryed in those monumental arms,
All we can wish, is, may his earth lye light
Upon thy tender limbs, and so good night.

The Surprisal, or Loves Tyranny.

There's no dallying with love
Though he be a child, and blind;
Then let none the danger prove;
Who would to himself be kind;
　　Smile he does, when thou dost play,
　　But his smiles to death betray.

Lately with the boy I sported,
Love I did not, yet love feigned;
Had no mistriss, yet I courted;
Sigh I did, yet was not payned,
   Till at last his love in jest
   Prov'd in earnest, my unrest.

When I saw my fair one first,
In a feigned fire I burn'd;
But true flames my poor heart pierc'd,
When her eyes on mine she turn'd;
   So a reall wound I took
   For my counterfeited look.

Slighted love his skill to show
Struck me with a mortall dart;
Then I learn'd that 'gainst his bow,
Vain are all the helps of art:
   And thus captiv'd found that true,
   Doth dissembled love pursue.

'Cause his fetters I disclaim'd,
Now the tyrant faster bound me
With more scorching bonds inflam'd,
'Cause in love so cold he found me;
   And my sighs more scalding made,
   'Cause with winds before they play'd.

Who love not then, O make no show;
Love's as ill deceived as fate,

Fly the boy, hee'l cogge and woe;
Mock him, and hee'l wound thee strait:
  They who dally, boast in vain;
  False love wants not real pain.

On the Eyes and Breasts of the Lady on whom he was inamoured.

Lady, on your eyes I gaz'd,
    When amaz'd
  At their brightnesse,
On your breasts I cast a look,
    No lesse took
  With their whitenesse;
Both I justly did admire
These all snow, and those all fire.

Whilest these wonders I surveigh'd,
    Thus I said
  In suspence,
Nature could have done no lesse
    To expresse
  Her providence,
Then that two such fair worlds might
Have two suns to give them light.

On an old Batchelour.

Mop-ey'd I am, as some have said,
Because I've liv'd so long a maid;

But grant that I should married be,
Should I one jot the better see?
No, I should think that marriage might   ·
Rather than mend me, blind me quite.

On Love.

Love scorch'd my finger, but did spare
The burning of my heart,
To tell me that in love my share
Should be a little part;
Little I love, but if that he
Would but that heat recall,
That joynt to ashes burnt should be,
E're I would love at all.

Vertue improved by suffering.

'Tis but the body that blind fortune's spight
Can chayn to earth, the nobler soul doth alight
Her servile bonds, and takes to heaven her flight.

So heav'n through dark clouds lightneth, whiles the
Is but a file to its bright splendor made;   (shade
So starrs with greater lustre might invade.

So sparkle flints when struck, so mettles find
Hardness from hammering, and the closer bind;
So flames increase, the more supprest by wind.

And as the grindstone to unpolish'd steel
Gives edge and lustre, so my mind I feel
Whetted and glaz'd, by fortunes turning wheel.

The Braggadochio Captain.

Whilst timorous *Ansa* led his martial band
'Gainst the invader of his native land,
Thus he bespake his men before the fight,
Courage (my friends) lets dine, for we to night
Shall sup, sayes he, in heaven; this having said,
Soon as the threatning ensigns were display'd,
And the loud drums and trumpets had proclaim'd
Defiance twixt the hosts, he, who ne're sham'd
At losse of honour, fairly ran away;
Who being ask'd, how chance he would not stay
And go along with them to sup in heaven,
Pardon me, friends, said he, I fast this even.

The choice of a Wife.

I would not have a wife with such a wast
As might be well with a thumb-ring imbrac'd;
Whose bony hips which out on both sides stick,
May serve for graters, and whose lean knees prick;
One who a saw doth in her back-bone beare,
Whose withered legs like kenes do appear;
Nor would I have her yet of bulk so grosse,
That weigh'd shee'd break the scales of th'market crosse,
A meer unfathom'd lump of grease, no, that
I do not rellish, give me flesh, not fat.

A Debtor to his Creditor.

Thou thinkest, th'hast shown thy self a mighty friend,
Because to me thou fifty pounds didst lend;

But if you rich, for lending, mayest be'said
· So great a friend, what I ? who poor repay'd.

On a vain fond Husband.

Thou wondrest thy wives ears should smell so ill,
They may thank thee, thou whisperest in them still.

On a Boy kill'd by the fall of an Ice-sickle.

Where *Thames* her waters through the bridge doth poure,
And th'upper buildings sweat with many a showre ;
A drop congealed to an ice-sickle
On a childs throat that stood beneath it fell ;
And when the poor childs fate dissolv'd it had,
Melted away in the warm wound it made ;
What may not cruell fate ? or where will not
Death find us out if water cut the throat ?

On the Statue of a Tyrant, which falling kill'd a Child.

Thy statue, sad usurper, doth present
　　To tyrants a sad document ;
Though marble, on its basis yet so fast
　　It stood not, but it fell at last,
And seems as when he liv'd, as cruell still,
It could not fall, but it must kill.

On a Widdow.

Fain shee'd have *Robert,* and who blame her can,
But hee'l not have her, and who'l blame the man ?

On one that wore a Leather Cap.

Whilst thou a kids skin cap put'st on
To hide the baldnesse of thy crown,
One jested handsomely who sed
Thou wear'st thy shooes upon thy head.

Ice and Fire.

Naked love did to thine eye,
Fairest, once to warm him fly;
But its purer flame and light
Scorch'd his wings, and spoyl'd his sight.

Forc'd from thence he went to rest
In the soft couch of thy breast,
But there met a frost so great
As his torch extinguisht strait.

When poor *Cupid* being constrain'd
His cold bed to leave complain'd,
  What a lodging's here for me
  If all ice and fire she be?

Counsel not to love.

He that will not love must be
My scholar, and learn this of me;
There be in love as many fears
As the summers corn hath eares.

Sighs and tears, and sorrows more
Then the sand that make the shoare;
Fiery colds, and freezing heats,
Fainting swounds, and deadly sweats,
Now an ague, then a feaver,
Both tormenting lovers ever:
Wouldst thou know besides all these
How hard a woman 'tis to please?
How crosse, how sullen, and how soon,
She shifts and changes like the moon,
How false, how hollow she's in heart,
And how she is in every part
How high she's priz'd, and worth but small?
Little thou't love, or not at all.

The Recantation.

Nay, let her go, can I endure all this?
Yet dye to doat upon a maidens kisse!
Is there such magick in her looks that can
Into a fool transfigurate a man?
Didst not thou love her? true, and she disdain
To meet thy vertue, let her meet her shame;
Were she as fair, as she her self would be,
Adorn'd with all the cost of bravery;
Could she melt hearts of flint, and from her eye
Give her beholders power to live or dye;
Id'e rather beg she would pronounce my death,
Then be her scorn, though that preserv'd my breath;

Rise heart, and be not fool'd! Sfoot, what a shame
Were it for thee to reinsence one flame
From the declining spark? dost thou not know
As she's a woman, her whole sex doth owe
To thine all honour? her false heart and pride
Dare not oppose thy faith, then turn high-tide,
And let her, since her scorn doth so deceive thee,
By her repentance strive again to please thee.

Inconstancy defended.

Leave fairest, leave, I pray no more
With want of love, or lightnesse charge me;
'Cause your looks captiv'd me before,
May not anothers now inlarge me?

He whose misguided zeal hath long
Pay'd homage to some stars pale light,
Better inform'd may without wrong
Leave that t'adore the queen of night.

Then if my heart which long serv'd thee
Will to another now incline,
Why term'd inconstant should it be
For bowing 'fore a richer shrine?

Censure those lovers so, whose will
Inferiour objects can entice,
Who changes for the better still,
Makes that a vertue you call vice.

The Reply.

Shall I hopelesse then pursue
A fair shaddow that still flyes me ?
Shall I still adore and woe
A proud heart that doth despise me ?
Yes, a constant love may so,
Yet 'tis but a fruitlesse show.

Shall I by the erring light
Of two crosser starrs still sail ?
That do shine, but shine in spight,
Not to guide, but make me faile ?
I a wandring course may steer,
But the harbour ne're come neer.

Whilst these thoughts my soul possesse,
Reason passion would o'resway,
Bidding me my flames suppresse,
Or divert some other way ;
But what reason would pursue,
When my heart runs counter too ?

So a pilot bent to make
Search for some unfound-out land,
Does with him his loadstone take
Sayling to the unknown strand ;
But sail he which way he will
The loadstone to the north poynts still.

The Vow.

By my life I vow
That my life art thou ;
By my heart, and by my eyes,
But thy faith denyes
To my juster oath t'incline,
For thou sayest, I swear by thine.

By this sigh I sweare,
By this falling teare,
By the undeserved paines
My grieved soul sustains,
Thou mayest now believe my moan,
They are too too much my own.

On a Maid in love with a Youth blind of one Eye.

Though a sable cloud benight
One of thy fair twins of light,
Yet the other brighter seems
As t'had rob'd his brothers beams,
Or both lights to one were run,
Of two starrs to make one sun :
Cunning archer ! who knows yet
But thou winkst my heart to hit ;
Close the other too, and all
Thee the god of love will call.

Love begotten by pitty.

'Tis true your beauties which before
Did dazle each bold gazers eye,
And forc'd even rebell hearts t'adore,
Or from its conquering splendour fly ;
Now shines with new increase of light,
Like *Cynthia* at her full most bright.

Yet though you glory in th'increase
Of so much beauty, dearest faire ;
They erre who think this great accesse,
Of which all eyes th'admirers are ;
Or arts or natures gifts should be,
Leave then the hidden cause from me.

Pity in thee, in me desire,
First bred (before I durst but ayme
At fair respect) now that close fire
Thy love hath fann'd into a flame,
Which mounting to its proper place
Shines like a glory 'bout thy face.

The Bag of a Bee.

To have the sweet bag of the bee
Two *Cupids* fell at odds,
And whose the pretty prize should be,
They vow'd to ask the gods ;

Which *Venus* hearing, thither came,
And for their boldnesse stript them,
And taking from them each his flame,
With myrtle rods she whipt them;
Which done, to still their wanton cryes,
When quiet grown sh'had seen them,
She kiss'd, and wip'd their dove-like eyes,
And gave the bag between them.

To make much of Time.

Gather your rose-buds whilst you may,
Old Time is still a flying;
And that same flower that smiles to day
Too morrow may be dying.

The glorious lamp of heaven, the sun,
The higher he is getting,
The sooner will his race be run,
And neerer to his setting.

That age is best which is the first,
When youth, and blood are warmer;
And being spent, the worse and werst
Times still succeed the former.

Then be not coy, but use your time,
And while you may, go marry;
For having lost but once your prime,
You may for ever tarry.

On the Picture of Icarus in Wax.

What once did unto thee impart
The means of death, by happy art
Now thee restores to life again ;
Yet still remember to refrain
Ambitious flights, nor soar too nigh
The sun of an inflaming eye ;
For so thou mayst scorch'd by those beams
In ashes dye, as once in streams.

The Farewell to Love, and to his Mistresse.

What conscience say, Is it in thee,
When I a heart had one,
To take away that heart from me,
And to retain thy own ?
For shame and pity now incline
To play a loving part,
Either to send me kindly thine,
Or send me back my heart ;
Court not both, for if thou dost
Resolve to part with neither,
Why yet to show that thou art just
Take me, and mine together.

A FAREWELL TO FOLLY.

Farewel, ye gilded follies, pleasing troubles ;
Farewel, ye honour'd rags, ye christal bubles ;
Fame's but a hollow eccho ; gold, poor clay ;
Honour, the darling but of one short day ;
Beauties chief idol, but a damask skin ;
State, but a golden prison to live in,
And torture free-born minds ; imbroydred trains,
But goodly pageants : proudly swelling vains,
And blood ally'd to greatness, is but loane,
Inherited, not purchast, not our own.
Fame, riches, honour, beauty, state, trains, birth,
Are but the fading blessings of the earth,
I would be rich, but see man too unkind,
Digs in the bowels of the richest mine.
I would be great, but yet the sun doth still
Levell his beams against the rising hill.

I would be fair, but see the champion proud,
The worlds fair eye, oft setting in a cloud.
I would be wise, but that the fox I see
Suspected guilty, when the fox is free.
I would be poor, but see the humble grasse
Trampled upon, by each unworthy asse.
Rich, hated; wise, suspected; scorn'd if poor;
Great, fear'd; fair, tempted; high, still envied more.
Would the world then adopt me for her heir;
Would beauties queen entitle me the fair;
Fame, speak me honours minion; and could I
With *Indian*-angels, and a speaking eye,
Command bare heads, bow'd knees, strike justice dumb,
As well as blind and lame, and give a tongue
To stones by epitaphs; be call'd great master
In the loose lines of every poetaster;
Could I be more than any man that lives,
Great, wise, rich, fair, all in superlatives:
Yet I these favours, would more free resign,
Then ever fortune would have had them mine.
I count one minute of my holy leisure,
Beyond the mirth of all this earthly pleasure.
Welcom pure thoughts, welcom ye careless groves;
These are my guests; this is the court age loves.
The winged people of the skies shall sing
Me anthems, by my sellers gentle spring.
Divinity shall be my looking-glass,
Wherein I will adore sweet vertues face.
Here dwells no heartless loves, no pale-fac't fears,
No short joyes purchast with eternal tears.

Here will I sit and sigh my hot youths folly ;
And learn to affect an holy melancholy :
And if contentment be a stranger, then
Ile ne'r look for it but in heaven agen.

———

AN INVITATION TO THE READER.

HAVING now fed thy youthfull frencies, with these
juvenilian fancies; let me invite thee (with myself)
to sing *Altiora peto*. And then to meet with this thy
noble resolution, I would commend to thy sharpest
view and serious consideration, the sweet cœlestial
sacred poems by Mr. *Henry Vaughan*, intituled *Silex
Scintillans*.

There plumes from angels wings, he'l lend thee,
Which every day to heaven will send thee.

(*Hear him thus invite thee home.*)

If thou wouldst thither, linger not,
    Catch at the place,
Tell youth, and beauty, they must rot,
    They'r but a case :
Loose, parcell'd hearts will freeze ; the sun
    With scatter'd locks
Scarce warms, but by contraction
    Can heat rocks ;

Call in thy powers; run, and reach
    Home with the light;
Be there, before the shadows stretch,
    And span up night;
Follow the cry no more: there is
    An ancient way
All strewed with flowers and happinesse,
.   And fresh as *May;*
There turn, and turn no more; let wits
    Smile at fair eyes,
Or lips; but who there weeping sits,
    Hath got the prize.

Outlandish Proverbs,

SELECTED

BY M^r. G. H.

———————

LONDON,
PRINTED BY T. P. FOR HUMPHREY BLUNDEN;
AT THE CASTLE IN CORNHILL.
1640.

Outlandish Proverbs.

1. Man proposeth, God disposeth.
2. Hee begins to die, that quits his desires.
3. A handfull of good life, is better then a bushell of learning.
4. He that studies his content, wants it.
5. Every day brings his bread with it.
6. Humble hearts, have humble desires.
7. Hee that stumbles and falles not, mends his pace.
8. The house shewes the owner.
9. Hee that gets out of debt, growes rich.
10. All is well with him, who is beloved of his neighbours.
11. Building and marrying of children, are great wasters.
12. A good bargaine is a pick purse.
13. The scalded dog feares cold water.
14. Pleasing ware, is halfe sould.
15. Light burthens, long borne, growe heavie.
16. The wolfe knowes, what the ill beast thinkes.

17. Who hath none to still him, may weepe out his eyes.

18. When all sinnes growes old, coveteousnesse is young.

19. If yee would know a knave, give him a staffe.

20. You cannot know wine by the barrell.

21. A coole mouth, and warme feete, live long.

22. A horse made, and a man to make.

23. Looke not for muske in a dogges kennell.

24. Not a long day, but a good heart rids worke.

25. Hee puls with a long rope, that waights for anothers death.

26. Great strokes make not sweete musick.

27. A caske and an ill custome must be broken.

28. A fat house-keeper, makes leane executors.

29. Empty chambers, make foolish maides.

30. The gentle hawke, halfe mans her selfe.

31. The devill is not alwaies at one doore.

32. When a friend askes, there is no, tomorrow.

33. God sends cold, according to cloathes.

34. One sound blow will serve to undo us all.

35. Hee looseth nothing, that looseth not God.

36. The Germans wit, is in his fingers.

37. At dinner my man appeares.

38. Who gives to all, denies all.

39. Quick beleevers neede broad shoulders.

40. Who remove stones, bruise their fingers.

41. All came from, and will goe to others.

42. He that will take the bird, must not skare it.

43. He lives unsafely, that lookes too neere on things.

44. A gentle houswife, marres the houshold.

45. A crooked log makes a strait fire.

46. He hath great needle of a foole, that plaíes the foole himselfe.

47. A marchant that gaines not, looseth.

48. Let not him that feares feathers, come among wild-foule.

49. Love, and a cough cannot be hid.

50. A dwarfe, on a gyants shoulder, sees further of the two.

51. Hee that sends a foole, means to follow him.

52. Brabling curres never want sore eares.

53. Better the feet slip then the tongue.

54. For washing his hands, none sels his lands.

55. A lyons skin is never cheape.

56. The goate must browse where she is tyed.

57. Who hath a wolfe for his mate, needes a dog for his man.

58. In a good house all is quickly ready.

59. A bad dog never sees the wolfe.

60. God oft hath a great share in a little house.

61. Ill ware is never cheape.

62. A cherefull looke, makes a dish a feast.

63. If all fooles had bables, wee should want fuell.

64. Vertue never growes old.

65. Evening words are not like to morning.

66. Were there no fooles, badd ware would not passe.

67. Never had ill workeman good tooles.

68. Hee stands not surely, that never slips.

69. Were there no hearers, there would be no back-biters.

70. Every thing is of use to a housekeeper.

71. When prayers are done, my lady is ready.

72. At length the fox turnes monk.

73. Flies are busiest about leane horses.

74. Harken to reason or shee will bee heard.

75. The bird loves her nest.

76. Every thing new, is fine.

77. When a dog is a drowning, every one offers him drink.

78. Better a bare foote then none.

79. Who is so deafe, as he that will not heare.

80. He that is warme, thinkes all so.

81. At length the fox is brought to the furrier.

82. Hee that goes barefoot, must not plant thornes.

83. They that are booted are not alwaies ready.

84. He that will learne to pray, let him goe to sea.

85. In spending, lies the advantage.

86. Hee that lives well is learned enough.

87. Ill vessells seldome miscarry.

88. A full belly neither fights nor flies well.

89. All truths are not to be told.

90. An old wise mans shaddow, is better then a young buzzards sword.

91. Noble houskeepers neede no dores.

92. Every ill man hath his ill day.

93. Sleepe without supping, and wake without owing.

94. I gave the mouse a hole, and she is become my heire.

95. Assaile who will, the valiant attends.

96. Whether goest griefe? where I am wont.

97. Praise day at night, and life at the end.

98. Whether shall the oxe goe, where he shall not labour.

99. Where you thinke there is bacon, there is no chimney.

100. Mend your cloathes, and you may hold out this yeare.

101. Presse a stick, and it seemes a youth.

102. The tongue walkes where the teeth speede not.

103. A faire wife and a frontire castle breede quarrels.

104. Leave jesting whiles it pleaseth, lest it turne to earnest.

105. Deceive not thy physitian, confessor, nor lawyer.

106. Ill natures, the more you aske them, the more they stick.

107. Vertue and a trade are the best portion for children.

108. The chicken is the countries, but the citie eates it.

109. He that gives thee a capon, give him the leg and the wing.

110. Hee that lives ill, feare followes him.

111. Give a clowne your finger, and he will take your hand.

112. Good is to be sought out, and evill attended.

113. A good pay-master starts not at assurances.

114. No alchymy to saving.

115. To a gratefull man give mony when he askes.

116. Who would doe ill ne're wants occasion. .

117. To fine folkes a little ill finely wrapt.

118. A child correct behind and not before.

119. To a faire day open the window, but make you ready as to a foule.

120. Keepe good men company, and you shall be of the number.

121. No love to a fathers.

122. The mill gets by going.

123. To a boyling pot flies come not.

124. Make hast to an ill way that you may get out of it.

125. A snow yeare, a rich yeare.

126. Better to be blinde, then to see ill.

127. Learne weeping, and thou shalt laugh gayning.

128. Who hath no more bread then neede, must not keepe a dog.

129. A garden must be lookt unto and drest as the body.

130. The fox, when hee cannot reach the grapes, saies they are not ripe.

131. Water trotted is as good as oates.

132. Though the mastiffe be gentle, yet bite him not by the lippe.

133. Though a lie be well drest, it is ever overcome.

134. Though old and wise, yet still advise.

135. Three helping one another, beare the burthen of sixe.

136. Old wine, and an old friend, are good provisions.

137. Happie is hee that chastens himselfe.

188. Well may hee smell fire, whose gowne burnes.

139. The wrongs of a husband or master are not reproached.

140. Welcome evill, if thou commest alone.

141. Love your neighbour, yet pull not downe your hedge.

142. The bit that one eates, no friend makes.

143. A drunkards purse is a bottle.

144. Shee spins well that breedes her children.

145. Good is the *mora* that makes all sure.

146. Play with a foole at home, and he will play with you in the market.

147. Every one stretcheth his legges according to his coverlet.

148. Autumnal agues are long, or mortall.

149. Marry your sonne when you will; your daughter when you can.

150. Dally not with mony or women.

151. Men speake of the faire, as things went with them there.

152. The best remedy against an ill man, is much ground betweene both.

153. The mill cannot grind with the water that's past.

154. Corne is cleaned with winde, and the soule with chastnings.

155. Good words are worth much, and cost little.

156. To buy deare is not bounty.

157. Jest not with the eye or with religion.

158. The eye and religion can beare no jesting.

159. Without favour none will know you, and with it you will not know your selfe.

160. Buy at a faire, but sell at home.

161. Cover your selfe with your shield, and care not for cryes.

162. A wicked mans gift hath a touch of his master.

163. None is a foole alwaies, every one sometimes.

164. From a chollerick man withdraw a little, from him that saies nothing, for ever.

165. Debters are lyers.

166. Of all smells, bread : of all tasts, salt.

167. In a great river great fish are found, but take heede, lest you bee drowned.

168. Ever since we weare cloathes, we know not one another.

169. God heales, and the physitian hath the thankes.

170. Hell is full of good meanings and wishings.

171. Take heede of still waters, the quick passe away.

172. After the house is finisht, leave it.

173. Our owne actions are our security, not others judgements.

178. Thinke of ease, but worke on.

179. Hee that lies long a bed his estate feeles it.

180. Whether you boyle snow or pound it, you can have but water of it.

181. One stroke fells not an oke.

182. God complaines not, but doth what is fitting.

183. A diligent shcoller and the master's paid.

184. Milke saies to wine, welcome friend.

185. They that know one another, salute a farre off.

186. Where there is no honour, there is no griefe.

187. Where the drink goes in, there the wit goes out.

188. He that staies does the businesse.

189. Almes never make poore orthus.

190. Great almes-giving lessens no mans living.

191. Giving much to the poore, doth inrich a mans store.

192. It takes much from the account, to which his sin doth amount.

193. It adds to the glory both of soule and body.

194. Ill comes in by ells, and goes out by inches.

195. The smith and his penny both are black.

196. Whose house is of glasse, must not throw stones at another.

197. If the old dog barke he gives counsell.

198. The tree that growes slowly, keepes it selfe for another.

199. I wept when I was borne, and every day shewes why.

200. Hee that lookes not before, finds himselfe behind.

201. He that plaies his mony ought not to value it.

202. He that riseth first, is first drest.

203. Diseases of the eye are to bee cured with the elbow.

204. The hole calls the thiefe.

205. A gentlemans grayhound, and a salt-box; seeke them at the fire.

206. A childs service is little, yet hee is no little foole that despiseth it.

207. The river past, and God forgotten.

208. Evils have their comfort, good none can support (to wit) with a moderate and contented heart.

209. Who must account for himselfe and others, must know both.

210. Hee that eats the hard shall eate the ripe.

211. The miserable man makes a peny of a farthing, and the liberall of a farthing sixe pence.

212. The honey is sweet, but the bee stings.

213. Waight and measure take away strife.

214. The sonne full and tattered, the daughter empty and fine.

215. Every path hath a puddle.

216. In good yeares corne is hay, in ill yeares straw is corne.

217. Send a wise man on an errand, and say nothing unto him.

218. In life you lov'd me not, in death you bewaile me.

219. Into a mouth shut, flies flie not.

220. The hearts letter is read in the eyes.

221. The ill that comes out of our mouth falles into our bosome.

222. In great pedigrees there are governours and chandlers.

223. In the house of a fidler, all fiddle.

224. Sometimes the best gaine is to lose.

225. Working and making a fire doth discretion require.

226. One graine fills not a sacke, but helpes his fellowes.

227. It is a great victory that comes without blood.

228. In war, hunting, and love, men for one pleasure a thousand griefes prove.

229. Reckon right, and February hath one and thirty daies.

230. Honour without profit is a ring on the finger.

231. Estate in two parishes is bread in two wallets.

232. Honour and profit lie not in one sacke.

233. A naughty child is better sick, then whole.

234. Truth and oyle are ever above.

235. He that riseth betimes hath some thing in his head.

236. Advise none to marry or to go to warre.

237. To steale the hog, and give the feet for almes.

238. The thorne comes forth with his point forwards.

239. One hand washeth another, and both the face.

240. The fault of the horse is put on the saddle.

241. The corne hides it self in the snow, as an old man in furrs.

242. The Jewes spend at Easter, the Mores at marriages, the Christians in sutes.

243. Fine dressing is a foule house swept before the doores.

244. A woman and a glasse are ever in danger.

245. An ill wound is cured, not an ill name.

246. The wise hand doth not all that the foolish mouth speakes.

247. On painting and fighting looke aloofe.

248. Knowledge is folly, except grace guide it.

249. Punishment is lame, but it comes.

250. The more women looke in their glasse, the lesse they looke to their house.

251. A long tongue is a signe of a short hand.

252. Marry a widdow before she leave mourning.

253. The worst of law is, that one suit breedes twenty.

254. Providence is better then a rent.

255. What your glasse telles you, will not be told by councell.

256. There are more men threatned then stricken.

257. A foole knowes more in his house, then a wise man in anothers.

258. I had rather ride on an asse that carries me, then a horse that throwes me.

259. The hard gives more then he that hath nothing.

260. The beast that goes alwaies never wants blowes.

261. Good cheape is deare.

262. It costs more to doe ill then to doe well.

263. Good words quench more then a bucket of water.

264. An ill agreement is better then a good judgement.

265. There is more talke then trouble.

266. Better spare to have of thine own, then aske of other men.

267. Better good afarre off, then evill at hand.

268. Feare keepes the garden better, then the gardiner.

269. I had rather aske of my sire browne bread, then borrow of my neighbour white.

270. Your pot broken seemes better then my whole one.

271. Let an ill man lie in thy straw, and he lookes to be thy heire.

272. By suppers more have beene killed then *Gallen* ever cured.

273. While the discreet advise the foole doth his busines.

274. A mountaine and a river are good neighbours.

275. Gossips are frogs, they drinke and talke.

276. Much spends the traveller, more then the abider.

277. Prayers and provender hinder no journey.

278. A well-bred youth neither speakes of himselfe, nor being spoken to is silent.

279. A journying woman speakes much of all, and all of her.

280. The fox knowes much, but more he that catcheth him.

281. Many friends in generall, one in speciall.

282. The foole askes much, but hee is more foole that grants it.

283. Many kisse the hand, they wish cut off.

284. Neither bribe nor loose thy right.

285. In the world who knowes not to swimme, goes to the bottome.

286. Chuse not an house neere an inne, (viz. for noise) or in a corner (for filth.)

287. Hee is a foole that thinks not, that another thinks.

288. Neither eyes on letters, nor hands in coffers.

289. The lyon is not so fierce as they paint him.

290. Góe not for every griefe to the physitian, nor for every quarrell to the lawyer, nor for every thirst to the pot.

291. Good service is a great inchantment.

292. There would bee no great ones if there were no little ones.

293. It's no sure rule to fish with a cros-bow.

294. There were no ill language, if it were not ill taken.

295. The groundsell speakes not save what it heard at the hinges.

296. The best mirrour is an old friend.

297. Say no ill of the yeere, till it be past.

298. A mans discontent is his worst evill.

299. Feare nothing but sinne.

300. The child saies nothing, but what it heard by the sire.

301. Call me not an olive, till thou see me gathered.

302. That is not good language which all understand not.

303. Hee that burnes his house warmes himselfe for once.

304. He will burne his house, to warme his hands.

305. Hee will spend a whole yeares rent at one meales meate.

306. All is not gold that glisters.

307. A blustering night, a faire day.

308. Bee not idle and you shall not bee longing.

309. He is not poore that hath little, but he that desireth much.

310. Let none say, I will not drinke water.

311. Hee wrongs not an old-man that steales his supper from him.

312. The tongue talkes at the heads cost.

313. Hee that strikes with his tongue, must ward with his head.

314. Keep not ill men company, lest you increase the number.

315. God strikes not with both hands, for to the sea he made havens, and to rivers foords.

316. A rugged stone growes smooth from hand to hand.

317. No lock will hold against the power of gold.

318. The absent partie is still faultie.

319. Peace, and patience, and death with repentance.

320. If you loose your time, you cannot get mony nor gaine.

321. Bee not a baker, if your head be of butter.

322. Aske much to have a little.

323. Litle stickes kindle the fire; great ones put it out.

324. Anothers bread costs deare.

325. Although it raine, throw not away thy watering pot.

326. Although the sun shine, leave not thy cloake at home.

327. A little with quiet is the onely dyet.

328. In vaine is the mill clacke, if the miller his hearing lack.

329. By the needle you shall draw the thread, and by that which is past, see how that which is to come will be drawne on.

330. Stay a little and news will find you.

331. Stay till the lame messenger come, if you will know the truth of the thing.

332. When God will, no winde, but brings raine.

333. Though you rise early, yet the day comes at his time, and not till then.

334. Pull downe your hatt on the winds side.

335. As the yeere is, your pot must seeth.

336. Since you know all, and I nothing, tell me what I dreamed last night.

337. When the foxe preacheth, beware geese.

338. When you are an anvill, hold you still; when you are a hammer strike your fill.

339. Poore and liberall, rich and coveteous.

340. He that makes his bed ill, lies there.

341. Hee that labours and thrives spins gold.

342. He that sowes trusts in God.

343. Hee that lies with the dogs, riseth with fleas.

344. Hee that repaires not a part, builds all.

345. A discontented man knowes not where to sit easie.

346. Who spits against heaven, it falls in his face.

347. Hee that dines and leaves, layes the cloth twice.

348. Who eates his cock alone must saddle his horse alone.

349. He that is not handsome at 20, nor strong at 30, nor rich at 40, nor wise at 50 will never bee handsome, strong, rich, or wise.

350. Hee that doth what hee will, doth not what he ought.

351. Hee that will deceive the fox, must rise betimes.

352. He that lives well sees a farre off.

353. He that hath a mouth of his owne, must not say to another; Blow.

354. He that will be served must bee patient.

355. Hee that gives thee a bone, would not have thee die.

356. He that chastens one, chastens 20.

357. He that hath lost his credit is dead to the world.

358. He that hath no ill fortune, is troubled with good.

359. Hee that demands misseth not, unlesse his demands be foolish.

360. He that hath no hony in his pot, let him have it in his mouth.

361. He that takes not up a pin, slights his wife.

362. He that owes nothing, if he makes not mouthes at us, is courteous.

363. Hee that looseth his due, gets not thankes.

364. Hee that beleeveth all, misseth, hee that beleeveth nothing, hitts not.

365. Pardons and pleasantnesse are great revenges of slanders.

366. A married man turnes his staffe into a stake.

367. If you would know secrets, looke them in griefe or pleasure.

368. Serve a noble disposition, though poore, the time comes that hee will repay thee.

369. The fault is as great as hee that is faulty.

370. If folly were griefe every house would weepe.

371. Hee that would bee well old, must bee old betimes.

372. Sit in your place and none can make you rise.

373. If you could runne, as you drinke, you might catch a hare.

374. Would you know what mony is, go borrow some.

375. The morning sunne never lasts a day.

376. Thou hast death in thy house, and dost bewaile anothers.

377. All griefes with bread are lesse.

378. All things require skill, but an appetite.

379. All things have their place, know wee, how to place them.

380. Little pitchers have wide eares.

381. We are fooles one to another.

382. This world is nothing except it tend to another.

383. There are three waies, the universities, the sea, the court.

384. God comes to see without a bell.

385. Life without a friend is death without a witnesse.

386. Cloath thee in war, arme thee in peace.

387. The horse thinkes one thing, and he that sadles him another.

388. Mills and wives ever want.

389. The dog that licks ashes, trust not with meale.

390. The buyer needes a hundred eyes, the seller not one.

391. He carries well, to whom it waighes not.

392. The comforters head never akes.

393. Step after step the ladder is ascended.

394. Who likes not the drinke, God deprives him of bread.

395. To a crazy ship all winds are contrary.

396. Justice pleaseth few in their owne house.

397. In times comes he, whom God sends.

398. Water a farre off quencheth not fire.

399. In sports and journeys men are knowne.

400. An old friend is a new house.

401. Love is not found in the market.

402. Dry feet, warme head, bring safe to bed.

403. Hee is rich enough that wants nothing.

404. One father is enough to governe one hundred sons, but not a hundred sons one father.

405. Farre shooting never kild bird.

406. An upbraided morsell never choaked any.

407. Dearths foreseene come not.

408. An ill labourer quarrells with his tooles.

409. Hee that falles into the durt, the longer he stayes there, the fowler he is.

410. He that blames would buy.

411. He that sings on Friday, will weepe on Sunday.

412. The charges of building, and making of gardens are unknowne.

413. My house, my house, though thou art small, thou art to me the Escuriall.

414. A hundred loade of thought will not pay one of debts.

415. Hee that comes of a hen must scrape.

416. He that seekes trouble never misses.

417. He that once deceives is ever suspected.

418. Being on sea saile, being on land settle.

419. Who doth his owne businesse foules not his hands.

420. Hee that makes a good warre makes a good peace.

421. Hee that workes after his owne manner, his head akes not at the matter.

422. Who hath bitter in his mouth, spits not all sweet.

423. He that hath children, all his morsels are not his owne.

424. He that hath the spice, may season as he list.

425. He that hath a head of waxe must not walke in the sunne.

426. He that hath love in his brest, hath spurres in his sides.

427. Hee that respects not, is not respected.

428. Hee that hath a fox for his mate, hath neede of a net at his girdle.

429. He that hath right, feares, he that hath wrong, hopes.

430. Hee that hath patience hath fatt thrushes for a farthing.

431. Never was strumpet faire.

432. He that measures not himselfe, is measured.

433. Hee that hath one hogge makes him fat, and hee that hath one son makes him a foole.

434. Who letts his wife goe to every feast, and his horse drinke at every water, shall neither have good wife nor good horse.

435. He that speakes sowes, and he that holds his peace, gathers.

436. He that hath little is the lesse durtie.

437. He that lives most dies most.

438. He that hath one foot in the straw, hath another in the spittle.

439. Hee that's fed at anothers hand may stay long ere he be full.

440. Hee that makes a thing too fine, breakes it.

441. Hee that bewailes himselfe hath the cure in his hands.

442. He that would be well, needs not goe from his owne house.

443. Councell breakes not the head.

444. Fly the pleasure that bites to morrow.

445. Hee that knowes what may bee gained in a day never steales.

446. Mony refused looseth its brightnesse.

447. Health and mony goe farre.

448. Where your will is ready, your feete are light.

449. A great ship askes deepe waters.

450. Woe to the house where there is no chiding.

451. Take heede of the viniger of sweet wine.

452. Fooles bite one another, but wisemen agree together.

453. Trust not one nights ice.

454. Good is good, but better carries it.

455. To gaine teacheth how to spend.

456. Good finds good.

457. The dog gnawes the bone because he cannot swallow it.

458. The crow bewailes the sheepe, and then eates it.

459. Building is a sweet impoverishing.

460. The first degree of folly is to hold ones selfe wise, the second to professe it, the third to despise counsell.

461. The greatest step is that out of doores.

462. To weepe for joy is a kinde of manna.

463. The first service a child doth his father is to make him foolish.

464. The resolved minde hath no cares.

465. In the kingdome of a cheater, the wallet is carried before.

466. The eye will have his part.

467. The good mother sayes not, will you? but gives.

468. A house and a woman sute excellently.

469. In the kingdome of blindmen the one ey'd is king.

470. A little kitchin makes a large house.

471. Warre makes theeves, and peace hangs them.

472. Poverty is the mother of health.

473. In the morning mountaines, in the evening fountaines.

474. The back-doore robs the house.

475. Wealth is like rheume, it falles on the weakest parts.

476. The gowne is his that weares it, and the world his that enjoyes it.

477. Hope is the poore mans bread.

478. Vertue now is in herbs and stones and words onely.

479. Fine words dresse ill deedes.

480. Labour as long liu'd, pray as ever dying.

481. A poore beauty finds more lovers then husbands.

482. Discreet women have neither eyes nor eares.

483. Things well fitted abide.

484. Prettinesse dies first.

485. Talking payes no toll.

486. The masters eye fattens the horse, and his foote the ground.

487. Disgraces are like cherries, one drawes another.

488. Praise a hill, but keepe below.

489. Praise the sea, but keepe on land.

490. In chusing a wife, and buying a sword, we ought not to trust another.

491. The wearer knowes, where the shoe wrings.

492. Faire is not faire, but that which pleaseth.

493. There is no jollitie but hath a smack of folly.

494. He that's long a giving, knowes not how to give.

495. The filth under the white snow, the sunne discovers.

496. Every one fastens where there is gaine.

497. All feete tread not in one shoe.

498. Patience, time and money accommodate all things.

499. For want of a naile the shoe is lost, for want of a shoe the horse is lost, for want of a horse the rider is lost.

500. Weigh justly and sell dearely.

501. Little wealth little care.

502. Little journeys and good cost, bring safe home.

503. Gluttony kills more then the sword.

504. When children stand quiet, they have done some ill.

505. A little and good fills the trencher.

506. A penny spar'd is twice got.

507. When a knave is in a plumtree he hath neither friend nor kin.

508. Short boughs, long vintage.

509. Health without money, is halfe an ague.

510. If the wise erred not, it would goe hard with fooles.

511. Beare with evill, and expect good.

512. He that tells a secret, is anothers servant.

513. If all fooles wore white caps, wee should seeme a flock of geese.

514. Water, fire, and souldiers, quickly make roome.

515. Pension never inriched young man.

516. Under water, famine, under snow bread.

517. The lame goes as farre as your staggerer.

518. He that looseth is marchant as well as he that gaines.

519. A jade eates as much as a good horse.

520. All things in their beeing are good for something.

521. One flower makes no garland.

522. A faire death honours the whole life.

523. One enemy is too much.

524. Living well is the best revenge.

525. One foole makes a hundred.

526. One paire of eares drawes dry a hundred tongues.

527. A foole may throw a stone into a well; which a hundred wise men cannot pull out.

528. One slumber finds another.

529. On a good bargaine thinke twice.

530. To a good spender God is the treasurer.

531. A curst cow hath short hornes.

532. Musick helps not the tooth-ach.

533. We cannot come to honour under coverlet.

534. Great paines quickly find ease.

535. To the counsell of fooles a woodden bell.

536. The cholerick man never wants woe.

537. Helpe thy selfe, and God will helpe thee.

538. At the games end we shall see who gaines.

539. There are many waies to fame.

540. Love is the true price of love.

541. Love rules his kingdome without a sword.

542. Love makes all hard hearts gentle.

543. Love makes a good eye squint.

544. Love askes faith, and faith firmenesse.

545. A scepter is one thing, and a ladle another.

546. Great trees are good for nothing but shade.

547. Hee commands enough that obeyes a wise man.

548. Faire words makes mee looke to my purse.

549. Though the fox run, the chicken hath wings.

550. He plaies well that winnes.

551. You must strike in measure, when there are many to strike on one anvile.

552. The shortest answer is doing.

553. It's a poore stake that cannot stand one yeare : in the ground.

554. He that commits a fault, thinkes every one speakes of it.

555. He that's foolish in the fault, let him be wise in the punishment.

556. The blind eate many a flie.

557. He that can make a fire well, can end a quarrell.

558. The tooth-ach is more ease, then to deale with ill people.

559. Hee that should have what bee hath not, should doe what he doth not.

560. He that hath no good trade, it is to his losse.

561. The offender never pardons.

562. He that lives not well one yeare, sorrowes seven after.

563. He that hopes not for good, feares not evill.

564. He that is angry at a feast is rude.

565. He that mockes a cripple, ought to be whole.

566. When the tree is fallen, all goe with their hatchet.

567. He that hath hornes in his bosom, let him not put them on his head.

568. He that burnes most shines most.

569. He that trusts in a lie, shall perish in truth.

570. Hee that blowes in the dust fills his eyes with it.

571. Bells call others, but themselves enter not into the church.

572. Of faire things, the autumne is faire.

573. Giving is dead, restoring very sicke.

574. A gift much expected is paid, not given.

575. Two ill meales make the third a glutton.

576. The royall crowne cures not the head-ach.

577. 'Tis hard to be wretched, but worse to be knowne so.

578. A feather in hand is better then a bird in the ayre.

579. It's better to be head of a lyzard, then the tayle of a lyon.

580. Good & quickly seldome meete.

581. Folly growes without watering.

582. Happier are the hands compast with yron, then a heart with thoughts.

583. If the staffe be crooked, the shaddow cannot be straight.

584. To take the nuts from the fire with the dogges foot.

585. He is a foole that makes a wedge of his fist.

586. Valour that parlies, is neare yeelding.

587. Thursday come, and the week's gone.

588. A flatterers throat is an open sepulcher.

589. There is great force hidden in a sweet command.

590. The command of custome is great.

591. To have money is a feare, not to have it a griefe.

592. The catt sees not the mouse ever.

593. Little dogs start the hare, the great get her.

594. Willowes are weake, yet they bind other wood.

595. A good prayer is master of anothers purse.

596. The thread breakes, where it is weakest.

597. Old men, when they scorne young make much of death.

598. God is at the end, when we thinke he is furthest off it.

599. A good judge conceives quickly, judges slowly.

600. Rivers neede a spring.

601. He that contemplates, hath a day without night.

602. Give loosers leave to talke.

603. Losse embraceth shame.

604. Gaming, women, and wine, while they laugh they make men pine.

605. The fatt man knoweth not, what the leane thinketh.

606. Wood halfe burnt is easily kindled.

607. The fish adores the bait.

608. He that goeth farre hath many encounters.

609. Every bees hony is sweet.

610. The slothfull is the servant of the counters.

611. Wisedome hath one foot on land, and another on sea.

612. The thought hath good leggs, and the quill a good tongue.

613. A wise man needes not blush for changing his purpose.

614. The March sunne raises but dissolves not.

615. Time is the rider that breakes youth.

616. The wine in the bottell doth not quench thirst.

617. The sight of a man hath the force of a lyon.

618. An examin'd enterprize, goes on boldly.

619. In every art it is good to have a master.

620. In every country dogges bite.

621. In every countrey the sun rises in the morning.

622. A noble plant suites not with a stubborne ground.

623. You may bring a horse to the river, but he will drinke when and what he pleaseth.

624. Before you make a friend, eate a bushell of salt with him.

625. Speake fitly, or be silent wisely.

626. Skill and confidence are an unconquered army.

627. I was taken by a morsell, saies the fish.

628. A disarmed peace is weake.

629. The ballance distinguisheth not betweene gold and lead.

630. The perswasion of the fortunate swaies the doubtfull.

631. To bee beloved is above all bargaines.

632. To deceive ones selfe is very easie.

633. The reasons of the poore weigh not.

634. Perversnes makes one squint ey'd.

635. The evening praises the day, and the morning a frost.

636. The table robbes more then a thiefe.

637. When age is jocond it makes sport for death.

638. True praise rootes and spreedes.

639. Feares are divided in the midst.

640. The soule needes few things, the body many.

641. Astrologie is true, but the astrologers cannot finde it.

642. Ty it well, and let it goe.

643. Emptie vessels sound most.

644. Send not a catt for lard.

645. Foolish tongues talke by the dozen.

646. Love makes one fitt for any work.

647. A pittifull mother makes a scald head.

648. An old physitian, and a young lawyer.

649. Talke much and erre much, saies the Spanyard.

650. Some make a conscience of spitting in the church, yet robbe the altar.

651. An idle head is a boxe for the winde.

652. Shew me a lyer, and ile shew thee a theefe.

653. A beane in liberty, is better then a comfit in prison.

654. None is borne master.

655. Shew a good man his errour and he turnes it to a vertue, but an ill, it doubles his fault.

656. None is offended but by himselfe.

657. None saies his garner is full.

658. In the husband, wisedome, in the wife gentlenesse.

659. Nothing dries sooner then a teare.

660. In a leopard the spotts are not observed.

661. Nothing lasts but the church.

662. A wise man cares not for what he cannot have.

663. It's not good fishing before the net.

664. He cannot be vertuous that is not rigorous.

665. That which will not be spun, let it not come betweene the spindle and the distaffe.

666. When my house burnes, it's not good playing at chesse.

667. No barber shaves so close, but another finds worke.

668. Ther's no great banquet, but some fares ill.

669. A holy habit clenseth not a foule soule.

670. Forbeare not sowing, because of birds.

671. Mention not a halter in the house of him that was hanged.

672. Speake not of a dead man at the table.

673. A hatt is not made for one shower.

674. No sooner is a temple built to God but the devill builds a chappell hard by.

675. Every one puts his fault on the times.

676. You cannot make a wind-mill goe with a paire of bellowes.

677. Pardon all but thy selfe.

678. Every one is weary, the poore in seeking, the rich in keeping, the good in learning.

679. The escaped mouse ever feeles the taste of the bait.

680. A litle wind kindles; much puts out the fire.

681. Dry bread at home is better then rost meate abroad.

682. More have repented speech then silence.

683. The coveteous spends more then the liberall.

684. Divine ashes are better then earthly meale.

685. Beauty drawes more then oxen.

686. One father is more then a hundred schoole-masters.

687. One eye of the masters sees more, then ten of the servants.

688. When God will punish, hee will first take away the understanding.

689. A little labour, much health.

690. When it thunders, the theefe becomes honest.

691. The tree that God plants, no winde hurts it.

692. Knowledge is no burthen.

693. It's a bold mouse that nestles in the catts eare.

694. Long jesting was never good.

695. If a good man thrive, all thrive with him.

696. If the mother had not beene in the oven, shee had never sought her daughter there.

697. If great men would have care of little ones, both would last long.

698. Though you see a church-man ill, yet continue in the church still.

699. Old praise dies, unlesse you feede it.

700. If things were to be done twice, all would be wise.

701. Had you the world on your chesse-bord, you could not fit all to your mind.

702. Suffer and expect.

703. If fooles should not foole it, they should loose their season.

704. Love and businesse teach eloquence.

705. That which two will, takes effect.

K K 2

706. He complaines wrongfully on the sea that twice suffers shipwrack.

707. He is onely bright that shines by himselfe.

708. A valiant mans looke is more then a cowards sword.

709. The effect speakes, the tongue needes not.

710. Divine grace was never slow.

711. Reason lies betweene the spurre and the bridle.

712. It's a proud horse that will not carry his owne provender.

713. Three women make a market.

714. Three can hold their peace, if two be away.

715. It's an ill councell that hath no escape.

716. All our pompe the earth covers.

717. To whirle the eyes too much shewes a kites braine.

718. Comparisons are odious.

719. All keyes hang not on one girdle.

720. Great businesses turne on a little pinne.

721. The wind in ones face makes one wise.

722. All the armes of England will not arme feare.

723. One sword keepes another in the sheath.

724. Be what thou wouldst seeme to be.

725. Let all live as they would die.

726. A gentle heart is tyed with an easie thread.

727. Sweet discourse makes short daies and nights.

728. God provides for him that trusteth.

729. He that will not have peace, God gives him warre.

730. To him that will, waies are not wanting.

731. To a great night a great lanthorne.

732. To a child all weather is cold.

733. Where there is peace, God is.

734. None is so wise, but the foole overtakes him.

735. Fooles give, to please all, but their owne.

736. Prosperity lets goe the bridle.

737. The frier preached against stealing, and had a goose in his sleeve.

738. To be too busie gets contempt.

739. February makes a bridge and March breakes it.

740. A horse stumbles that hath foure legges.

741. The best smell is bread, the best savour, salt, the best love that of children.

742. That's the best gowne that goes up and downe the house.

743. The market is the best garden.

744. The first dish pleaseth all.

745. The higher the ape goes, the more he shewes his taile.

746. Night is the mother of councels.

747. Gods mill grinds slow, but sure.

748. Every one thinkes his sacke heaviest.

749. Drought never brought dearth.

750. All complaine.

751. Gamsters and race-horses never last long.

752. It's a poore sport that's not worth the candle.

753. He that is fallen cannot helpe him that is downe.

754. Every one is witty for his owne purpose.

755. A little lett lets an ill workeman.

756. Good workemen are seldome rich.

757. By doing nothing we learne to do ill.

758. A great dowry is a bed full of brables.

759. No profit to honour, no honour to religion.

760. Every sin brings it's punishment with it.

761. Of him that speakes ill, consider the life more then the words.

762. You cannot hide an eele in a sacke.

763. Give not S. *Peter* so much, to leave Saint *Paul* nothing.

764. You cannot flea a stone.

765. The chiefe disease that raignes this yeare is folly.

766. A sleepy master makes his servant a lowt.

767. Better speake truth rudely, then lye covertly.

768. He that feares leaves, let him not goe into the wood.

769. One foote is better then two crutches.

770. Better suffer ill, then doe ill.

771. Neither praise nor dispraise thy selfe, thy actions serve the turne.

772. Soft and faire goes farre.

773. The constancy of the benefit of the yeere in their seasons, argues a Deity.

774. Praise none to much, for all are fickle.

775. It's absurd to warme one in his armour.

776. Law sutes consume time, and mony, and rest, and friends.

777. Nature drawes more then ten teemes.

778. Hee that hath a wife and children wants not businesse.

780. A shippe and a woman are ever repairing.

781. He that feares death lives not.

782. He that pitties another, remembers himselfe.

783. He that doth what he should not, shall feele what he would not.

784. Hee that marries for wealth sells his liberty.

785. He that once hitts, is ever bending.

786. He that serves, must serve.

787. He that lends, gives.

788. He that preacheth giveth almes.

789. He that cockers his child, provides for his enemie.

790. A pittifull looke askes enough.

791. Who will sell the cow, must say the word.

792. Service is no inheritance.

793. The faulty stands on his guard.

794. A kinsman, a friend, or whom you intreate, take not to serve you, if you will be served neately.

795. At court, every one for himselfe.

796. To a crafty man, a crafty and an halfe.

797. Hee that is throwne, would ever wrestle.

798. He that serves well needes not ask his wages.

799. Faire language grates not the tongue.

800. A good heart cannot lye.

801. Good swimmers at length are drowned.

802. Good land, evill way.

803. In doing we learne.

804. It's good walking with a horse in ones hand.

805. God, and parents, and our master, can never be requited.

806. An ill deede cannot bring honour.

807. A small heart hath small desires.

808. All are not merry that dance lightly.

809. Curtesie on one side only lasts not long.

810. Wine-counsels seldome prosper.

811. Weening is not measure.

812. The best of the sport is to doe the deede, and say nothing.

813. If thou thy selfe canst doe it, attend no others helpe or hand.

814. Of a little thing a little displeaseth.

815. He warmes too neere that burnes.

816. God keepe me from foure houses, an usurers, a taverne, a spittle, and a prison.

817. In hundred elles of contention, there is not an inch of love.

818. Doe what thou oughtest, and come what come can.

819. Hunger makes dinners, pastime suppers.

820. In a long journey straw waighs.

821. Women laugh when they can, and weepe when they will.

822. Warre is deaths feast.

823. Set good against evill.

824. Hee that brings good newes knockes hard.

825. Beate the dog before the lyon.

826. Hast comes not alone.

827. You must loose a flie to catch a trout.

828. Better a snotty child, then his nose wip'd off.

829. No prison is faire, nor love foule.

830. Hee is not free that drawes his chaine.

831. Hee goes not out of his way, that goes to a good inne.

833. There come nought out of the sacke but what was there.

834. A little given seasonably, excuses a great gift.

835. Hee lookes not well to himselfe that lookes not ever.

836. He thinkes not well, that thinkes not againe.

837. Religion, credit, and the eye are not to be touched.

838. The tongue is not steele, yet it cuts.

839. A white wall is the paper of a foole.

840. They talke of Christmas so long, that it comes.

841. That is gold which is worth gold.

842. It's good tying the sack before it be full.

843. Words are women, deedes are men.

844. Poverty is no sinne.

845. A stone in a well is not lost.

846. He can give little to his servant, that lickes his knife.

847. Promising is the eve of giving.

848. Hee that keepes his owne, makes warre.

849. The wolfe must dye in his owne skinne.

850. Goods are theirs that enjoy them.

851. He that sends a foole expects one.

852. He that can stay obtaines.

853. Hee that gaines well and spends well, needes no count booke.

854. He that endures, is not overcome.

855. He that gives all, before hee dies provides to suffer.

856. He that talkes much of his happinesse summons griefe.

857. Hee that loves the tree, loves the branch.

858. Who hastens a glutton choakes him.

859. Who praiseth Saint *Peter*, doth not blame Saint *Paul*.

860. He that hath not the craft, let him shut up shop.

861. He that knowes nothing, doubts nothing.

862. Greene wood makes a hott fire.

863. He that marries late, marries ill.

864. He that passeth a winters day escapes an enemy.

865. The rich knowes not who is his friend.

866. A morning sunne, and a wine-bred child, and a latin-bred woman, seldome end well.

867. To a close shorne sheepe, God gives wind by measure.

868. A pleasure long expected, is deare enough sold.

869. A poore mans cow dies rich mans child.

870. The cow knowes not what her taile is worth, till she have lost it.

871. Chuse a horse made, and a wife to make.

872. It's an ill aire where wee gaine nothing.

873. Hee hath not liv'd, that lives not after death.

874. So many men in court and so many strangers.

875. He quits his place well, that leaves his friend there.

876. That which sufficeth is not little.

877. Good newes may bee told at any time, but ill in the morning.

878. Hee that would be a gentleman, let him goe to an assault.

879. Who paies the physitian, does the cure.

880. None knowes the weight of anothers burthen.

881. Every one hath a foole in his sleeve.

882. One houres sleepe before midnight, is worth three after.

883. In a retreat the lame are formost.

884. It's more paine to doe nothing then something.

885. Amongst good men two men suffice.

886. There needs a long time to know the worlds pulse.

887. The ofspring of those that are very young, or very old, lasts not.

888. A tyrant is most tyrant to himselfe.

889. Too much taking heede is losse.

890. Craft against craft, makes no living.

891. The reverend are ever before.

892. *France* is a meddow that cuts thrice a yeere.

893. 'Tis easier to build two chimneys, then to maintaine one.

894. The court hath no almanack.

895. He that will enter into Paradise, must have a good key.

896. When you enter into a house, leave the anger ever at the doore.

897. Hee hath no leisure who useth it not.

898. It's a wicked thing to make a dearth ones garner.

899. He that deales in the world needes foure seeves.

900. Take heede of an oxe before, of an horse behind, of a monke on all sides.

901. The yeare doth nothing else but open and shut.

902. The ignorant hath an eagles wings, and an owles eyes.

903. There are more physitians in health then drunkards.

904. The wife is the key of the house.

905. The law is not the same at morning and at night.

906. Warre and physicke are governed by the eye.

907. Halfe the world knowes not how the other halfe lies.

908. Death keepes no calender.

909. Ships feare fire more then water.

910. The least foolish is wise.

. FINIS.

T. DAVISON, Lombard-street,
Whitefriars, London.